13-10

SLAVE AND FREEMAN

Geo L Knap

SLAVE AND FREEMAN

THE AUTOBIOGRAPHY OF
GEORGE L. KNOX

Edited with an Introduction by

WILLARD B. GATEWOOD, Jr.

THE UNIVERSITY PRESS OF KENTUCKY

Library of Congress Cataloging in Publication Data

Knox, George L   1841-1927.
  Slave and freeman, the autobiography of George L. Knox.

  Bibliography: p.
  Includes index.
  1. Knox, George L., 1841-1927. 2. Afro-Americans—
Indiana—Biography. I. Gatewood, William B. II. Ti-
tle.
F535.N4K557   977.2'004'96073   [B]   78-21058
ISBN 0-8131-1384-9

Scholarly publisher for the Commonwealth,
serving Berea College, Centre College of Kentucky,
Eastern Kentucky University, The Filson Club,
Georgetown College, Kentucky Historical Society,
Kentucky State University, Morehead State University,
Murray State University, Northern Kentucky University,
Transylvania University, University of Kentucky,
University of Louisville, and Western Kentucky University.

Editorial and Sales Offices: Lexington, Kentucky 40506

CONTENTS

To
VICTORIA KNOX PORTER
granddaughter of George L. Knox

PREFACE

By the 1890s George L. Knox was generally recognized as the most prominent black citizen in Indiana. Born a slave in Tennessee, he migrated to Indiana shortly before the end of the Civil War and settled in Greenfield where he embarked upon a career as a barber. In time he expanded his barbershop, purchased real estate, participated in local politics, and acquired a wide circle of acquaintances, including the poet James Whitcomb Riley. After eighteen years in Greenfield, Knox moved to Indianapolis where he resided from 1884 until his death in 1927. In Indianapolis he operated a large and well-equipped barbershop in the heart of the city. A conspicuously successful black businessman closely identified with a variety of religious, civic, and racial organizations, he was best known, perhaps, as the owner and publisher of an influential black newspaper and as an active member of the state organization of the Republican party. Throughout his life Knox consistently maintained that only through work, thrift, personal morality, and self-help would black Americans succeed in their struggle for first-class citizenship. Convinced that his own career provided abundant evidence in support of the validity of such a formula, he decided to publish his autobiography in serialized form in the weekly editions of his newspaper.

Ultimately his "success story" appeared in fifty-four chapters, ranging in length from a few brief paragraphs to several columns set in small type. On occasion the availability of space in a particular edition of his paper obviously dictated chapter lengths. It also appears that each installment of the autobiography was published as soon as Knox had written it. As a result, in two instances when he later recalled experiences which he considered significant but which had been omitted from the narrative already published, he incorporated them into two chapters and allowed these chapters to appear out of chronological sequence. For the sake of clarity and continuity, the edited version of the autobiography has abandoned the numerous and often meaningless chapter divisions and instead has been divided into three sections, each of which encompasses an important segment of Knox's career. The material contained in the two chapters which originally appeared out of sequence has been inserted at chronologically appropriate points in the narrative. Throughout, an effort has been made to identify individuals, incidents, and institutions mentioned in the text of the autobiography. The introduction, which attempts to place Knox in historical perspective, devotes especial attention to his career during the period after 1894 which is not covered in the autobiography.

Numerous individuals provided valuable assistance in the editing of this work. I am especially indebted to librarians and archivists at Indiana State Library, Ohio Historical Society, University of Arkansas, and Duke University. Various officials of Wilson County, Tennessee, made it possible for me to consult important records in the courthouse in Lebanon. Nan Woodruff of the Booker T. Washington Papers was extraordinarily helpful in ferreting out the Washington-Knox correspondence. Two of my colleagues, James S. Chase and Randall B. Woods, read the manuscript and gave me the benefit of their counsel. John Hope Franklin not only offered perceptive suggestions and criticisms regarding the manuscript but also located various members of the Knox family. My debt to him is immeasurable. Knox's great-granddaughter, Sister Francesca Thompson, OSF, offered encouragement and graciously responded to my numerous inquiries. Barbara Lineberger, who typed and retyped the manuscript displayed extraordinary patience and an uncanny ability to decipher my copy. My wife, Lu Brown Gatewood, maintained a constant interest in this project and is in large measure responsible for its completion.

W. B. G.

INTRODUCTION

A T THE AGE OF FIFTY-FOUR GEORGE L. KNOX, THE PREEM-
inent black citizen of Indiana, decided to publish his autobiography. For a year beginning in December 1894, virtually every issue of
his weekly newspaper, the *Indianapolis Freeman*, included one or more
chapters of his "Life as I Remember It—As a Slave and Freeman." Although Knox indicated that the account of his life would appear in
book form shortly after its serialization in the *Freeman*, no such volume was published. He may have been discouraged by the unflattering
references to the account, which appeared in a few black journals,[1] but
he obviously did not abandon the idea. More than a dozen years later
he was busily engaged in preparing an updated version for publication.
The advance publicity described it as the story of a life "well spent in
the service of God, race and church."[2] Again, for reasons unknown,
an autobiographical volume failed to appear. Since Knox remained an
active force in Afro-American life for more than three decades after the
publication of his life story in the *Freeman* in 1894-1895, it is unfortunate that these decades are not covered in his extant writings. Clearly,
however, that portion of his autobiography which does survive was
written at a time when he had reached the pinnacle of his prestige and
influence. Between 1888 and 1896 he acquired substantial wealth, purchased a newspaper, and served twice as a lay delegate to the General
Conference of the Methodist Episcopal Church and twice as an alternate delegate-at-large from Indiana to the Republican National Convention. Prominent in numerous civic and racial uplift organizations
within the black community, he counted among his friends and acquaintances a host of famous Americans of both races, including businessmen, bishops, senators, poets, and a president of the United States.

On September 18, 1895, several months before the appearance of
the last installment of Knox's autobiography, Booker T. Washington
delivered the famous address in Atlanta which thrust him and his formula for race relations into national prominence.[3] Knox's autobiography and Washington's address had much in common. Although the
two men differed in educational background, religious concerns, and
techniques of political involvement, their ideological assumptions and
outlook on racial matters were almost identical. Both exuded optimism even in the face of devastating adversity and persisted in the belief that self-help, personal morality, industry, the acquisition of prop-

erty, and adjustment to a segregated society constituted the only feasible means for black Americans to advance. As former slaves whose successes were of the Horatio Alger variety, both found in their careers justification for their formulas of racial progress. That blacks could overcome the prejudice against their race through productive, upright lives was a theme that pervaded Knox's autobiography as well as Washington's Atlanta Address and his *Up from Slavery* published in 1901. Since Knox was quick to perceive how thoroughly and eloquently Washington had articulated his own views, his newspaper was among the first to endorse the Atlanta Compromise and to accept the principal of Tuskegee Institute as the spokesman for black America. Knox ultimately came to occupy an important place within the so-called Tuskegee Machine, an intricate, nationwide network of individuals and institutions loyal to Washington and his philosophy.

George L. Knox was born a slave on September 16, 1841, in Wilson County, Tennessee. Located near the center of the state a few miles east of Nashville, it formed a triangle bounded by the Cumberland, Stones, and Caney Fork rivers and was made up largely of small farms rather than large plantations. At the time of Knox's birth Wilson County contained a total population of 24,460, a quarter of which consisted of slaves. These slaves were concentrated largely in the hands of a few owners; seventy-four individuals in 1840 owned almost 40 percent of all slaves in the county. In addition to corn, wheat, and tobacco, the county also produced many hogs, sheep, and horses. Sawmilling was important, especially around Lebanon, the county seat, while Statesville, a town eighteen miles to the southwest, boasted several cotton mills and a wood manufacturing establishment.[4] Statesville reached its zenith about 1835, and according to one observer in the 1880s had "retrograded" ever since.[5] Knox spent his early years in Statesville and its environs. In fact, he was twenty-one years old before he saw the world beyond the immediate vicinity of his birthplace.

Little is known of his early life and family other than the scant information contained in his autobiography and a few references in public addresses. He was one of three children belonging to Charles and Nancy Fisher Knox. His mother, described as a "mulatto woman," was apparently born free but was sold into slavery following the death of her mother. His father, though always a slave, was on occasion referred to as a "Baptist preacher."[6] By 1847 both parents were dead, leaving Knox, his older sister, Huldah, who was eight, and his younger brother, Charles, who was four. On numerous occasions Knox mentioned the fact that his family enjoyed a privileged status within the slave hierarchy because of the "special consideration" shown them by their owners.

Although Knox was never reticent to proclaim his affection for the whites whom he served as a slave, none of his public statements revealed their identity. But by supplementing the information contained in his autobiography with data from various county court records and the federal census, it is possible to establish that he and his family belonged to John Knox, a planter of means, who had settled near the site of Statesville in the closing years of the eighteenth century. Despite Knox's claim that "old master" possessed "many slaves," an inventory of John Knox's estate reveals that at the time of his death in 1846, his slave property consisted of two male and two female adults and seven children, a total of eleven slaves ranging in age from fifty years to four months. As Knox indicated in his autobiography, when "old master" died, his slaves were taken to Statesville and sold at public auction; but because Knox's parents had been favorites of their owner, his heirs were determined that their slave children should not be sold to the slave traders. The legal documents describing the settlement of John Knox's estate indicate that two residents of Wilson County purchased the two adult male slaves and that his son, R. A. Knox, not only acquired the slave boys, George and Charles, for the nominal sum of $2.00 but also assumed charge of the remaining slaves, including their sister Huldah, with instructions to "see . . . [them] out for victuals and clothes."[7]

If John Knox was the person to whom Knox referred in his autobiography as "old master," it is considerably more difficult to establish the identity of the individual described as "young master." At first glance it would appear to be R. A. Knox, since he acquired Knox and his younger brother at the estate sale in 1847, but certain other evidence brings that assumption into question. R. A. Knox, for example, is not listed in the census of Wilson County for either 1850 or 1860, but W. C. Knox was a thirty-four-year-old merchant in States-

5

ville who owned a single slave, a nineteen-year-old male.[8] This description coincided with that of the "young master" given in Knox's autobiography, and the age of the male slave was exactly that of Knox in 1860. However, Knox's suggestion that his "young master" belonged to the Eighth Tennessee Cavalry (sometimes called Fourth Tennessee Cavalry) does little to clarify the situation, because both R. A. and W. C. Knox were members of this regiment. W. C. Knox, however, belonged to Company D of that regiment, made up only of men from Wilson County and commanded by Captain James M. Phillips to whom George Knox, the slave, was assigned as a body servant. R. A. Knox belonged to Company G of the same regiment which consisted of recruits from Rutherford and Cannon counties.[9] Interestingly enough, though, Knox's account indicates that the wife of his "young master" was from Rutherford County, which he mistakenly refers to as "Reliford county."

Although Knox occasionally incorporated references to his experiences as a slave in his public addresses, these contribute little to establishing the identity of his "young master." In an Emancipation Day speech in 1894, for example, he described his childhood and then told of returning to his birthplace in Tennessee many years after the Civil War to visit his former master who was, at that time, practically destitute.[10] It is not clear from the address whether Knox was referring to his first visit "back home" in 1883, the second in 1887, or the third in 1891 when he brought his invalid sister to Indianapolis to live with his family.[11] So far as establishing the identity of his "young master" is concerned, it makes little difference because W. C. Knox had died in 1866;[12] therefore, the former master to whom he alluded in this speech was obviously R. A. Knox.

In an address in 1920, Knox again described his experiences as a slave and a visit he made to his former master after the Civil War:

> Back in the days of slavery, my master had a large number of slaves, my family being the favorite of the owners. When the old master died, we were all sold, but to keep my sister, brother and myself from being sold to Negro traders and taken south . . . I, a little fellow of three years, was bought by my young master for $300 and his sister bought my brother and sister. That kept us in the family. The war came on after that and I was freed. Then, I came to Indiana. After being away from

6

home for twenty six years, I returned to see my people. I found my former master in need. He said to me: "I have been made poor. Everything has been taken from me. I am now seventy-six years old. I can never make it any more." I said to him: "Do you remember at your father's sale your sister bought my sister and brother and you bought me? I have gone north and have been blessed. That act was bread cast upon the water to be gathered many days after. As long as I have one dollar, half of it is yours." From that time on he wrote to me for clothes and I helped him as long as he lived.[13]

Although the "former master" in this account was apparently R. A. Knox, the reference to $300 as the price paid by the "young master" stands in sharp conflict with the nominal sum mentioned in the documents relating to the settlement of "old master's" estate. Yet, Knox consistently stated that he was bought for $300.[14] The paucity of documentation relating to his early life simply makes it impossible either to corroborate or to deny the validity of his assertion. Because of the factual accuracy of his autobiography in regard to virtually all important matters, it scarecely seems appropriate to dismiss this bit of information as a figment of Knox's imagination. It may well be that he has reference to a sale other than that described in the records concerning the settlement of "old master's" estate which in turn may shed some light on the identity of "young master." If for example R. A. Knox, who purchased him and his brother Charles for $2.00 in 1847, later sold him to W. C. Knox for $300, Knox could legitimately allude to each, within different contexts, as his master. Therefore, the "young master" of the autobiography may refer to W. C. Knox and the "former master" whom Knox visited after the Civil War may refer to R. A. Knox.

In either case, it seems beyond contradiction that a certain bond of affection developed between the "young master" and his slave. Knox often characterized his owner as a humane, almost indulgent, master, citing in particular his intervention to protect him from corporal punishment and rejection of an offer of $1,600 in gold for him when he was sixteen years old. His master's wife even remarked that her husband seemed more solicitous of the slave's welfare than of her own. In referring to his master in 1894, Knox recalled: "he was always good to me."[15]

7

Despite the leniency of his "young master," Knox by no means escaped the dehumanization and cruelty of the slave system. His autobiography vividly evokes the pathos of a young slave's life, especially in those passages describing his rare visits with his brother and paternal grandmother and pleas to his master to be taken away from a farm where he had been hired out. That he would be "sold South" and permanently separated from the surviving members of his family was a constant source of dread and fear. And his "young master," however indulgent, never allowed Knox to forget his state of dependence. "When I left my master during the war," Knox later recalled, "he said to me that I would come back, that I could not take care of myself. He told me that so often that I had just about concluded it was so."[16] But his ingenuity, resourcefulness, and unwavering optimism enabled him to survive the strictures of slavery and the confusion of war to succeed as a free man.

Since Knox's master was for a time a schoolteacher, he had little use for the labor of a strong, young male slave. Therefore, he hired out Knox to work, first on the farm of a "pious Presbyterian" family, then on a plantation owned by a locally prominent physician. He worked briefly for a tanner before returning to the household of his master late in the 1850s, when the latter quit teaching to open a store in Statesville. Anxious to "be given a prestige over other slaves by not having to go on the farm to work," Knox temporarily satisfied his ambition by serving as an apprentice to a shoemaker in Statesville. But when his master closed his store and resumed teaching school, his slave was again hired out as a farm laborer. At the outbreak of the Civil War, however, Knox was working at a sawmill located across a small stream from Statesville.

When Knox's master joined a Confederate volunteer unit and went off to war, the occasion was one of sadness for both master and slave. The young slave, separated from his "only friend," accompanied his mistress to the home of her parents in south-central Tennessee where they remained for about a year. At the expiration of his twelve-month enlistment period in 1862, his master resumed teaching school in Wilson County. Pleased to be back in familiar surroundings, Knox was hired out as a bootmaker and for a time did a brisk business in orders from Confederate soldiers. But the encroachment of Union

8

troops into the vicinity of Wilson County late in 1862 and early 1863 brought the war home to both slave and master. When his master returned to Confederate military service early in 1863, he took his slave with him and arranged for him to become a body servant of Captain James M. Phillips, the commander of Company D of the Eighth Tennessee Cavalry. Allowed to visit home shortly afterward, Knox decided never to return to the "rebel army." In May 1863, after bidding his sweetheart farewell, he led a party of slaves including his brother Charles into Union lines near Murfreesboro. The death of Charles within a few weeks left Knox with no family except his sister whom he would not see again for almost two decades.[17]

Always adept at making himself useful, he was at one time or another a cook, nurse, servant, messenger, and teamster with the Fifty-seventh Indiana Infantry[18] as it, along with other Union forces, converged on Chattanooga. Knox was in the midst of the fighting around that city late in 1863, serving first as a servant to Captain John F. Monroe of the Fifteenth Indiana Infantry. Following the death of Captain Monroe from wounds received at Missionary Ridge, he went to work for Lieutenant William G. Humphreys of the Fifty-seventh Indiana and later for Captain Addison Dunn of the same regiment. "Shut out from home," Knox decided that he should make his way north. An opportunity to "go North" came early in 1864 when Captain Dunn, having been granted a furlough, took Knox to Indiana with him. Despite the racial prejudice he encountered there, he was convinced that an ambitious black man was more likely to prosper in Indiana than in the South, and he remained in Indianapolis when Captain Dunn left to rejoin his regiment in Tennessee.

With the departure of the captain in April 1864, Knox was on his own in a strange city. He first secured employment with Judge Elijah B. Martindale, one of the most prominent citizens of Indianapolis, but soon quit for a better paying job at the Bates House, the city's leading hotel. Starting as a yardman, he so impressed the proprietor that he soon became head porter. But eager to learn a trade he left the hotel before the end of 1864 to take a job in a barbershop owned by Reuben Gibbs, a well-known black barber. Recognizing that "the colored barber was the big man in the social and business world of his race,"[19] he persuaded Gibbs to allow him to become a "cub barber" in his shop. All the while, he lived frugally and managed to save enough from his earnings to invest in a barbershop opened by a group of barbers in Kokomo, Indiana. For the first three months of 1865 he remained in Kokomo perfecting his skill as a "tonsorial artist." Returning to Indianapolis in March, he continued to pursue his trade and prospered for a time owing to the presence of a large number of free-spending soldiers who had returned home from the war. Knox accumulated sufficient capital to lease a barbershop in the Sherman House, an Indianapolis hotel, a move that proved to be financially disastrous because the lease was fraudulent. His losses left him "dead broke" just as he was engaged to be married to Aurilla Harvey,[20] the daughter of Preston and Martha Harvey, who had migrated from North Carolina to Howard County, Indiana, in 1844. Preston Harvey, a man of means, apparently had no intention of allowing his daughter to marry a man without regular employment.

Convinced that barbershops in Indianapolis would suffer a serious decline in business as the returning soldiers depleted their muster-out pay, Knox investigated the possibility of opening a shop of his own in a nearby small town. His choice was Greenfield, the county seat of Hancock County. Why he chose Greenfield is not altogether clear. At the time of his arrival the only black residents of the town were the family of Irvin Hunt, a veteran employee in a local newspaper office. In all probability the reason Knox selected Greenfield was that many of those soldiers of the Fifty-seventh Indiana whom he had known during the war resided in the town or nearby. Their friendship not only proved to be a boon to his barbering business but also served to insulate him from some of the racial prejudice among white citizens in the locality.[21]

On October 4, 1865, a month after Knox opened his sparsely furnished barbershop in Greenfield, he married Aurilla Harvey, an educated, industrious woman who not only assisted her husband in learning to read and write but also remained a constant source of support and strength for him. The couple first boarded with the Hunts, but after Knox's barbering enterprise became established, they purchased a modest home. Their first child, a son named William Walter was born in 1867; the second, a daughter named Nellie, arrived two

10

years later; and the third, also a son, Elwood, was born in 1871.[22]

The atmosphere in Greenfield in the fall of 1865 scarcely indicated a bright future for the town's newest black residents. As Knox indicated in his autobiography, "prejudice was very high." The so-called Negro Question, especially as it related to suffrage, schools, and federal Reconstruction policies was the subject of highly emotional debates in which the white citizens of Hancock County tended to divide along party lines. The Democrats who had a slight majority viewed Negro suffrage "a noxious heresy of Eastern fanatics" and considered the admission of blacks to public schools as a dangerous move in the direction of social equality between the races. The local Democratic journal, *The Hancock Democrat*, whose blatantly racist editorials specialized in denouncing "Negro equality," was unalterably opposed to the Civil Rights Act of 1866, the Fifteenth Amendment, and the domination of southern states "by ignorant and depraved negroes." The editor of the *Democrat*, William Mitchell, was as certain that his Negro employee, Irvin Hunt, was content "for white people to govern the country" as he was that the white Republicans of Hancock County were guilty of the grossest hypocrisy in their support of the freedman's cause. Among the most influential Republicans in Greenfield during Knox's residence there were Adam L. Ogg, a Civil War veteran and a pension attorney, John W. Jones, an attorney and realtor, and Nelson Bradley, a banker,[23] all of whom befriended the black barber and shielded him from the more vicious forms of racial prejudice.

During his first years in Greenfield, Knox avoided politics and concentrated on proving himself worthy of the respect of leading whites of both parties. He worked long hours and catered to the vanities of his white clientele. His business soon outgrew the crude facilities of his original shop, whereupon he leased a room on Gooding Corner in the heart of Greenfield opposite the county courthouse. The move resulted in even greater business; Knox soon added a second chair and employed a black barber to assist him. By the time he left Greenfield in 1884, his shop was a commodious establishment with a barber's pole, four chairs, and fixtures which made it the equal of "any shaving parlor in Eastern Indiana." A corner of the shop contained cases displaying an assortment of fine cigars and bottles of his own "hair restorative" guaranteed to cleanse the scalp of "dandruff and other impurities." Except in winter, tables containing flower and garden plants lined the street outside the shop.[24]

The location of the barbershop in the center of town as well as Knox's engaging personality and skill as a barber made his establishment a popular gathering place for the most influential white citizens of Greenfield and Hancock County. Knox cultivated their friendship, listened attentively to their conversation, and won their confidence and esteem. In time he became the confidant of many locally prominent individuals, including such political leaders as Adam Ogg, William J. Sparks, and Ephraim Marsh. Even William Mitchell whose newspaper was hostile toward every legislative effort to protect the civil rights of blacks respected Knox and generally referred to him as "our handsome and gentlemanly tonsorial friend."[25] Among the most prominent residents of Greenfield was the Riley family. Both Reuben A. Riley, a respected attorney and the town's first mayor, and his son James Whitcomb Riley, who became famous as a poet, were special friends of the black barber. As a teenager, the younger Riley was a regular visitor in the barbershop where he learned much about the Hoosier dialect that was later used in his verse. One of Riley's poems, entitled "Local Politician from Away Back" and published in 1887, contained a specific reference to Knox's barbershop.[26]

Although Knox succeeded in widening his circle of friends among the local elite and in building up his barbering trade, he was well aware that his illiteracy constituted a major obstacle to the realization of his ambitions. Despite the frustrations involved in overcoming this handicap, he persisted in his efforts, aided by his wife, until he had mastered the alphabet. In 1870 he was largely responsible for organizing a Sunday school for blacks under the auspices of the Methodist Episcopal Church. Thomas Snow, an eccentric English shoemaker in Greenfield, who became superintendent of the Sunday school, devoted as much time to teaching reading and writing as to religious instruction. Taking advantage of Snow's "lessons," Knox mastered simple exercises in reading and writing. Supported by his influential white friends, he secured the establishment of a public school for the fifteen black children of Greenfield in 1873. Although concern for the education of his own children undoubtedly lay behind his efforts, Knox himself benefited from the public school. Black teachers boarded in his home and one of these, Calvin B. Gilliam, contributed significantly to his education by having him recite lessons at night.[27]

By the mid-1870s Knox had acquired the rudiments of an education. Thereafter, he read widely in various types of literature and took advantage of any opportunity to improve his literary skills. In 1874 he organized a "colored debating society" which included black men from Greenfield as well as other towns in Hancock County.[28] Although Knox ultimately enjoyed a wide reputation as a forceful, articulate public speaker, the deficiencies of his formal education never wholly disappeared. His autobiography, produced less than a quarter of a century after he was first introduced to the alphabet, indicates the nature of the problems that continued to plague his prose.

During his residence in Greenfield, Knox proved to be as enthusiastic in promoting the cause of religion among black citizens as the cause of education. The origin of his interest in religious affairs is by no means clear, but conceivably his father who was a slave preacher may have been responsible or perhaps he was influenced by the "pious Presbyterian family" to whom he was hired out as a slave. Regardless of the source of his religious concerns, Knox envisioned the church as a principal instrument for the moral uplift of his race—a theme that he reiterated in addresses and writings throughout his life. The success of the Sunday school led to a demand for a church, since the town had no place for blacks to worship. Inclined "to take hold of undeveloped affairs and build them up," Knox was the key figure in organizing a black congregation which affiliated with the predominantly white Methodist Episcopal Church (Northern Methodist). So long as he remained in Greenfield, Knox maintained a constant interest in this church, known as the Second Methodist Church, and labored ceaselessly to increase its membership. In 1881 he organized and managed a week-long camp meeting which featured well-known preachers and attracted large audiences made up of whites as well as blacks. For the next several years he sponsored and coordinated similar revivalistic meetings. Knox took great pride in the spiritual and financial successes of these enterprises, viewing them as evidence of his managerial skills.[29]

The interest that Knox displayed in religion and personal economic advancement was equaled only by his passion for politics. Not until the

13

early 1870s, however, did he assume an active role in the political life of Greenfield. For a half dozen years, he observed political contests, listened to the conversations of his white patrons, learned to read and write, and established himself as a responsible member of the community. Although Knox was never allowed to forget that he was a black man, the Negro Question no longer figured as prominently in party struggles of Hancock County as it did when he first settled there. "A Republican from principle and not for revenue," he supported the faction of the party headed locally by Captain Adam Ogg, who relied upon him to keep the small bloc of black voters in the county loyal to Republicanism. In performing this task Knox was always careful to avoid any action likely to alienate whites. On occasion he addressed racially mixed audiences at political rallies in nearby towns and regularly served as an adviser to the inner council of the Hancock County Republican organization.

But Knox's most important "campaign work" during elections took place in his barbershop as he went about his daily routine of shaving and cutting the hair of politicians of both parties and all factions. Because he enjoyed their confidence, they were inclined to talk freely about party affairs. Conversations with his Democratic patrons inevitably produced information which he undoubtedly made available to his Republican allies. Moreover, as Greenfield's leading barber Knox was on friendly terms with a cross-section of the male populace and occupied an advantageous position to gauge the drift of political sentiment and to ascertain issues likely to affect voting behavior. His astuteness as a political observer greatly enhanced his value to the local Republican organization. Knox himself took considerable pride in the accuracy of his predictions regarding election results. In 1880 the local Democratic journal characterized him as a real power in Hancock County Republican circles, claiming that he, Ogg, and John W. Jones constituted the party's ruling triumvirate.[30]

That Knox was selected to attend a National Conference of Colored Men which met in Nashville, Tennessee, in May 1879 was testimony to his rising prominence. He was one of eleven black men who represented the state at the Nashville meeting. The purpose of the gathering was to consider the exodus of blacks from the South to Kansas, Indiana, and other western states. Fully aware of the oppressed

14

condition of black Southerners, Knox expressed sympathy for them and defended their right to move to any locality they desired. At the same time he pointed out the practical difficulties certain to result from any large-scale migration. He desired, above all, to do nothing which would intensify the racial animosity of whites and thereby worsen the plight of blacks, in the North as well as in the South. In the course of an address to the convention, Knox declared: "There is an impression abroad that the Northern delegates have come here to take away the colored people in the southern states from their homes. This is not so." These remarks prompted shouts of "take him out" from a few spectators in the galleries.[31] Of far greater significance, however, was the hostility directed toward him upon his return home.

When Negro emigrants from North Carolina appeared in Indiana, Democrats charged that the exodus was a political plot fomented by white Republicans and their black henchmen. According to Democratic sources, Knox's former employer, Judge Martindale of Indianapolis, was the mastermind of the plot.[32] Although Hancock County actually attracted few emigrants, several black families from North Carolina did arrive in Greenfield late in 1879. Local whites were quick to register their opposition, and the *Hancock Democrat* mounted an editorial campaign against the exodus which assumed a racist tone not evident since the late 1860s. It directed its fire at Ogg, Jones, and other white Republicans as well as their black ally, Knox, and accused them of being involved in "an outrageous and damnable plot to flood Hancock County with pauper negroes from the South, hoping thereby to aid their party in the coming campaign." Citing Knox's attendance at the Nashville convention, the *Democrat* accused him of having "been engaged in an effort to scare southern negroes from their comfortable southern homes for the advancement of the [Republican] party here in the North." From the outset Knox vigorously denied that he was in any way connected with any Republican emigration scheme or that he had ever encouraged southern blacks to settle in Hancock County. Such denials failed to convince the editor of the *Democrat* who continued to heap abuse upon him and strongly hinted that his complicity in the Republicans' "damnable plot" would bring about his financial ruin. A Greenfield correspondent, writing in the *Indianapolis Journal* in January 1880, claimed that the editor of the *Democrat* professed "the

15

most intense hatred of the negro" and "poured out the very dregs of his wrath upon Mr. G. L. Knox, a colored barber, who has lived here ever since the war, and who by industry and economy has accumulated considerable property and who in every moral quality is as much the superior of his maligner as can be imagined."[33]

For a time certain Democrats in Greenfield did attempt to exert economic pressure upon Knox. At the height of the agitation over the emigrant question he encountered competition from a white barber who opened a "shaving parlor" in the Guymon House, the town's leading hotel, which became known as the "Democratic barbershop."[34] But if, as Knox claimed, his enemies expected to put him out of business, their efforts proved wholly unsuccessful. Because most of his prominent friends, Democrats as well as Republicans, remained loyal to him throughout the controversy, he continued to prosper and even enlarged his barbershop. By 1883 the agitation over black emigrants from the South had subsided and even the *Hancock Democrat* abandoned its harassment of Knox.

Although Knox successfully withstood the outburst of prejudice aimed at him during the controversy over emigration, he decided in 1884 to leave Greenfield for Indianapolis. The latter was a relatively large city with a rapidly growing black population which had already reached more than 6,500. Throughout his residence in Greenfield, Knox was a frequent visitor to the city and over the years had established important contacts within its black community. In his autobiography he explained his decision in terms of his conviction that he had "outgrown" Greenfield and could come nearer realizing his ambitions in a larger city. In another context he suggested that a desire to insure his children "superior educational advantages" prompted him to make the move.[35] But it also seems likely that his periodic encounters with overt racial prejudice, especially during the emigration crisis, made him acutely aware of the peculiar vulnerability of an ambitious black man in a small, virtually all-white town.

Whatever motives may have prompted Knox to leave Greenfield, his years there constituted a highly significant phase of his career. Greenfield, in fact, provided him with the experience necessary for achieving prominence in Indianapolis and in the national Afro-American community. Arriving in the small Indiana town as a penniless, illiterate ex-slave, Knox became within two decades a literate, prosperous, and respected citizen. By 1884 he had established a thriving barbershop, acquired some real estate, and perfected the entrepreneurial skills which underlay much of his later success. Because of his leadership in establishing and maintaining a church for Greenfield's black citizens, he became widely known among the "colored contingent" in the Methodist Episcopal Church. Equally important in preparing him to assume a larger role in public affairs was the apprenticeship in politics which he served during his residence in Greenfield. In an age of fierce political struggles and in a place characterized by vigorous two-party rivalry, he learned the intricacies of politics from veteran experts in the art. Although whites came to look upon him as the spokesman for Hancock County's small black constituency, his political role was by no means limited to activities within the black community. Through his personal relationship with Ogg and other white Republicans he came to occupy a position within the party that allowed him to exert a more general influence. But the price of his position was acquiescence in the overruling power of whites.

By the time Knox left Greenfield in 1884 he had developed a formula of race relations which underwent only slight modification during the next four decades. It was a formula shaped in large part by his own experiences first as a slave and later as a black barber dependent for his livelihood upon the patronage of whites. If he escaped the harsher aspects of slavery in Tennessee through the influence of a humane master, his initial success as a free man in Indiana owed much to the support of his white friends in Greenfield. Shunning the "lower elements" of both races, Knox identified with the "best white people" and so thoroughly internalized their own petit bourgeois values that his views on most important questions, including race, closely resembled those of his white models. An optimist who refused to succumb to either bitterness or despair, even in the face of racial prejudice directed specifically at him, he believed that obstacles to the progress of blacks would be eliminated in the same degree that blacks demonstrated a capacity for patience, industry, economy, and virtuous living. A sense of his own elite status is evident throughout his autobiography. Indeed, he viewed himself as belonging to a small group of blacks who through their own initiative had lifted themselves "out of the

17

depths" and achieved a measure of security and material success which separated them from the black masses by a wide chasm.

Although Knox opposed restrictions on the economic opportunities and civil rights of black citizens, he renounced "social equality" and accepted segregation as the price of peace between the two races. An accommodationist who could be deferential toward whites without being obsequious, he was always conscious of the nuances and subtleties involved in the complex web of race relations. Eschewing what he called "fancy theories," Knox preferred to deal in the "practical realities" of the racial situation which in his opinion required blacks to employ protest tactics sparingly and avoid giving needless offense to the "dominant race." Militancy rarely characterized either his action or language except in his pursuit of such themes as self-help and virtuous living. He often referred to the "unity of the races"—the mutuality of interest between blacks and whites—and consistently employed words such as *brotherhood, love*, and *harmony* in discussing relations between whites and blacks.[36]

On March 1, 1884, Knox and William Bibbs, a well-known black barber in Indianapolis, opened a shaving parlor in that city on South Meridian Street in a room recently vacated by Western Union Telegraph. Despite predictions that a "country barber" like Knox was certain to fail in a big city, the barbershop proved to be an extraordinarily prosperous venture.[37] Before the end of his first year in Indianapolis, he expanded its facilities and regularly employed six barbers. Determined to provide the city with a shaving parlor equal to any in either Chicago or Cincinnati, Knox arranged to lease the Bates House Barbershop located in the hotel in which he had served as porter more than twenty years earlier. Although he retained his South Meridian Street shop, he devoted most of his attention to the new establishment and spared little expense in renovating and furnishing it. The new Bates House Barbershop which opened on April 18, 1885, surpassed anything Indianapolis had ever possessed in the way of tonsorial parlors. One observer described it as "a thing of beauty" and its owner as a "good businessman" who conducted everything "in first class style." Equipped with the latest barbering fixtures, ten chairs and fifteen ornate baths, it was likened to the elegant "harem of an Eastern caliph." In 1891 Knox added a Ladies' Hair Dressing Department, known as the Ladies' Annex, and purchased the YMCA Barbershop which he operated in conjunction with the Bates House Barbershop. In the following year he leased the barbershop in the Grand Hotel and as in the case of the Bates House staffed it with a complete corps of black barbers. For fifteen years beginning in 1902 he managed the barbershop in the Denison House, another well-known Indianapolis hotel.[38]

In the late nineteenth and early twentieth centuries the ownership of barbershops, especially those located in cities, provided black men such as Knox with one of the few nonprofessional avenues for achieving status and wealth. Many of his contemporaries who occupied positions of leadership in the black community had begun as barbers. Among the most notable of these were two wealthy insurance executives, John Merrick of Durham, North Carolina, and Alonzo Herndon of Atlanta, Georgia, founders of the North Carolina Life Insurance Company and Atlanta Life Insurance Company, respectively. But the individual whose career more nearly resembled that of Knox was George A. Myers of Cleveland, Ohio. Unlike Knox, Myers had been born free in Baltimore and had spent his life in various large cities. In 1888 he assumed direction of the Hollenden Barbershop in Cleveland which, like Knox's Bates House Barbershop, was connected with a leading hotel, the Hollenden House. Through the income and contacts provided by his barbershop, Myers became a civic leader in Cleveland's black community and an influential member of Senator Marcus A. Hanna's Republican organization.[39]

Although a few black barbers did succeed in maintaining a policy of accepting both black and white customers, most accommodated public opinion and established a de facto color line. Those with a white clientele were rarely willing to "risk serving blacks because they feared this would 'drive the white trade away.' " Despite their adherence to a policy of segregation, black barbers increasingly encountered competition from both native and foreign-born barbers. Even though their decline in Indianapolis was not so dramatic as in some other cities, it was nonetheless substantial. In 1890, for example, blacks constituted 34 percent of the barbers in Indianapolis while in 1910 they made up less than 23 percent.[40]

19

Perhaps it was evidence of Knox's tenacity that for more than three and a half decades he possessed one or more barbershops in Indianapolis which, regardless of his other enterprises, remained the principal source of his income. By the mid-1890s his shops provided employment for more than fifty blacks. "Considering the number of people who get their support through his enterprises," a Negro newspaper remarked, "we feel justified in saying that Mr. Knox is doing good work for the race." Because he employed only black barbers, another Negro journal claimed in 1892 that he deserved "well of the 'craft' everywhere, for the colored barber, like the Indian, has been for a number of years slowly driven toward the setting sun, by the hordes of white barbers who have sprung up like mushrooms in a damp atmosphere."[41] A few years later, a black journalist noted that Knox was "solving the race problem, not by talking alone but by doing something practical."[42] By the 1890s Knox devoted himself primarily to the managerial aspects of his barbering and other enterprises and rarely assumed a position behind the barber's chair except to shave patrons of especial prominence such as James Whitcomb Riley, his friend from Greenfield who had become a famous poet, and the principal businessmen of Indianapolis who appreciated his industry and entrepreneurial skills as well as his tonsorial artistry. Knox especially cultivated the friendship of prominent Republicans such as Lew Wallace, Roger R. Shiel, and Benjamin Harrison who were regular patrons of his barbershops. His acquaintance with the city's business and political elite was a factor of critical significance in his rapid rise to prominence in Republican affairs.

Within a decade after moving to Indianapolis, Knox had become the city's most conspicuously successful black businessman.[43] His wealth was insignificant compared to that of many whites who patronized his barbershops, but it was sufficient to place him far above most of the city's black population. Although he maintained a simple life-style and was quick to condemn blacks for frittering away their modest resources on frivolities, he did provide generously for his wife and children. The Knoxes resided in a commodious house, employed a maid, and traveled extensively.[44] Gradually, they assumed a place among the black elite of Indianapolis which in the 1880s and 1890s consisted of the Bagbys, Elberts, Christys, Thorntons, McCoys, Hills, and a few other families. Most of these families were the descendants of free Negroes or of slaves who had escaped north many years before Emancipation. Characterized by a relatively high level of education, they furnished the black community with teachers, journalists, physicians, and attorneys who dominated its social, cultural, and political affairs.[45] Despite the fact that his wife belonged to this group, members of the elite at first looked askance at Knox himself. Some spoke disparagingly of his "deficiency" in formal education; others viewed him as an unsophisticated rustic; and still others opposed his accommodationist attitude toward race relations.[46] But his success in business and increasing popularity with influential whites tended to quiet such objections and paved the way for him to become a leader within the black community.

As much as any other institution, the church provided Knox with the means for assuming such a role. Soon after arriving in Indianapolis, he joined Simpson Chapel Methodist Episcopal Church and remained closely identified with it for more than four decades. Like the church that he organized in Greenfield, Simpson Chapel was within the jurisdiction of the Lexington Conference, an all-black organizational subdivision of the predominantly white Northern Methodist Church. Organized in 1869 at the request of the Negro members of the Kentucky Annual Conference, the new conference which ultimately embraced black congregations in Kentucky, Indiana, Ohio, Michigan, Wisconsin, Minnesota, and portions of Illinois remained under the general supervision of a white bishop. Simpson Chapel Church, established in 1874, became one of the most influential congregations within the Lexington Conference. A succession of well-known black clergymen including Marshall W. Taylor, Louis M. Hagood, and Edward W. S. Hammond occupied the Simpson Chapel pulpit. From the mid-1880s on, Knox was its most conspicuous layman. Long active in its Sunday school and largely responsible for the construction of a new church building in the 1890s, he represented the congregation in quarterly and district conferences on numerous occasions.[47]

In 1888 Knox was elected a lay delegate from the Lexington Conference to the denomination's quadrennial General Conference which met that year in New York. Reelected to the same position two years later, he traveled to Omaha where, as in New York, he actively participated in the deliberations of the church's governing body and served as a lay spokesman for the Negro members of the conference who functioned as a "black caucus" concerning matters of particular interest to Negroes. At the General Conference in New York he delivered an impassioned address in defense of extending the tenure of Methodist ministers from three to five years, favored making the Committee on Prohibition a standing rather than a special committee because of "the monster of alcohol," and vigorously opposed a measure he believed would subvert the original purpose of the denomination's Freedman's Aid Society. In Omaha he was largely responsible for the election of his friend Edward W. S. Hammond as editor of the *Southwestern Christian Advocate*, the church paper published for its Negro membership. At neither conference was his name prominently linked with efforts of the "black caucus" to secure the election of a Negro bishop, although he appears to have supported the idea. He later became an enthusiastic participant in the movement and lived to witness the election of two Negroes to the episcopacy in 1920.[48]

Knox could scarcely have been unaware of the criticism leveled against those blacks who chose to remain in the predominantly white Methodist Episcopal Church rather than abandoning it for one of the black Methodist denominations. Typical of such criticism were editorials in the *New York Freeman* denouncing blacks within the Northern Methodist Church as a "class of cringing Negroes" who were always "dodging and sliding" in order to satisfy both whites and blacks.[49] Knox was always quick to defend those blacks in the Northern Methodist Church, and, as for himself, he was certain that he could do more for his race by retaining his membership in it than by affiliating with one of the black Methodist groups.[50] Nothing perhaps better exemplified his racial philosophy than his membership in a segregated all-black subdivision of a white denomination. Such an arrangement was a practical demonstration of Booker T. Washington's famous analogy of the relationship between the hand and the fingers to describe the relationship between blacks and whites—"separate as the fingers in all things purely social," yet "one as the hand in all things essential to mutual progress."

Although the church was always one of Knox's central concerns, it was by no means his only interest outside those of a purely economic or political nature. Not long after moving to Indianapolis he joined the Douglass Literary Society, one of the city's best-known black cultural organizations, and later served as its president for six successive terms.[51] Both his familiarity with the Bible and his reading in ancient history and classical literature were evident in his oratory, which in the fashion of the day tended to be florid and verbose. A skilled debater and perennial master of ceremonies at special events, such as visits to the city by Frederick Douglass and Booker T. Washington, Knox figured prominently in virtually all cultural, social, and charitable movements in the city's black community from the late 1880s until his death. A member of the Odd Fellows and various other fraternal orders, he also actively participated in the Afro-American League and the Anti-Lynching League and in 1895 was a sponsor of the Colored Benevolent Society, a subdivision of the Indianapolis Charity Organization. Always interested in the Christian training of youth, he was one of the founders of the Colored Branch of the Indianapolis YMCA, which he served for a time as president. In recognition of his service Madame C. J. Walker, a wealthy manufacturer of cosmetics for blacks, commissioned a well-known artist to paint a portrait of him which for years hung in the Colored YMCA Building.[52]

In view of his strong commitment to the Republican party and his previous political activities, it was natural that Knox should become involved in politics in Indianapolis. In general, he employed the same tactics that he had used in Greenfield: he assiduously courted the favor of prominent white Republicans, especially those who patronized his barbershops; at the same time he established himself within the black community through his success as an entrepreneur and as an active participant in church and civic affairs. Despite the overt resentment of some veteran black politicians in Indianapolis who viewed him as an interloper, Knox increasingly assumed a role in party affairs which relegated them to the status of "back numbers." By the early 1890s and for years afterwards, he was generally recognized as the preeminent black Republican in Indiana. Although he was frequently mentioned as a candidate for the state legislature and occasionally boomed for federal posts such as minister to Haiti and register of the treasury, he never held any public office. His was the role of a "black Warwick," who exercised power and influence bestowed upon him by the white Republican hierarchy.[53]

Knox won the confidence of party leaders during a period of political uncertainty in the late 1880s and early 1890s. Confronted by rumblings of discontent and threats of political independence by parts of the black constituency,[54] white Republicans were quick to appreciate the value and services of so reliable a black man as Knox, a prosperous, honorable citizen who preached party regularity and shared many of their views on public issues. In return for his labors to keep black voters loyal to the party of Lincoln, the Republican hierarchy provided Knox with the means of functioning as a political broker within the black community where his influence was often decisive in determining strategy and in the distribution of patronage. The arrangement that came to exist between Knox and the white Republican elite closely resembled what has been termed "clientage politics, or patron-client politics" in which middle-class blacks "fashioned personalized links with influential whites for a variety of socio-political purposes."[55] The support that Knox received from Roger R. Shiel, John K. Gowdy, and other key figures in Indiana Republicanism tended to lend substance to his claims of political leadership in the black community.

Such claims, however, encountered strong challenges from various black Republicans who had previously acted as spokesmen of racial interests. In particular the *Indianapolis World*, a black weekly owned and edited by Levi Christy, resented references to Knox as "*the* colored man in this town."[56] The *World*, launched as a Republican paper, assumed an independent position in 1888 and ultimately embraced the Democratic party four years later. In 1892 it led the attack on Knox, claiming that he had been "thrust forward as the leader of Negroes" by white Republicans. The *World* condemned the party leadership for overlooking the services of such veteran black Republicans as Dr. S. A. Elbert and J. S. Hinton in order to "pile up honors on Mr. Knox who has never done the party any service because he could not for lack of ability to do so."[57] Even those friendly to Knox admitted that "his growing proportions" in party affairs had alienated important elements in the black community because of the widespread belief that he was a leader of blacks chosen by whites.[58]

As proof that Knox did not qualify as a "race leader," his enemies called attention to the fact that he ran a "colorline barbershop" which refused service to blacks. "A man who runs a business where he discriminates against his own people," the *World* declared, "has no right to pose as a leader of his race." In its view Knox was a "white man's nigger."[59] Although the same journal had lauded him a few months earlier for providing employment for many blacks in his barbershops, it nonetheless maintained that the racial policy of those establishments disqualified him for a position of political leadership. For a decade beginning in 1892 the question of Knox's "colorline barbershops" provided a convenient weapon for those opposed to his racial philosophy or envious of his position within the Republican party structure. Although he once was quoted as denouncing the charge as "a lie," the fact was that he did operate barbershops for "whites only."[60] Since Knox believed that the prevailing racial atmosphere allowed him no alternative if his barbering establishments were to prosper, he rationalized that criticism of his policy emanated only from those blacks "with nothing substantial to offer" but fanciful theories. "Negroes who engage in business of any kind," he once remarked, "are usually criticized most severely by Negroes who are incapable of engaging in any kind of business for themselves."[61]

Despite the fulminations of his critics, it was obvious by 1892 that Knox, more than any other black Republican, enjoyed the confidence and support of the state's party leaders. In May 1892 the *Indianapolis News*, a leading white daily, noted that he seemed "to be coming into prominence by lumps."[62] Within the first six months of that year he added the Grand Hotel shop to his barbering enterprises, was reelected a delegate to the General Conference of the Methodist Church, and purchased the *Freeman*, an independent black weekly with Democratic proclivities which he transformed into a staunchly Republican journal. But more indicative of his growing political stature was his appointment to the State Republican Central Committee—the "first Afro-American thus honored in Indiana"[63]—followed shortly afterward by his selection as an alternate delegate at-large to the Republican National Convention. Though chosen as an alternate, Knox actually functioned as a full-fledged delegate when Stanton J. Peelle, a recent appointee to the court of claims decided not to attend the convention. At the convention in Minneapolis, Knox attracted considerable attention for his eloquent defense of Benjamin Harrison whose bid for renomination encountered serious opposition from various elements within the Republican party, including some blacks. He used his influence to keep the "black and tan" delegations from the South loyal to the president and to thwart the activities of an unofficial group of Negro Republicans from Indiana who came to the convention to demonstrate their support for James G. Blaine. Whenever it was charged that the president was not favorably disposed toward blacks, the Harrison managers would arrange for Knox to meet the individual making the charge and engage him in debate.[64] Following the renomination of Harrison, Knox took an active part in the campaign. Aside from speeches delivered in various parts of Indiana, he used his newly acquired newspaper to extol the virtues of Harrison and the Republican party.

On July 1888 the *Freeman* had been launched by Edward E. Cooper, an unabashed political opportunist, who began the paper as an advocate of political independence and ultimately committed it to the support of the Democratic party. Though an imaginative and resourceful editor who made the *Freeman* a showpiece of Negro journalism, described as the "Harper's Weekly of the Colored race," Cooper possessed little business finesse. Because he lived in such "swell" style and spent far more on the newspaper than advertising and circulation receipts warranted, he was chronically in debt. Within a few years the paper was heavily mortgaged. Among those who held mortgages on the *Freeman* was Knox, who finally purchased it in 1892 when Cooper could no longer ward off his creditors.[65] Cooper remained on the staff of the paper for a few months, but its political affiliation changed immediately. As soon as Knox purchased it, the *Freeman* threw its support behind the Harrison campaign and thereafter for more than thirty years remained loyal to the national Republican party.

Although Knox again served as an alternate delegate at-large to the Republican National Convention in 1896 and continued to maintain close contact with the Republican leadership in Indiana for some years, his role in party politics was never as visible or significant as it had been in 1892. Beginning in the mid-1890s, the Republican party in the state became increasingly indifferent to the Negro vote; the margin of its victories was sufficiently large that it no longer felt compelled to cultivate black voters, and indeed many white Republicans came to view the party's black constituency as a distinct liability.[66] Unfortunately, Knox's autobiography ends with the political campaign during the fall of 1894 and therefore does not provide a chronicle of his reactions to this drift in Republican politics in Indiana which became obvious shortly thereafter. But from various other sources it is possible to ascertain how he adjusted to the new situation. Clearly, he did not suddenly abandon the Republican party and for a time insisted that blacks should place politics lower on their list of priorities. According to an editorial in his newspaper in 1900 which obviously reflected his views, "education, respectability and worth are the shibboleths; politics incidentally." Politics was "not a god to be worshipped above everything else" especially since "more downright good" accrued "to the race from other sources."[67]

That Knox encouraged blacks to place less emphasis on political activity did not mean that he forsook politics. Despite an inclination to embrace an optimistic view of "the progress of the race" and to reject the Democratic party as a feasible alternative for black voters, he grew increasingly resentful of the indifference of Indiana Republicans toward the political aspirations of Negro citizens. For reasons that are not clear this resentment came to focus on Jesse Overstreet, who had first been elected a Republican congressman from the Indianapolis district in 1894. The two men had both served on the State Republican Central Committee two years earlier and Knox had vigorously supported Overstreet until about 1903. In the following year he announced his intention to challenge Overstreet by running as an independent for his congressional seat—a decision strenuously opposed by his friend Booker T. Washington. While Knox emphasized that he was not fighting the Republican party but rather a particular white Republican in whose district blacks held the balance of power, he nonetheless declared: "The time has come when the Negro should cease to be a subservient tool of any party and should make himself an independent factor. If we go on year after year supporting a party whose representatives in office do nothing substantial toward the advancement of our race, because they look upon our support as a matter of course, we never will achieve any tangible results ourselves. Everybody will respect us more if we think and act for ourselves."[68] Knox denounced Overstreet for ignoring his black constituents, not so much for excluding them from political patronage, but rather for his failure to support causes which "in a broader sense" contributed to the "advancement of our race." Specifically, he castigated Overstreet for his refusal to support a measure to reduce the congressional representation of those southern states which disfranchised black citizens.[69]

While Knox was circulating a petition in an effort to get his name on the ballot as an independent, Archibald A. Young, Overstreet's campaign manager, released a statement charging that Knox's candidacy was a "Democratic trick." Young maintained that Knox had decided to enter the race only after a lengthy conference with Thomas Taggart, the former mayor of Indianapolis who had recently become chairman of the Democratic National Committee. Another Overstreet partisan, William E. English, declared that Taggart had "gone a' niggerin' " and was last "seen in the vicinity of Knox." Even Roger R. Shiel, a white Republican with whom Knox had been closely allied in the early 1890s, attributed his candidacy "to the fact that he was getting old." Knox, like many other blacks in Indianapolis, respected Taggart but categorically denied Young's charge in a sworn affidavit. At any rate, the leading white Republicans in the city, as well as many prominent blacks, some of whom still harbored resentment against Knox for preempting their places in the party structure, vigorously opposed him, claiming that he could not possibly win and that his candidacy would only split the Republican vote and insure the election of a Democrat. In addition to using their considerable financial resources to thwart Knox's candidacy, the Overstreet forces repeatedly impugned his personal integrity by claiming that he was in the pay of the Democrats. It was also charged that the congressman's partisans attempted to apply economic pressure upon Knox both by urging whites not to patronize his barbershops and by encouraging blacks to resist the "white only" policy maintained by these establishments.[70]

Although Knox acquired six times the required number of signatures on his petition, the County Board of Election Commissioners, made up of two Republicans and one Democrat, voted two to one not to allow his name to appear on the ballot unless he proved that each signature was that of a legal voter. In view of the fact that the board's

28

decision was made only two weeks before the election date, the stipulation requiring him to validate each name was tantamount to denying his petition. Convinced that the decision was wholly unjust and contrary to all precedent, Knox took the matter to court seeking a writ of mandamus to force the placing of his name on the ballot. But when Overstreet's forces managed to prolong the proceedings so that it was impossible for the court to render a decision in time to meet the deadline for the printing of the ballots as established by law, Knox chose to abandon his legal struggle. At his request the court dismissed the suit. On November 7, 1904, the day before the election, Knox issued a statement describing his treatment at the hands of Overstreet's "henchmen" as "an outrage upon all self-respecting Negroes throughout this city." Although Overstreet was reelected, Knox was correct in claiming that he could no longer rely upon Indianapolis's black voters for solid support. On election day, many blacks, unwilling to vote Democratic and angered by the Republican congressman's treatment of Knox, went to the polls with "pasters"—tabs containing Knox's name—which they pasted on the ballot over the name of Overstreet.[71] When four years later Overstreet suffered a stunning defeat, Knox maintained that his efforts in 1904 had been vindicated.

Knox's abortive attempt to run for Congress as an independent marked a turning point in his relations with the Republican party. The so-called Brownsville affair in 1906 which prompted President Theodore Roosevelt to dismiss two battalions of black soldiers without honor posed additional difficulties for so loyal a party man as Knox. The shifting editorial position of his newspaper during the prolonged agitation over the affair pointed up his dilemma: despite his reluctance to attack a Republican president, he was nonetheless unwilling to defend the dismissal of the black troops. Whatever his misgivings about the outcome of "this ugly muddle" or his disappointment with Roosevelt's intransigence, he counseled black Americans to remain loyal to the "party of Lincoln" in presidential elections and to support Roosevelt's handpicked successor, William Howard Taft, in 1908.[72]

Although Knox himself continued to support the Republican ticket in national elections and regularly attended the party's national conventions as a spectator, he encouraged black voters in Indiana to demonstrate their political independence in state and local contests. The extent of Knox's alienation from the state Republican organization became evident in 1907 when he and Indiana Congressman James E. Watson shared the platform at an Emancipation Day celebration in Anderson. Immediately following a brief address in which he expressed contempt for the racist antics of Senator Benjamin R. Tillman of South Carolina, Watson left before the conclusion of the ceremonies. Knox used the time allotted to him to denounce Watson's behavior as typical of northern white Republicans, that is, their practice of engaging in rhetorical battles against southern racists within the safe confines of political stumps north of the Mason-Dixon Line rather than with legislative action in Congress and their habit of speaking to black audiences and fleeing before the conclusion of the program in order to avoid fraternizing with individual Negroes.[73]

During the next decade Knox found little in the performance of the Republican party in Indiana to inspire the confidence of the state's black voters. Although he endorsed Republican candidates for national office and was enthusiastic about the nomination of Warren Harding for president in 1920 because of his stand against lynching, his advocacy of independence in local and state politics by that date had prompted widespread speculation regarding his real party affiliation. Rumors to the effect that he was a "democrat in disguise" had become so common by April 1920 that Knox felt compelled to set the record straight. In a speech at Penick Chapel AME Church in Indianapolis, he denounced such rumors as "false and mischievous," as the work of his political enemies. "Ever since I was 16 years of age," he declared, "I have been with my people in all that it means to stay with one's people." For him racial loyalty meant loyalty to the historic tenets of the Republican party. "I am," he concluded, "a more true republican than all my critics put together. I am, and have always been, a republican." Because of his loyalty to what he perceived as the party's original principles, he was all the more concerned about the drift of Indiana Republicanism which in his view had increasingly demonstrated that it was "out of sympathy with its colored adherents." He therefore called upon the state's Republican leaders in 1920 to abandon the "nefarious practice of ignoring its colored followers" lest they sap the party of its strength and reduce it to minority status. The rise of the Ku Klux Klan early in the decade served only to deepen his disillusionment with

30

Republican leadership at all levels. Finally, in 1924, when the Klan had become a power in Indiana Republicanism, he called upon black citizens to support the Democratic ticket, nationally as well as locally.[74]

From the late 1890s on, Knox devoted his attention primarily to his barbershops, church affairs, and, especially, his newspaper. The *Freeman* was essentially a family enterprise whose financial operations were under the direct control of Knox and his son Elwood. Under their ownership and management it moved to larger quarters in 1893 and proclaimed itself "a national race paper." Its profusely illustrated pages regularly included literary and historical essays, columns devoted to the interests of homemakers, farmers, and mechanics, and correspondence from black communities, large and small, from Georgia to California. The *Freeman* contained little "patent matter," ready-made copy purchased by weeklies primarily for the purpose of adding national and international news. Knox took great pride in the amount and quality of original composition which appeared in his journal. A few years after he assumed direction of the *Freeman*, it began to devote more attention to sports and theatrical news and introduced a page entitled "The Waiter" edited by W. Forrest Cozart, organizer of the Afro-American Headwaiters' Mutual Benefit Association in 1899. By the second decade of the twentieth century theatrical news took up as much as one-fourth of each edition of the *Freeman*, making the newspaper an indispensable source of information about black actors, theatrical companies, music, and musical organizations in the era. For a time a subsidiary of the Freeman Company, known as E. C. Knox and Company and described as "music publishers of Indianapolis," specialized in the publication of songs popular on the black theatrical circuit. That Edward Thompson Knox, the stepson of Elwood, was a well-known actor with the Lafayette Players may have contributed to the *Freeman*'s interest in theatrical and musical matters.[75]

Although the *Freeman* retained the format begun by Cooper, the financial aspects of its operation underwent a thoroughgoing reorganization under Knox. Not the least of the changes occurred in the job-printing department of the Freeman Publishing Company, which Knox transformed into a highly profitable enterprise. Under his direction both advertising receipts and subscription sales increased dramatically. In keeping with its claims as a "national race paper" the *Freeman* attracted advertisements from sources far beyond Indianapolis or even Indiana. Theatrical companies and various manufacturers of cosmetics for blacks were among the more frequent advertisers in the paper. In addition to periodic subscription campaigns, Knox kept several "traveling agents" in the field, especially in the South, in an effort to build up circulation in the section of the country where a majority of blacks resided. On occasion such agents served both as subscription and advertising salesmen and as reporters. For a time Knox had an arrangement with Pullman porters whose runs passed through Indianapolis, to pick up and distribute the weekly editions of the *Freeman*. Late in the 1890s the newspaper began to provide more extensive coverage of growing black communities in northern cities and ultimately established bureaus in several such cities. For more than a dozen years Richard W. Thompson, a veteran journalist closely identified with Booker T. Washington who formerly lived in Indianapolis, served as the *Freeman*'s correspondent in Washington, D.C. His weekly reports from the nation's capital were especially rich in political news of interest to blacks. By the turn of the century the *Freeman* boasted that it possessed the largest circulation of any black journal in America. By its own calculations the paper had a weekly circulation of 16,000 in 1903. This figure had risen to 20,000 a decade later. The black press generally agreed that the *Freeman* was one of the most important black publications in America and that its annual Christmas editions which usually consisted of twenty or more pages constituted "Negro journalism at its best."[76]

Following the departure of Cooper in 1892, a succession of talented writers including Allison Sweeney, Julius Cox, and W. Milton Lewis served as editors of the *Freeman*. But their editorials always reflected Knox's philosophy and views on public issues. Because his views coincided so completely with those of Booker T. Washington, it is not surprising that the *Freeman* became one of the earliest and most persistent journalistic advocates of the Tuskegee philosophy. In commenting on Washington's Atlanta Address in 1895, it was effusive in its praise of the man as well as his speech. "What wonderful equipoise of mind and judgment rare," it concluded, "to have made a speech with no offensive words for whites or blacks."[77] From 1895 on, Knox and the *Freeman* remained closely allied with Washington; it endorsed his formula of race relations, defended him against critics in the black community, and repeatedly proclaimed that "if the Negro will be saved, he must save himself."[78] Like Washington, Knox remained steadfast in his conviction that the South was "the field of the Negro's future progress." He consistently opposed any mass exodus of blacks out of the South to either the North or the West and condemned "back-to-Africa" movements whether advocated by Bishop Henry M. Turner in the 1890s or Marcus Garvey in the 1920s. No less strident were his criticisms of those blacks given to lawlessness and vagrancy who, in his opinion, added immeasurably to the existing burdens of the whole race. Among the favorite editorial themes of the *Freeman* were discourses on "the colored men in business" which extolled the virtues of work, the acquisition of wealth, and "clean living."[79]

Not content with mere words, Knox was one of the first to make substantial investments in the black-owned Fidelity Savings and Loan Association established in Indianapolis in 1892 and was a director of the Frederick Douglass Life Insurance Company which, launched in 1913, claimed to be the "first insurance company ever organized by colored men in Indiana." Long active in the Negro National Business League, which Washington founded in 1900 and headed until his death fifteen years later, Knox served the organization in various official capacities, including that of first vice president. Visits to Tuskegee, itself a showpiece of black enterprise, served to strengthen his conviction that "the brightest future of the race" lay in pursuing Washington's approach.[80]

For a decade and a half after 1895, Knox used his newspaper to promote Washington's "industrial idea" and to focus attention on his personal achievements. The *Freeman* regularly published material supplied by Washington and followed his suggestions regarding subjects worthy of editorial comment. Because Knox consistently sought to protect "every interest of Dr. Washington's,"[81] he refused to publish anything that reflected adversely upon the Tuskegean and his philosophy. "We have often cut out many damaging articles concerning Dr. Washington and the Institute," he wrote in 1911.[82] Fully aware of the value of Knox's support, Washington repaid his loyalty by heavily

33

advertising Tuskegee Institute in the *Freeman* and by lending other types of financial aid. Although his newspaper had been supporting Washington enthusiastically since the Atlanta Address of 1895, it was not until six years later that Knox requested a contribution. "If you feel that our services in your behalf are of any material interest and if you desire to assist us . . . ," Knox wrote Washington in January 1901, "we will be pleased to accept your check for any amount you think we are entitled."[83] Washington responded with a check for five dollars. Thereafter, Knox periodically received subsidies from Tuskegee, the largest being eighty dollars to "cover expenses of the Holiday [Christmas] edition" of 1903. On at least one occasion, in 1905, he obtained a loan of $150 from Washington.[84] Because of the relationship between Washington and the *Freeman*'s owner, W. E. B. Du Bois characterized Knox as one of the pro-Tuskegee "bribe-takers" among black publishers, who stifled all criticism of Washington in return for financial support. Whatever the validity of Du Bois's charge, there is no evidence that Knox, like certain other black publishers, ever became financially dependent upon Tuskegee.[85]

Nor is it correct to assume that no differences existed between Knox and Washington. Despite pronouncements about the secondary importance of politics, Knox never attempted to obscure his political activity as Washington did. In fact, he was inclined to boast publicly of his role in party affairs. Nor is it likely that Washington would have been as bold as Knox was in 1896 in demanding the removal of legal restrictions against interracial marriage in Indiana. But this is not to imply that Knox was always consistent in his approach to the "race problem." Notwithstanding his enthusiasm for vocational training and criticism of the "inflated notions about education" held by the opponents of Washington, he regretted what he viewed as the erosion of the "old literary spirit" and spoke approvingly of "an aristocracy of letters."[86] And while outspoken in his condemnation of lynching and various forms of discrimination, Knox denied any interest in "social equality" and in 1897 strongly opposed a bill to abolish racially segregated schools in Indiana. Actually he was in large part responsible for the failure of the measure. Although he condemned the bill on the grounds that it would result in the closing of black schools which in turn would subject black "children of tender age to the hardships of traveling long distances" to attend mixed schools, his main concern was that the measure would result in a displacement of black teachers.[87] At times Knox assumed the position of a thoroughgoing accommodationist and at others one that seemed to place him among the more militant elements of the black community. On occasion he was altogether capable of pursuing both simultaneously.

From the mid-1890s to about 1904 Knox's utterances on racial concerns exhibited an accommodationist tone that prompted some anti-Washington elements to describe him as belonging to that species of "fawning 'race leaders' " who were "capable of heaping insult on their own people for a grin from a white man."[88] Although such descriptions were scarcely justified, some of his pronouncements seemed so far removed from reality that they invited ridicule. For example, an editorial in his newspaper late in 1899, at a time when others spoke of the precarious condition of blacks in America, declared: "Take it all in all there is but little reason [for Negroes] to be dissatisfied with conditions in this country. All phases of the race problem are in a more satisfactory stage of solution. It behooves the race to contend for greater rights in a spirit consonant with the age, recognizing the fact that the little besetments are the mile-stones that punctuate the way to the ultimate good."[89]

Late in 1901 Knox elaborated upon his racial philosophy in a lecture entitled "The American Negro and His Possibilities" which he delivered in Memphis, Atlanta, and various other cities in the South. A revised version of the lecture later appeared in *Twentieth Century Negro Literature*, a large volume of essays on "vital topics" written by "one hundred of America's greatest Negroes." In his lecture-essay Knox argued that slavery had been "a redeeming institution to the American Negro" who, "thrown upon his own resources," was well along the way toward sharing in the nation's wealth. Despite "the lowering clouds and muttering thunders of the present," he predicted a bright future for the race if only its masses could "be prodded up" to the standards set by Crispus Attucks, Booker T. Washington, and other leaders of the race. While he did not deny the existence of racial discrimination, he was convinced that the Negro masses failed to take advantage of those opportunities which were open to them and appeared to "be hedged about by a wall of indifference." The result was that the whole race, especially "the better Negro," suffered from the "slothfulness and lawlessness of some of its members." Nor, in his opinion, was the white man solely responsible for the prevalence of racial prejudice; Negroes themselves, especially "the new Negro," who had never experienced slavery and knew "only freedom," helped to increase prejudice and discriminatory laws because of his "indolence and vice." "No respectable class of men, white or black," he declared, "is going to be governed by a hoodlum element." Until the black masses learned the value of persistence, "courageous work," and moral character, they would bear the brunt of prejudice. That neither Booker T. Washington nor the class of blacks to which he belonged had been disfranchised was offered as proof of his contention that as Negroes in general emulated Washington's example of self-help, good citizenship, and the purposeful life, they too would escape the lash of prejudice. But for the race to rise to the full height of its possibilities, Knox maintained, each Negro must be "proud of his race and color" and recognize at the same time the necessity of learning to live in harmony with "his white brother." Unity of the races was no less important than racial unity, and those blacks who responded to discrimination and prejudice by displaying hate and bitterness toward whites exposed the race to a "whirlwind of destruction."[90]

Although Knox never completely abandoned the philosophy he articulated early in the twentieth century and consistently boasted that the *Freeman* was "the most conservative and modest in policy" of all black newspapers, he did modify his position on occasion, generally in the direction of a more forthright stand in defense of Negro rights. In his view Afro-Americans were more American than African and were entitled to all rights and privileges enjoyed by other citizens of the United States. Because Negroes had lived in America for almost as long as whites and had contributed to the making of the nation, Knox considered as altogether undesirable schemes designed to locate black Americans in separate, segregated territories or to transport them "back to Africa." For example, he described Moses Madden's proposition in 1920 to create an all-black state along the Rio Grande River as "an unmistakable attempt at Jim Crowing our people." But to the end of his life he disavowed any intent of making "inroads on the white people in a social way." Although he opposed laws prohibiting marriage between black and white, he was convinced that responsible citizens of both races should use their influence to discourage such marriages. Afro-Americans, Knox insisted, were not interested in "social equality," which was a bogus issue raised periodically by whites; rather black citizens were preeminently concerned with securing "equal justice."[91]

From 1917 until his death a decade later Knox raised his voice in behalf of various causes designed to secure such justice for black citizens. He repeatedly reprimanded the Republican party for ignoring its black constituency; spoke out vigorously against the revived Ku Klux Klan which came to occupy a dominant place in Indiana politics in the early 1920s; crusaded for better housing for the burgeoning black populations of northern cities; urged the passage of the Dyer federal antilynching bill in 1920 on the grounds that states had demonstrated their inability or unwillingness to stop the lynching evil; spoke approvingly of Monroe Trotter's National Equal Rights League in 1917; and endorsed the National Association for the Advancement of Colored People seven years later, urging Negroes of Indianapolis to unite under the banner of this organization.[92] But as always, Knox balanced his calls for racial unity with those for a unity of races, for the establishment of bonds of friendship between blacks and whites.

Amid the racial eruptions in 1919 Knox called upon blacks to exercise "much discretion" and to maintain "a sober and intelligent disposition toward the opposite race." While freely admitting that the oppression of blacks lay at the root of the "racial flare-ups," he nonetheless believed that cooperation and communication between "responsible" whites and blacks were essential to the prevention of continual race warfare. He consistently maintained that the existence of such cooperation in Indianapolis had spared the city of bloody riots like those in Chicago, Washington, and elsewhere.[93] In 1920, at the age of seventy-nine, he spearheaded a drive to create a fund for the orphaned son of a white man who had drowned while attempting to rescue two black children. In his remarks to a black audience convened to establish the fund, he declared: "I have always loved the white man. I have loved him from my infancy and as you can see that has been a long time." To substantiate this profession of love for whites, he told once again the story of his childhood in slavery and his indebtedness to a benevolent master.[94]

Despite his advanced age, Knox remained in remarkably good health. The years seemed to have enhanced his physical appearance. More portly than in his youth, he nonetheless stood erect with his broad shoulders thrown back and his head of snowy white hair tilted in a way that suggested self-confidence and pride. Always impeccably attired in dark, conservative suits and broad-brim hats, Knox was a familiar figure on the streets of Indianapolis, a man known and respected by peoples of all races and classes. Testimony to his unique status was his appointment in 1914 by Mayor Joseph E. Bell to a committee of five to distribute among various charities the monies derived from the operation of movie houses on Sunday. Although Knox sold his last barbershop in 1920 and allowed his son Elwood to assume greater responsibility for the management of the *Freeman*, he continued to devote attention to the paper and to fill numerous speaking engagements throughout the country. On a single day early in October 1920, for example, he presented an address on "Great Men" to the Douglass Literary Society and "a ringing political speech" at the local Republican headquarters in Indianapolis. For more than three decades he was a conspicuous figure at the annual meetings of the Afro-American Press Association, an organization in which he held various offices. He was also active in the Old Settlers' Club which restricted its membership to the families of black citizens who had resided in Indianapolis for thirty years or more. It was an exclusive organization which served to set the old residents apart from those who began to arrive in the city in increasing numbers after 1910.[95]

By that date two of Knox's children had died, William in 1892 at the age of twenty-five and Nellie in 1904 at the age of thirty-six. His wife Aurilla remained active in religious and civic affairs until about 1900 when her health began to deteriorate rapidly. Despite visits to California and Florida in "search of health," she failed to regain her strength and was for some years a semi-invalid. She died in 1910 at the age of sixty-five. Four years later, Knox married Mrs. Margaret Nickens, a socially prominent widow in Indianapolis. Always a devoted family man, he took great pride in his surviving son, Elwood, and was indulgent toward his grandchildren, Victoria and especially his namesake, George L. Knox, who was born in 1917.[96]

In World War I, as in the Spanish-American War,[97] Knox rallied to the defense of the flag and called upon all blacks to "declare themselves promptly on the side of their country." Although the war with Spain had failed to bestow upon Negroes the "rich harvest" which Knox envisioned, he nonetheless pursued a similar theme in 1917-1918, describing the conflict as holding "great hope for us—the Negroes of America" and reminding blacks that "everything considered," they had "very much to be thankful for" in the United States. Popular as a "patriotic" speaker throughout the war, Knox extolled the bravery of black men, urged the appointment of as many Negroes to military commissions "as can qualify," and advised blacks to purchase war bonds to demonstrate both their civic loyalty and their financial good sense. Early in the summer of 1918 he was among thirty-one prominent black men who attended a conference in Washington at the request of Emmett Scott, the special assistant to the secretary of war, who formerly had served as Booker T. Washington's secretary. This group drafted a "Bill of Particulars," recommending specific measures necessary to insure the solid support of the black community for the war effort.[98]

Following World War I, Knox's principal enterprise, the *Freeman*, fell upon lean days in large part because of spiraling inflation and stiff competition from newspapers more attuned to the interest of the black community in the "new era." Evidence that all was not well with the *Freeman* appeared first late in 1917 when Knox attempted largely in vain to increase the number of local subscribers by expanding his coverage of news among blacks in Indianapolis and environs. Since his purchase of the newspaper, he had taken great pride in its "national" circulation. By World War I other, more "up-to-date," journals such as the *Chicago Defender* had emerged as serious competitors on the national scene. To revive the circulation of the *Freeman* within Indianapolis, Knox employed an experienced journalist from New Orleans, Gabriel Stanley, and placed him in charge of local news in October 1917 and launched a much publicized subscription campaign which offered a Briscoe automobile as the prize for the person selling the largest number of subscriptions. In mid-June 1918 the "*Freeman* distribution truck" made its first appearance on the streets of the city. Despite these efforts, the *Freeman* made few inroads into the local circulation of its principal competitor, the *Indianapolis Recorder*, which had consistently specialized in the coverage of city and state news. In August 1920 the high cost of paper forced a reduction in the format of the *Freeman* and an increase in its price. The financial strain was all the more acute because Knox had gone into debt to purchase up-to-date printing equipment. Throughout the early 1920s the paper continued publication but even with its more modest format it often operated at a deficit. Finally, in January 1926, the *Freeman* suspended publication, and Knox entered a plea of voluntary bankruptcy. Its debts were listed at $6,000 while its assets amounted to only $700. The Negro press generally noted with regret the passing of what the *Cleveland Gazette* called "one of our oldest publications."[99]

Undaunted by the demise of the *Freeman*, Knox at the age of eighty-six traveled to North Carolina and Virginia to assist black editors in those states with subscription campaigns. On August 24, 1927, while visiting his old friend John Mitchell, editor of the *Planet*, in Richmond, Virginia, he suffered a paralytic stroke. Rushed to St. Phillip's Hospital he died later the same day. Following funeral services at his beloved Simpson Chapel on August 29, the throng of mourners moved to Crown Hill Cemetery where he was buried. The press, black and white, noted the passing of "the dean of Negro publishers"[100] whose personal philosophy was summarized in a statement which had appeared on the masthead of the *Freeman:* "If a newspaper does not take a cheerful, hopeful and constructive view of things, it is not a healthful force in the community. This paper exists to render service to society. It will not become rabid, yellow or truculent."[101] In spite of the strictures imposed upon him by a segregated society and the criticism from blacks who disagreed with his philosophy of race relations, Knox never succumbed to bitterness or despair and remained firm in his conviction that a bright future awaited Afro-Americans.

PART ONE

From Slavery to Freedom:
TENNESSEE, 1841-1864

M Y FATHER'S NAME WAS CHARLES KNOX AND MY MOTH-
er's Nancy Fisher. They were married about 1838. Although
my mother was born free, when my grandmother died, she was sold
into slavery. No one had the courage to take up her cause, so she
remained in slavery entailing the curse upon her children. My father
had always been a slave. There were three children, the oldest a girl
named Huldah,[1] and two boys, Charles[2] and George L., myself. I was
born Sept[ember] 16, 1841. I retain but a faint recollection of my
mother, my father dying about two years and a half following her de-
cease. When I was about three years old my old master died. He
owned many slaves and as was the custom of that country, had to be
sold. We were taken to a small town by the name of Statesville [Ten-
nessee],[3] where the Negro-traders gathered from every part of the
country to buy slaves to take further South and sell. It was a sad time
for those to be separated, perhaps forever. Mothers were sold from
their babes, husbands and wives were rent asunder, traders examining
them as they might have done horses, looking into their mouths and
testing the limbs of men and women alike, while the cry of the auc-
tioneer and the moan of the poor slaves, who were to be sold, added a
picturesque sadness to the scene. Our family was more fortunate than
the others owned on the place, in that "old master" always seemed desirous to extend us special consideration. We were sold to the children
of our old master. One of my young mistresses bought my sister, the
other my brother, while my young master bought myself, I being so
small that my father held me on the auction block while I was sold. As
others did not want to bid against the children, I was knocked off to
my young master[4] for $300. Not being a married man, he made his
home with his sister, hiring me out for my board and clothes. There I
stayed for five or six years, bound to a family, who were strict Presby-
terians and very pious, especially the older members. They did not allow me to pick up an ax on the Sabbath day or do any kind of work.
They kept me very close. There were times for months that I was not
permitted to leave the place. When I was given leave of absence, generally on Sabbath evenings, it made me so glad that I would run most
of the way to the place I was going. I would visit my brother or
grandmother, and when my leave of absence had expired my heart became heavy and sad to think that I had to return to the plantation there

to remain for another six months. If I happened to make one misstep I would not be given the privilege to go again perhaps for a year. While I was bound out, I learned to do all kinds of farm work. I never made but one trade in my life, and that was with a white boy who lived on the place. He had an old blind mare he used to haul rails up and down the hill. I gave him the only five cents I had on earth to let me ride and drive that old blind mare one afternoon. After our day's work was done I begged him to give me my five cents back, it being the only one I had ever had. I did not know when I would get another. He finally gave it back to me and plagued me about it so much that I vowed I never would ask again to be released from a trade I had made, which vow I always kept.

One time my master being a guest at the plantation where I was hired, in the morning when he came out on the porch to bathe his face, I slipped up to him and in a low tone begged him to take me away, as I did not want to live there any longer. He therefore took me back to Statesville, about three miles from where I had been sold and hired me out to one Dr. H. Knight.[5] My new employer lived in the town and owned a plantation. He placed me on the farm to work, where I stayed about one year. This was another hard place. They did not allow me to go on the streets, but kept me very close. After his father's death, my master taught school until he went into the mercantile business. In the meantime I was hired out to a man by the name of Daniel Boyd,[6] who put me at the tanner's trade, but which I did not finish. About this time my master married a poor girl, who had always had plenty, but for some reason my new mistress, who had never owned slaves, and I did not get along very well. I was next bound out to learn the shoe maker's trade and felt very proud that I was going to be a boot and shoe maker. It seemed to me that I would be given a prestige over the other slaves by not having to go on the farm to work, as I would be enabled to live in town. My master sold out his dry goods store and went into the country to teach school, so he hired me out again. I lived there about two years. One day when they were cutting wheat in June and something did not go to suit them I was brought up to be given a whipping. My master had always said when I needed a whipping to give it to me. I ran away in the mountains and stayed there about a day. My master had gone to court that day about seventeen miles away, so they told my mistress that they had undertaken to whip me and I had run away, and wanted to know what they had better do. She informed them that my master thought more of me than he did of her and that they had better be a little careful. Then they sent for me to come in out of the woods. I got off by being struck two licks. Everything went smoothly then and after awhile we moved back to town again. This was in 1856, at which time I was set to learning the shoe maker's trade.

I recall a significant incident, as marking the premonition of coming changes, felt by the master classes, which happened when I was about sixteen years old, setting the whole community agog. Many of the colored people were inclined to trade and speculate. One of the things traded was a bugle which was gotten by a man by the name of Wash Smith. That was about five weeks before the Christmas week— a season of great pleasure and rejoicing among the slaves—it being the custom to give them that whole period between Christmas and New Year. The rumor got out that the slaves were going to rise and kill all the white people. I was staying at home and slept in my master's house. He asked me when the Negroes were going to rise. I said to him "what is that." It was something I had never heard of before in my life, and he said "they were going to rise up and kill all the whites." I said "I had not heard anything about it." He said, "is it not a fact that Wash had bought that bugle to sound the alarm for all the colored people to rise up." I told him that he had gotten the bugle in a trade. A meeting was called and the patrollers were started out in every district. If they caught a colored man out without a pass they hit him a certain number of licks on his back. As Christmas approached the excitement grew. The colored people were not allowed to leave their master's place unless they could give an account of themselves. The more the question was discussed the greater the excitement became. About two weeks before Christmas orders were issued that no colored man was to leave his master's premises unless sent for the doctor. If when their nightly visits were made, the patrollers failed to find the slaves at home they were to go back the next day and hit them thirty-nine licks with a raw cow-hide on their bare backs for being absent the night before. Orders were issued that two colored men were not to be seen talking together. They were not even allowed to talk to a poor white man for fear that they would take the Negro's part and aid him in the uprising. About four days before Christmas one Dr. McConnigan[7] who had been out in the country to see a patient, brought back the report that one of the leading Negroes in that part of the county had been captured and had been given five hundred licks. A report was circulated that there was a box of knives and pistols secreted in a hay and fodder stack, and a lot of guns in another stack and the excitement became very great. Orders were at once issued that the Negroes should not be permitted to leave their cabins at all.[8]

About the close of the holidays the excitement quieted down, and the colored people were restored their usual privileges. The patrollers rode now only on Saturday night, as that was the time the slaves were allowed a certain liberty. We began to talk over the great wrong that had been done, and the oppression that had been heaped upon us. Many wondered what would next take place and how they could stand such oppression. I was given a chance to speak and said "that in the midst of all the oppression, I could feel that freedom was not far away." About that time [in 1856] Fremont and Buchanan were running for President. The election was held, Fremont was defeated and Buchanan elected; then a gloom fell over our pathway, and freedom seemed further away than ever. Time passed on, and another campaign period was reached. We heard that a man by the name of Abraham Lincoln had been nominated by the "black Republicans," and on all sides he was cursed and reviled as a "darkey" and "nigger" lover.

In the town where I lived, Statesville, Lincoln received but one vote,[9] and I felt it would be impossible to elect him. When, however, the news reached us that he was really elected, the cloud seemed to move from our pathway, and we felt that freedom was coming. From a commercial standpoint the effect of the election of Lincoln was marked. The value of slave property began at once to fall. The excitement ran high and slave owners stood ready to dispose of their property at greatly reduced prices, until finally they could not sell at all. We heard that all the Southerners had resigned their positions in Congress. Then the Southerners began to congregate in the streets and talk war.

I stopped my shoe-making for a while and began engineering in a saw mill. I worked there until about the time the war broke out. The mill was right across the creek from the town and I could see the crowds as they congregated to discuss the coming struggle. In April they resorted to their fifes and drums in calling for volunteers. They were anxious that the poor whites should go to war. They would say to them that the "Yanks" and "Abe" Lincoln wanted the "niggers" to marry their daughters and rob them of their wives. In this way they soon raised a company. The whole business became confused one day, so they took a notion that they would send to Lebanon [Tennessee] and have Bob Hatton[10] come out and make them a speech. He had resigned his seat in Congress and returned home. He came and in his speech said he would not advise anyone to go to war, but he said that as for himself he was going. They concluded that they would go too. The rich men who had money bought brown jeans and made suits for the military company and put red stripes up the pants and round the coats. Just before they got ready to go, some one said that red would draw fire from the cannon so they tore it all off.

At this time I had quit the saw mill business and gone to work in the tan yard. One morning as I and a man by the name of Wash Smith were walking up the street a boy hissed a bull dog on him, the brute biting him. As he turned back I picked up a boulder and knocked the dog down. That caused another commotion. I went to my work, but Smith stayed to explain. The lady of the house went to bed from nervous prostration because I had struck her dog. They had us arrested. My master said he would spend $500 before I should be struck a lick. He had on his uniform getting ready to go to the army. That made him much more dear to me to think he would stand by me when so many men were deserting their slaves. This was about the latter part of April [1861]. The time had now arrived for the volunteers to leave their homes, and the girls promised that if they would go and fight and save their slaves that they would marry them when they returned home. The wealthy men promised to care for the families of the poor. Just before the soldiers got ready to leave, Capt. [Albert G.] Carden[11] made a speech to his company and told them that one southern man could run five northern men by just leveling his gun at them, that the Yanks were cowards. Some one added, it would be a breakfast spell. An older man replied that if they got through by dinner they would be doing well. Sunday morning we had orders to go. It was a sad sight. Mothers, fathers and sweethearts separating perhaps forever. I had orders to take my mistress to her father about fifty miles away. I had never been but about seventeen miles away from home in my life. I was twenty-one and had never heard a locomotive whistle and had never seen a steam car. After I had reached Murfreesboro, in company with my master, I began to realize my condition. They had all had their cry and I had to have mine. We went out about three miles from Murfreesboro and stopped there for about three days, but on Monday morning I took my master to the depot so he could take the cars and go to Nashville. We bid each other good-bye and we both shed tears. I felt that my only friend was gone; I began to think he would be killed and that I would be sold and carried away to the south. On my return home I accompanied my mistress to her father to stay until my master returned from the war. This was in Reliford county[12] where the slave-holders were very wealthy, some of them owning as high as 600 slaves. I heard the horn blow every morning at four o'clock and saw the slaves start out to their work to return about nine o'clock to get a piece of corn bread and bacon.

They called this part of Tennessee young Mississippi. It was here that I saw the first bull-whip. It was made of rawhide and had something like a forked end with a knot tied in it. They used it to whip the slaves, the forked end to split the hide. As we traveled on and before concluding our trip, we passed slave-holders living in splendor. When we got fifty miles away from home, I felt that the north never could whip the south. We stayed here for one year, as all the soldiers of the south were called for one year. Time passed on; the first Bull Run fight took place,[13] the Confederates winning a great victory. It was freely said that General [Winfield] Scott was too old to manage the Union Army, then another cloud came over my pathway. Nov[ember] came and Thanksgiving services were held. Rev. Dr. Moore preached. He spoke of their divine cause and charged the Yankees with not believing in any religion. He charged them with being polygamists and that they had burned the Bible and danced over its ashes. He preached a wonderful sermon about the victory they would gain. They had another fight soon after Thanksgiving at Fisher's Creek, Ky.,[14] the Union troops whipping, and some of the boys who went out so brave got so badly scared that they ran away and never stopped until they got home. My mistress was taken sick and I was called to fetch the doctor—the same doctor that preached the sermon. I had to show my sympathy for the south in order that they would not mistrust me. I wanted to tell the old doctor about the rebels being whipped so bad, but was at a loss how to broach the subject. I finally made a virtue of necessity, and blurted out that another fight had taken place, adding the Yankees had whipped. I knew that that would be bad news to him after preaching that Thanksgiving sermon, and the look that settled upon his face was a study. Time passed on; the fight commenced at Ft. Donaldson.[15] News came that the rebels were gaining the day. The fight went on, and about a week we heard that the Union army had whipped the rebels and were driving them back. The women began to get frightened; they had been told that the Union people had no respect for sex and that all kinds of depredations would be committed. They began to talk about what they would do with their sugar and meat. Some of them took it to the grave yard and buried it there. My master's wife's people were not much in sympathy with the slaveholders as they did not have slaves. I listened to hear what they would say, and they thought that they would all suffer alike. One evening the governor[16] passed in an omnibus and four horses making his way south. That caused the excitement to still grow higher. A little later on in the evening here come a man with a lot of horses and slaves making his way south. One of the white men asked the colored men what the news was. They said the Yankees were coming. This seemed to terrorize the community, and the wonder was what they would do with their slaves. They had been told that the Yankees had horns and were perfect heathens. By and by the Yankees came into that part of the country. They found them to be much nicer than their own soldiers, and they treated everybody more courteously.

My master now had served his time out for one year; he came home; they saw that they had made a mistake in taking one-year soldiers. The Confederate Congress passed a law, saying that all men who had served a year and were thirty-six years old could go home. [D. C.] Buel[l] and [Braxton] Bragg had made their great race across Tennessee and we went back to our home again. A law having been passed that all school teachers could stay at home, my master began teaching school,[17] while I went back to the shoe-making bench. One evening I overheard my master say that he had been offered $1500 in gold for me and now he could not get $500 in Confederate money. He also said if the Yankees came back any more he would take George and put him in front of the rebel army where the Yankees could not get him. This was in January, 1862. I made boots and sold them to the rebel soldiers as high as $16 a pair. I was working at my trade right along then. During the time the Stone River fight[18] was going on, in December '62; the slave-holders would go down to the battle-field and when their side seemed to be successful you could hear them yell and order the slaves around. They would go down the next day, and as it seemed the Union troops were winning, they would come back and say, "will you do so and so," and were as kind as could be to their slaves. On Sunday morning they gathered in the little town to hear the news. A man was seen coming down the road on a horse just as hard as he could ride. Some one asked him what the news was, and he said "the army is moving on to Murfreesboro and we have been defeated." This news just suiting me, I would go from house to house to deliver it, adding, "how bad it was that the Yankees had whipped us again." I put on as long a face as possible, but I was secretly rejoicing at the success of the Union army.

What was called the Conscript Act[19] was now put in force, and took everybody—school teachers, preachers and everybody that had been exempted before. It took in my master. He went to the rebel army again, this being in 1863. In March he came back and this time took me with him. So many of the southern boys had rich parents that they sent their slaves to wait on them. This so burdened the army that a law was passed, prohibiting any from having servants but officers. My master then put me with Capt. Phillips[20] as his servant as he could not have one; this was to keep me with the rebel army so that the Yankees could not get me; he was afraid he would lose me.

My master took me into the rebel army for safe keeping, and my first observation and experience with organized slave oligarchy was in a little town about twelve miles from home named Milton.[21] Here we entered the picket line of the rebel army, and the men who fought with Morgan, [Nathan Bedford] Forrest and Phillips were adventurous and daring fellows. This town, Milton, has since then become famous for lynching Negroes. We left Milton, passed through Woodbury and in the evening entered the camp of Captain Phillips. This

50

command was known as Phillips' Battalion. I cooked and waited upon my master and Captain Phillips also. Some few of Captain Phillips' men I knew, but the members of the other battalions I did not know. This was at a time when the masters could not do much to protect their slaves, and they feared they were about to lose all of them.

Day after day went on. Evenings, after I had gotten through with my work, I would take a walk around camp to see what was going on. The rebels at this time were very rough, swearing and cursing at every Negro they thought would be glad to leave them to go to the Yankees. They went out one day and captured some Union soldiers, and with them were a couple of colored men. Of course the rebels were very rough to these fellows because they felt they had been trying to get away from them. In order to save themselves from being severely punished, they declared they had been taken away from the rebels against their wishes by the Yankees. I was talking with them one day, and asked them what kind of a time they had while with the Yankees. They said they had a very good time and that the Yankees were in favor of giving us our freedom. I asked them if they liked it well enough to go back again. They said the first chance they got, they expected to. I would see them every day and we would talk over the situation. The rebels asked them if they liked to be with them; they replied yes, and insisted they did not want to get away; however the first opportunity that presented itself they made their escape.

We could see the Union troops in camp upon the top of the hill. The rebels were all the time cursing and swearing the Yankees would not fight. One day about 12 o'clock, General [Joseph] Wheeler and his staff came by and stopped at headquarters, and talked awhile. Of course, everybody who could stood around him to get a view of the great Southern General, of whom they had heard so much. I felt very low in spirits that day and did not care to see him myself, but the other colored boys went to see him. He was dressed in grand military elegance, and the boys talked about his manners, soldierly air, etc.

Every day the "Rebs" would send out "foragers," but as the Union troops had passed through this part of the country, it had made provisions very scarce. I was still lonely, and would, whenever I had the opportunity, seek the two colored men, who were laying plans to escape to the Yankees. I and the colored men had a talk one evening

51

and they thought they would go on that night, and so they did. The next morning when the roll was called, they came up missing. The "Rebs" then declared that they would never let another "nigger" go that had once been with the Yankees. This occurrence made them very angry and abusive to those who did not go. They felt that their colored men were not as safe as they should be. A few more days the Union troops moved on the rebel forces. The attack was rather unexpected, and if you ever saw an excited troop of soldiers it was those rebels. They were very much excited and feared being captured. That, however, was my greatest desire. I reasoned this way: If I were captured and taken away by the Yankees, and not satisfied, I could come back and the rebels would have nothing against me.

The fight did not last more than half a day, but the Union soldiers were driven back. The rebels felt sure and always believed that those two colored men, who had escaped, carried the news to the Union army and gave them information as to how strong they were. It was a cavalry fight on the "bushwhacking" order—fight and then run away. If a rebel soldier saw a colored man have on a good hat and he had an old one, he would drive up and take it off his head, throw his old hat at him and gallop away. After one month's experience in the rebel army I left it.

After I had been in the rebel army about one month and went through all the hardships that came up, I asked my master one day if I might not go home. I knew the time to ask him was when he was the most confident of success. When he thought that the Confederate army would be successful, then he was willing that I might go home. One day his company went foraging, so while they were cooking dinner and fixing to have a good time, the Union army at an unexpected moment rushed in and captured a lot of their horses and men, shooting some of the men. I had not yet forgotten my master's orders and one of the boys had to take a horse back that he had borrowed. I told him that my master said that I might go back home the first opportunity I had when there was anyone going back. He said all right. I saddled up my little filly and we started back home about eight o'clock in the morning, while they were still out fighting. It rained very hard and we traveled all day over the hills and across the mountains and we finally reached home. Everybody had gone from the country except the women and children, and I felt almost that the day of jubilee had come. I went to work on a farm. One day we were plowing and we seen a lot of Union soldiers coming and a great band of slaves following them. That night I concluded that I would go with the Yankees myself. When I got to town I found many of my acquaintances ready to go too. We had all met at Daniel Boyd's to lay out plans to leave. About this time a young lady for whom I had the greatest regard, came in and asked me what I was going to do. I replied nothing, but she said, "you are fixing to go away aren't you?" I said, "yes I am going with the Yankees to-night." She asked me not to go and began to cry.

When I saw her crying, I said, "I will not leave you until I have to." I went back to work next day and everything went well for about a month. One day when I was plowing my master came riding up, and I noticed he seemed worked up and out of patience. He said he did not condemn me for coming home, but thought I should have apprised him of my intent. I reminded him he had promised to let me come. He said he had come after me to go in the army again. He said the army was going to move and he was going to take me with him. I insisted I did not want to go, but he declared I must. He said that if I stayed here, the Union army would come and take me and he would lose me. He told me to saddle my filly and take it to the blacksmith shop to be shod as we would start to the army the next day. This was in May, 1863. I had my nag shod and returned home. My mistress, in the meantime, had ham and bread enough cooked and other provisions to last us two or three days while we were on our way. It was a rainy, damp evening in May and we were sitting by the side of an old-fashion[ed] fire place. I went in for the last time to remonstrate against going. I said to him that I did not want to go, and he replied that I must go. He said, "you wanted to go the first time," and I answered, "so did you want to go at first, but the last time you did not want to but they run the conscript and made you." He replied, "yes, and I am going to make you go this time." I replied I was like the fellow, "if I must, I must, but I hated it mighty bad."

I turned on my heels and looked at him for the last time. From that moment my mind was made up to run away. I sought my brother to tell him that I was going away, but he was not at home. I left word

53

there with a colored girl where he could find me. This was about the middle of May '63. I went to a place where a slave lived by the name of John Bigles.[22] I knew he had kept my cousin who had run away so I went to his house. I saw him, and he told me he could take care of me, but I would have to go to his wife's house. He told me that I would have to stay under the cabin floor where he kept my cousin. I said all right and about day-break before the children got up I went in under the floor. I could not sit up, and could do nothing but turn over and lay there all day. His wife who was a considerate soul kept a sharp lookout and passed what food I had through the floor to me. There was no basement to the house and it rested very close to the ground. I stayed there all day Thursday and Friday. There was an old colored lady on the place who told everything she knew. Had she known I was under there she would have told the whole neighborhood. They did not let her know anything about it. I could hear her talking about looking under the house to see if she could find some missing hens. I knew if she saw me I would be a "gonner."

Friday night I emerged from my hiding place, and John [Biggles] and I took a walk to talk over the situation. I told him that I had plenty of money to pay my way and him for whatever he did. I declared I could not stay under that house another day, so we arranged I should stay in the woods all day and at the house at night. On Sunday morning I went to my hiding place. About ten o'clock while sitting back in the bushes talking with a friend we noticed a couple of men coming on horseback as hard as they could ride. They proved to be the young masters of the man who was talking to me. They kept on, not observing us, until they reached the cabin. They went in and looked all about, under the house and everywhere. Some lady had told them she had seen their slave making his way toward the Yankees and they thought they would take him back. I stayed in that place until the following Sabbath. It was a desolate place and there was only one old man in that neighborhood and I could see him pass once in a while through that long dreary week. I would take a walk in the evenings on top of the hills and I would come out on a projecting rock and stand there and look for miles around and see the smoke as it would raise up and settle as though it would hide from the gaze of heaven the iniquity beneath. If I could have given utterance to my thoughts, it seemed I could have melted this wicked nation to tears. One may imagine how long the days were sitting there with not a solitary soul to speak to, hour after hour.

About the middle of the week my master sent one of his company home, with orders if I came back to capture and bring me to the rebel army. I had made up my mind to never go back. I could look from my hiding place and see the wheat fields that were just beginning to head. This was my second Sabbath in my new hiding place. I was always afraid of snakes, scorpions and lizards, and on Sunday morning they were thick there. The sun was shining very beautiful that morning, the birds were singing, and the hill was so steep that all I had to do was to lean over and view the panorama of teeming life beneath. I would look above when I heard a noise, only to be greeted by the snakey gaze of a coal black serpent about eight feet long. He would stop and lick his forked tongue out at me as though challenging my right to remain where I was. The reptiles were very thick and the exceeding quietness made them very bold. I lay over against the side of the hill and dropped into a troubled sleep. It seemed there was a snake in my bosom. I jumped about five feet and yelled like a wild man. When I found it to be but a dream I quieted down and looked to see if I had been discovered. No one had seen or heard me. I had been told the Sabbath before that the young lady who had wept at my departure was coming to see me. I sent her word that I did not think it safe for her to come as it might cause me to be discovered.

My brother came again and the same Ben Hill bringing word that my master said that George had either to go with him or the Yankees. I told my brother, who had concluded to accompany me, to get ready and come back and we would start that night. I had been waiting for the Union army to come by that I might get with them, word having come, however, that the Yankees were making their way back to Murfreesboro. The man who had been keeping me, and his uncle, about sixty years old, said they were going too and we decided to make the start at seven o'clock that Sunday night. I knew the country pretty well. It was about twenty-five miles from Murfreesboro. [John Hunt] Morgan's men and the bushwhackers were scouring the country in every direction, and this made it very dangerous. We started on our journey and as we come to the little villages we would turn aside and go around them. It seemed to me that all the dogs were loose and all the people up. As the Union army had passed that way that day, I gave orders that we would carry sticks, looking like guns, so we would be taken for soldiers, no one would tackle us. We heard that the bridge across Stone[s] River had been burned. When we come to the banks and viewed the burning bridge, our way looked dark and forbidding. I threw my head down and studied a minute which way to turn. We selected the left as the Union army had crossed that way and we passed over dry shod. We jumped and clapped our heels with satisfaction. We had traveled about eighteen miles. The picket line was about five miles out. We had heard that they did not allow anybody to pass and repass and the next thing was, how we were to get in, and what we would say when we got to the lines. I was to be the spokesman. Day had just begun to break; just about five miles out we struck a picket. He called us to halt and asked, "who comes there?" I said, "black men!" He permitted us to advance and said it was very fortunate for us that he was on guard; that a picket on guard the night before had heard a cow come along and shot her. The orders were very strict not to let any one pass. This was the first guard five miles out from Murfreesboro. He said he could not take us in to camp as he had no one to relieve him. That was just before sun up, and at that time of the year the mornings were very cool. He asked us if we had any tobacco. About eight o'clock in the morning the officer of the day came around. I asked him if he could take charge of us. He said that he could not take charge of us as the orders had been issued that no slaves were to be allowed harborage who were leaving their masters. He said that we could go to the cavalry's pickets at headquarters as the officers wanted to hire some waiters. I found that to be a kind of come-off. However, we went to the picket headquarters, but no one seemed to want to take us.

It was about ten o'clock in the day so they gave us our breakfast of "hard tack," coffee and "sow belly." This was our first meal inside the Union lines. We walked around there a while and no one seemed to want to claim us. About a half mile away was the infantry picket line. They said we could go up there and they would tell us where to go. As we were marching on, dressed in brown jeans, we had the appearance of rebels, scattered and going through the woods. This aroused the suspicion of the picket and they began to fumble their guns as though

56

ready to shoot. I ordered the boys to get together and march in the road or we would be shot. When we got there they asked us where we came from. I told them that our masters were in the rebel army and we were making our escape in order that we might join the Union army. They said they could do nothing for us, but would send a guard to go with us into the infantry picket headquarters. When we got there they said the orders were very strict and they dared not to take charge of us. The headquarters were in an old gin mill. This now was about half past eleven in the day. They then detailed a guard and took us to Gen. Geo. Waggoner's[23] headquarters. When we got to the general's headquarters he interrogated us in regard to leaving home, and why we had left. I told him my master was in the rebel army, in open rebellion against the Union.

He told the guard to take us over to the quartermaster's headquarters. It was twelve o'clock. Just about this time they were sweeping the quarters and they handed each one of us a brush and told us to begin sweeping. We had been traveling all night, marched twenty-five miles and this had made us very sore in our legs. Everybody was sweeping. At twelve o'clock the pickets would go out to shoot their guns off, while the drums were beating and flags waving, and the soldiers were marching to and fro, so we felt just about like a country dog in town for the first time.[24] Our masters had been telling us all the time that the Yankees wanted to get us and sell us in Cuba as slaves. I overheard a couple of Yankees saying, "There is a big fellow up there (he had reference to one of Jennings' slaves) that we could get $2,000 for in Cuba." To my great surprise there stood a man with a great long wagon whip, striking as though he would strike at some one. As I came by my brother sweeping, seeing this man with the whip, I said in a low tone, "It seems that our master's words are about to come true." At length the sweeping was all done, and the whip was laid away. I afterwards found out that that whip was all for mischief. Tired, and in the midst of strangers, all new faces to us, I began to reflect. I said to my brother in a low tone as I passed him, "this is hell isn't it." He said, "it is." However, I concluded if we had made our bed hard, we would lay on it, and never go back until we were taken or times were better. My brother went over into the 57th regiment[25] and got employment there. The old man, Moses Beagles [Biggles], was sixty years old. They gave him the job of cooking, and gave John Beagles [*sic*] and myself a job as teamsters. My team [of mules] was as large as horses. We took charge of our teams and commenced hauling around Murfreesboro.

Now we were right in the midst of army life. I, being away from home fifteen months once before, was better prepared to stand it than the rest. They began to get homesick. I told them to cheer up and be men and not get discouraged. I said, "don't you know if you go home you will get your backs cut all to pieces?" We had been there about a month. My brother took sick and was carried to the hospital. I took care of my team and waited on him the best I could. The nurses there did not take very good care of him. There were many sad sights in the hospital. I witnessed a very sad one. An old gentleman and a younger man were lying side by side; they had been lying there about two weeks, and I began to ask them questions. The old man said that the younger man was his son and he had not seen him for twenty years, and he had laid side by side with him two weeks before recognizing him, curse of slavery, separating parents from their children and vice versa. The next day my brother died. This made me very sad and threw a gloom over my pathway. My heart was filled with grief to such an extent that I shall not undertake to describe it. He was buried there. This left me alone. The only brother I had dead and gone from me. I felt the people at home would blame me for taking him away to his death.

Gen. [William S.] Rosencrans was waiting for the roasting ears [of corn] and peaches to mature so that he could have something for his army to feed on before he moved. One night about twelve o'clock we received marching orders. We started on our march from Murfrees-boro to Chattanooga by the way of Talahoma [*sic*]. When we got to Talahoma we stopped there for a day or two. There the Union army had captured a lot of rebels[26] and I went around to see if I knew any of them. I saw the son of old man Ayers[27] who[m] I used to work for. He asked me where I was going. I told him I was going on with the Union army. We got the news when we were there that John Morgan was making his raid through Indiana and Ohio.[28] One of the teamsters was a white man, and I said to him that I hated Morgan to go among the Union people and kill them off. He said he was glad of it; I asked him why, and he said that he had an uncle there who was as big a rebel as any of them, and that he wished they would take every horse he had and burn his barns. This was my first knowledge of a division of sentiment in the North.

Years after when in attendance at the Annual Reunion of the 57th Indiana Regiment, I was called upon to make a speech; responding I related what had passed between a white man and myself about John Morgan. While I was telling it I noticed some one move out in front of me and he waited there eagerly until I had finished speaking, when he said, "I am the boy who was talking to you about my old uncle in Ohio." Then and there we had a reunion of our own, aside from the general show.

We continued our march toward Chattanooga. The armies had passed on and the wagons had to follow; and as we went along we saw many new graves along the road. We knew then that marching meant a tramp through the valley of death. We got through to Pelham [Tennessee], and stopped there for a while. I took sick and doctored every way I could trying to cure myself. The old man who made the trip with us took sick and I suppose died, for I never saw him any more.

On Sunday morning we began our march to Warner's Ridge;[29] it was so steep that the soldiers helped to pull the wagons up. We went into camp about dark, and the next day we started out and marched all day on top of the ridge. In the evening we began to go down. We commenced going down, the hill was very steep, and although we locked all the wheels of the wagons, the mules nearly pulled them over. When we were near the bottom my wagon broke down, and we stopped there about two or three days. I was still sick and went to the doctor, and in a few days I was well again. Then we went out foraging and brought in roasting ears and peaches, and made peach cobbler, and I enjoyed myself eating peach cobbler. One day there was a great alarm in camp. They said the rebels were coming and I was sure we were all going to be captured, but it turned out to be a false alarm. Then we had orders to march again and go up another hill, and just as we had got to the foot of the hill, John, who had kept me under his house and fed me in the mountains, came to me and said, "George, I am going home." I said, "What is the matter with you, you have lost your reason haven't you?" I told him if he wanted to be a baby he could go back home. He said he was going back, and I told him he was liable to be killed before he got back, but he said he was going back. I told him to go, and when he got back to say he left me in Schotcha Valley,[30] and that "I am never coming back until the times are better, and can be a freeman."

As we wound our way up the hill, I had to stop my team and wait, and as I looked down in the Valley I could see the smoke as it would settle from the camp fire; and as I would look away across the mountains, no one ever knew how my heart was filled with sadness and loneliness. As I would think that I was the only one left out of four, I would look down the valley again while the tears began to roll down my cheeks. I said to myself, "Cheer up, it can't always be thus, there is something better awaits me." We finally reached the top of the ridge and stayed there about a week waiting for the army to come around. It was very dry and in August, and we hardly had water for man or beast, and were out of all kinds of rations except some crackers. We were living on roasting ears. One evening when we were hard up for rations, (they issued four ears of corn to each soldier) one man died and I heard one of the boys say you could go over in [the] Indiana [regiment] where the dead man had lived and get his corn. We were then about five miles from Chattanooga upon the mountain. They lost trace of the rebels there, so they began to throw shells and feelers, trying to find where the enemy were, and one day they struck a nest of them. The next news we heard was that we had thrown shells into Chattanooga and driven them out of the town. I had orders with other teamsters to take our wagons and go to Chattanooga. We started our teams down the mountain. It was dark and dreary looking, and we had just about two feet of space to the edge of the precipice. Just above us was about three or four hundred feet of rock or stone, and had we fallen we would have gone down amidst the panthers and wild cats. I unloaded my wagon at the ferry and then went back for another load; before we got back it was daylight. We loaded up our wagons and came down again. Then we went back and crossed over on the ferry boat and drove into the town waiting for orders to move. My wagon being the first to enter.

I overheard some colored women talking, and I supposed it was for my benefit, as I was with the army. I heard one of them say that "I told Misses this morning that I was not going to milk any more cows, the Yankees have come and I am free now." I said to them, "You had better stay with your mistress until the war is over"; that it was hard times in the army, and you had better stay at home. They said the year of jubilee had come and there was no more milking of the cows. As I drove on the main street of Chattanooga, I went into a house. It seemed to be a deserted hotel, and there were a lot of rebel clothes. I selected a white coat with a blue collar, blue cuffs and brass buttons. This was my uniform. The army had come over in advance of us, and I had orders to take my team and go out foraging. As I was driving along I said to myself "I cannot see why Bragg retreated from here." I felt that he moved out for the purpose of drawing us into a trap. This was in September. That day while I was out hauling, they began to fight. I heard the roaring of cannon, and said to the men who were with me that we were going to have a hard time, because the rebels knew what they were doing when they vacated the place. So we captured a rebel out there, who seemed to be scared and excited, and took him into camp. The fight went on; that was on Thursday and Friday; also on Saturday they had a very hard fight. General Rosencrans came back into town and said he had been wounded in the fight. Some of the people who had been out with him said that Gen. Rosencrans had just come into the city. I did not understand what he had come back for. I said that I believed they were whipping us, and so it was. Not long before 12 o'clock I had orders to take my team and go down near the foot of Lookout Mountain. There they were bringing the rebels back, shot, wounded and bleeding. I kept hauling baggage that evening for Warner's brigade.[31] I afterwards learned that Warner's men came up there with their seven shooters.

A lieutenant from an Illinois regiment was detailed to see what caused the dust in the distance. Gen. [George H.] Thomas thought that the enemy had gotten behind us. The excitement was running very high. The soldiers were trying to get away, the bridges were crowded and I kept hauling until night. The next morning I was given orders with others to go down to a planing mill near the foot of the mountain to haul some lumber. This was [a]bout ten o'clock in the day. The rebels had placed a signal man on the mountain, and the Union forces shelled him out because he was getting the situation of

61

our army. Our army was not in a condition to be viewed by the enemy as we had been cut to pieces on Sunday at Chickamauga, falling back to Chattanooga. Houses were torn down to build breastworks, leaving the furniture exposed. I recall a sad sight: A white woman walking down the street gathered up a chair that had been thrown out when her house had been torn down, as though she had resolved if she never had anything else in the world she would have that rocking chair. She seemed to be so very sad—her house torn down over her head, and she turned out a wanderer.

While we were hauling lumber we had occasion to pass a temporary hospital and there we saw the limbs of the wounded soldiers being amputated and thrown to one side, as though they had been cut off so many cattle. On Monday evening we began hauling whiskey. We would knock the head of a barrel out, take half of the whiskey out and fill the barrel up with water. We hauled it out and gave it to the soldiers. It gave them courage and made them feel more like war after the fatigue of fighting many days. Gen. Rosencrans would ride around the lines and tell the boys to hold out twenty-four hours, and they would be reinforced, and they would cry out that they would hold out twice twenty-four hours. So they were kept up on the whiskey and water for several days. Our army there was completely defeated and demoralized. If the rebels had known, they had but to move upon us. The rebels were laying back waiting, and our army was hoping for reinforcements. I was hauling provisions from one warehouse to another and from the depot. I was detailed to go out foraging and bring in corn, potatoes and other things to feed the soldiers. One evening away up the Tennessee Valley while we were out foraging we went into camp. About two miles and a half from camp we went out to see if we could buy some potatoes, chickens and such things. We intended to take the chickens to Chattanooga and sell them. We went to a house, two of us were colored and two white. There were no men folks about the house. We asked the women if we could buy some potatoes and chickens as they had plenty of them around; this was about fifty miles up the Tennessee Valley from Chattanooga. They refused to sell and refused to take greenbacks. I with the white men had some Confederate money. They said they would take Confederate money from the white soldiers, but they said they would not sell to the "nigger" for no

62

kind of money. They went to get the potatoes for the white soldiers, so my comrade and myself went around the house and helped ourselves. I was a pretty scientific hand myself, in taking chickens off the roost; this I learned while in the army. I would place a plank right at the breast of the chicken, and it would step off the roost on the board, and in this way I could lift them down and drop them in the sack. We grabbed a big rooster and he squawked and the women and dogs turned toward us, and we broke and ran to camp.

The next day, Sunday, I had orders to go to a certain barn, and the lady came out of the house and said that the Yankees had no business there. I said that we had orders to come and get anything we could lay our hands on and that she had no right to interfere with the affairs of the army. Just then I stuck my head out of the covered wagon and she exclaimed, "I thought you was a nigger!" I said, "nigger or no nigger, we are going to have this corn to take to Chattanooga to feed our stock on." Then we started back. It would sometimes be so dark that we could not see our hands before us, and in crossing the pontoon bridges, and some places had we made a step too far either way we would have been thrown in the river. When we reached camp we would give up all of the corn we had except enough to feed our mules. While the rations were so scarce I have seen soldiers come up where the mules were feeding and ask for an ear of corn. As we would be driving out sometimes the mules would get so hungry they would cry like children. I have seen horses and mules starve at the stake in Chattanooga. I was detailed to go hauling dead animals, mules, horses and cows that had starved to death. For six weeks I did that and have hauled as many as thirty-six a day. They were dumped in the river, but the soldiers drank the water just the same.

Gen. Rosencrans had been superceded by Gen. [Ulysses S.] Grant. One evening it was raining. I heard a horseman coming by that I found to be Gen. Grant and his staff. On another day I had orders to go over across the river to do some hauling, and as I was up on a high hill I was then in full view of Mission Ridge and Lookout Mountain where the rebel soldiers were camped. When I looked and seen all this I said to one of my fellow teamsters that I did not believe that Gen. Grant or any one else could whip the rebels from the position they held. About this time an order came that all teamsters that were not sworn soldiers were to give up their teams and enter the army.

This I did not prefer to do under the condition of things; I did not like to give up my team. I went to the 15th Indiana regiment, Col. Woods, [32] and hired to a captain by the name of Monroe.[33] This was about three days before the Missionary Ridge fight.

One day about one o'clock the whole army had orders to fall in, and the regimental colors were flying and the music began to play.[34] This meant that Gen. Grant had gotten ready to make a move and the word came FORWARD! As we went marching on, while the music played, and the balls whizzed around us, Col. Wood's division took a position and drove the rebels out of the trenches; the shot and shell were flying thick; this was now about sundown. All became quiet and Gen. Grant had his army throw up breastworks that night for miles around. As we were laying there in the line of battle we could hear the soldiers cheering as they were fighting. We could see [General Joseph] Hooker's men as they drove the rebels back on Lookout Mountain. As they drove the enemy back and were making their charges, our whole army raised a yell, then right off to our right you could see a kind of a beach where the rebels were camped thick. Next morning when we got up they were all gone. This made us feel some better.

A peculiar incident took place while the fight was going on. The rebels threw over one of the long slugs which came within about ten feet of a colored fellow and it plowed up the ground, and his mouth flew open, and a plug of tobacco fell to the ground. I never before saw a chew of tobacco knocked out of a man's mouth in that way. At 12 o'clock I took dinner to Capt. Monroe, the man I was waiting on. He knew they had to go into battle at 2 o'clock and he was so nervous that he could not eat. I believe he felt he would be killed before we could get up Mission Ridge. At two o'clock the whole army was to make a charge. In the morning Gen. Grant had been placing them in every direction. This alarmed the rebels. We charged down through an open field and routed the rebels from their breastworks. Gen. Grant sent his couriers in every direction. They went over the breastworks and up the hill after them. Gen. Geo. Wagner led his brigade up on horse back and of this fight we could see every movement, it was so plain. We followed right on up and I came across Capt. Monroe who had been shot. It was now getting about sundown. It was very clear that day, and towards evening the frost fell and made it very hard on the wounded soldiers on the battlefield. I carried Capt. Monroe off on a stretcher. We carried many of the wounded off the field and laid them around the fire, waiting for the ambulance to come and haul them back to Chattanooga. I heard one poor boy calling for his mother, but his voice became fainter and fainter; soon death put an end to his suffering.

I got an ambulance and took Capt. Monroe back to the temporary hospital in Chattanooga. The floor was covered with wounded soldiers. Some of the nurses in the midst of this suffering would stop to write letters home to their friends and tell them the news. I wondered how they could write in the midst of all that suffering. The surgeon was busy removing bullets and waiting on the wounded soldiers. The house was cold and I would heat bricks and put to the soldiers' feet. The soldiers not knowing my name would call, "O darkie! O, darkie! O darkie!" This they did to designate me from the other nurses, who did not give them the attention I did. I do not know how many soldiers were there. I do not remember sleeping any, I was so busy. I could always tell when one was going to die. He would begin to get deathly sick and vomit. The next morning they were hauled out and thrown into the dead house. It did not seem so hard to us then as it does now. I have seen a man shot dead just for taking a board. A man's life was not much in the army. About three o'clock the next day I called the doctor to Capt. Monroe and asked him if he could do anything for him. He said he had been badly shot and nothing could be done for him. He said, "raise him up," and I did so, but Capt. Monroe then asked me to lay him down, and before I could do so he died in my arms. He had a wife who lived in Indianapolis, but I was never able to locate her. There was a fellow in the hospital pretending to be nursing who I found was there for the purpose of robbing the wounded and dead soldiers. When Capt. Monroe died[35] I took his watch and money, and this fellow came to me and wanted to help count the money.

He said that there was about $30.00 and to let him take care of it. I refused and we came near having a fight over the captain's dead body. I gave the money to one of the men who was not wounded so bad. Shortly after, I quit the hospital for outside service. I left the 15th Indiana and joined the 57th, going to work for Lieutenant Humphrey[s] of Co. A.[36] Some of the regiments had gone into battle with 600 men and came out with 75; some with 800, coming out with 200. I think the 26th Ohio came out with 75 men. The day after the battle we buried the dead. Lieutenant Humphreys was a brave fellow: his home was in Madison, Ind. When I came North I met him here several times. The army had orders to move through East Tennessee, as Gen. [James] Longstreet was going that way. We struck out and marched about three miles in a swamp, but finally found a place to go into camp. We resumed our hard march, and many a soldier would march all day, only to die at night. In that part of the country we could get nothing but buckwheat flour, which made the soldiers sick. For about three days and nights we had nothing but parched corn and not enough of that. We marched about twenty-five miles each day, between 50,000 and 100,000 men. The advance moved about two o'clock in the afternoon. The other divisions would begin to move about six in the morning, going into camp about nine at night.

It came our turn to go into camp about ten o'clock one night. It was very dark. Where the army had been moving there were a great many dead horses, and it was a very hard matter to get water without getting it off of some dead animal. I went to where I heard the water roaring and gurgling and filled my canteen for our evening coffee. The next morning I went down to get some more fresh water and about thirty rods from where I got my water the night before there lay a dead horse, wedged in tight as a drum head, and his legs sticking out of the water. This was the kind of fresh water we had.

We had a fifer in the 40th Indiana who never ceased playing, especially in the evening. When the army would be tired and worn out he would strike up his fife to encourage us on our weary tramp. We had been on a march about four weeks and had not seen a woman. One afternoon about three o'clock as we were marching by a large frame building a woman came out and stood on the door-step. It was the prettiest sight our eyes had rested on for weeks. I never will forget how she was dressed. She had on white cuffs and collar and a white apron and a kind of dove colored dress. The boys in front cheered and saluted her as an emblem of civilization. The enthusiasm and joy of the moment was contagious and was taken up by the whole moving mass

66

of men. We were then getting near to Knoxville. On our march there we passed through the town[37] where Andy Johnson lived. There we saw where "Andy" kept his tailoring shop. At that time he was exiled from home. We went into camp on the banks of the river of Loudon on that cold New Year's of '64. We stayed about two weeks and did everything we could to keep warm. We entered Knoxville and went into camp on College Hill. Here we had to lay down in the mud and rain. The next morning they moved us on again. We marched across the river and made our march up to Dandridge, a little village of about fifty or seventy-five inhabitants. This was about ten o'clock in the morning and we went into camp again. I supposed that we would camp there for the night, but Longstreet's army was laying side by side with us, and we undertook to cross the river on wagons and the Longstreet men began to throw shells at us. In the struggle we captured a few of their men. About sundown I started my fire to get supper, as I supposed I would have plenty of time, but a line of battle was formed right across the fire I had made by a German regiment. Commands were given in German, and I could not understand what they were saying. We had orders to move on the side of the hill. I afterwards found out that we were getting in shape to retreat; that Longstreet's army was about to get in our rear.

Provision was scarce and the road was covered with ice. We marched all night. I came pretty near being captured. As the army was passing on, I sat down on the corner of the fence to rest a few minutes, and being tired and fatigued went to sleep while the army kept coming. The wagon train had passed. I heard strange voices. The men came driving the cattle, and the rebels being right behind them, they had to run to keep from being captured. This was about three o'clock in the morning. I ran for miles, trying to catch up with my command. I did not catch up that night. I overtook some fellows that had almost given up to be captured. They had built up a fire and a rear guard came up and made us hustle out. I did not catch up with my command until late in the day. I never went to sleep again on a march; it learned me a lesson. This was in February '64.

The weather had now turned very pleasant, so we remained in camp on the banks of the Loudon. I saw men so hungry that they ate the pure leaf lard without bread or anything else. Our rations there for six men was a handful of meal with a little beef. Henry Garrett drove an ox team, hauling meat, and his team moved so very slow, that the report came that he had been captured, but he was not. He now lives in Hancock County, Ind. Tom Orr, a quarrelsome fellow, and I were great friends. Tom thought he was a good man and I thought I was a pretty good man. So one evening we got into a wrestling scrap; I threw him three times. This caused a great lot of fun as Tom thought he was the best man in the whole regiment. About this time the question came up of re-enlisting for three more years in the war. That question was agitated and the officers made speeches to the men, and encouraged them to re-enlist. They told them they would give them $2.00 and a thirty days' furlough to come home. They first said they would not do it. They kept agitating it and they begin to re-enlist, one by one. The thought of getting to go home and having a thirty day's furlough was the only thing that encouraged them. Col. Leonard[38] had the regiment drawn up in line and made a speech to them, saying that all who wanted to go back with $2.00 would turn and march towards Chattanooga. About half of the regiment moved off and the other half stood. The colonel told them they might all go over across the river and stay with the others before they started back that night. That evening nearly the whole regiment re-enlisted.

The second brigade was pretty near all going to re-enlist and I began to think about myself. I had heard so many good things about the North. I was shut out from home and had no place to go and I began to talk around and some of the boys said if they were me they would go North. I told them I was willing to go, but I was afraid we would have trouble at Louisville. We had gotten back to Chattanooga. I had changed my company. Capt. Dunn[39] of Indiana said he would take me North if I would return back South with him. I said all right. We took the cars for Nashville. We got there in the morning and put up at the Maxwell Hotel. We had bean soup for breakfast and bean soup for dinner. We stayed there until about two o'clock in the day and took the train for Louisville. We got there and they put us in the barracks. While we were there, the officers felt a little high-toned and left their companions and went up town and stopped at the hotels. This angered the men and they knocked out windows and committed other acts.

About half past twelve we had orders to march on the ferry and cross to Jeffersonville, Ind. I felt a crisis was upon us and I grew quite nervous. The lieutenant colonel came aboard and said all the colored men would have to come off. Capt. Dunn said to me, "give me my carpet sack," and it seemed to me that he spoke as if he cared more for his carpet sack than for me. Some men on the boat swore that they would kill the first "nigger" they saw on Indiana soil. We were put off the ferry about half past eleven in the day. The ground was covered with snow. I had loaned one or two of the boys in the company about $40.00 and they were to pay me when we arrived in Louisville, but the orders were not to pay them until they crossed to Jeffersonville. This only left me with about $10.00 and in a strange town and that town Louisville.

They detailed Adjutant Smith[40] to look after our interest. He went to the commander of the post to try and obtain passes for us. He returned after he had been gone about an hour. I said to one of the boys he had bad tidings for us, for I could see from the manner in which he carried himself. He said he thought he would get us across, but he would have to have all of our names. We gave him our names and he went back only to return and tell us that he did not believe he could get us across at all. He also said we would all have to go down to the general's headquarters. I was leading them and we went about three squares. The adjutant told us that he would overtake us. I said, "halt men, we are sold!" I thought that the adjutant had played a trick on us, and by sending us off there would get rid of us. What made me think this was in slave times they would take hogs and mules and horses South, and they would take slaves along to drive them. When the trader would make a trade he would sell the mule and driver altogether. They would tell him that he, the slave, could drive them over and then come back; but he never got back home again. This is why you see so many "ads" for lost relatives in the columns of The Freeman.[41]

PART TWO

Citizen of Indiana:
SMALL-TOWN BARBER
AND POLITICIAN, 1864-1884

I N COMPANY WITH MY COMMAND, I HAD REACHED LOUIS-
ville, with signs of trouble ahead of us. Well we were marched on
down the street and made a turn towards the quarters. The Major had
not overtaken us yet, so we went in and found the general there. He
said, "do you remember what Adjutant Smith was talking about?" I
said, "yes sir." He interrogated us as to how we left home. I told him
our masters had gone to the rebel army and wanted to take us, but we
did not want to go and ran off. So he passed the whole eleven of us.
He gave orders to his daughter to write passes for eleven of us and put
our names in a large envelope. We went down to the river and met
some stragglers that had got left from our command who made especial boast that they would kill the first colored man they saw on Indiana soil. I was afraid we might get hurt as we were not armed; however, I hired a wagon and we went to the depot. When I got there our
train was gone. All the time these stragglers were swearing they
would kill the first "nigger" on Indiana soil. The time had come for
something to be done. There were men in the crowd old enough to be
my father, scared nearly to death. I was scared as bad as any of them,
but did not let on. One of our persecutors walked about ten paces and
turned; I showed fight. He then turned and left us, swearing he would
kill the next "nigger" he saw. I saw I had my man conquered and I
hollored and told the others I had him and that they might come out
from behind the depot where they had hid.

Now we were in the free state for the first time in our lives. The
conductor passed by and said "boys, you are left, but I will bring you
up in single file." That was usually an army term when they were going to use us pretty rough, and it excited us a great deal, but we afterward learned that he meant all right. Just about dark the train backed
up and all of us got on the cars. It was the first passenger car I ever saw
in my life. It seemed strange to me, but it was comfortable. They had
moved the soldiers to the freight car. About eleven o'clock in the
night we overtook the soldiers again. The conductor said "here is your
regiment." We all got off the cars and had to get in box cars where
there was no fire, and the soldiers were all on a spree, having a big
time, some fighting and some threatening to kill.

We came on and the next day landed at Indianapolis. Everything
seemed strange to me. The land seemed to be so level and most of the

houses seemed to be so small. In slave times they always had one large house, where the white people lived and around it were a lot of cabins where the colored people lived, so when I looked out and saw but one house and that a small one, it seemed odd to me. When we landed at the depot we were all marched down to the barracks on South West street. There we went into quarters and stayed a short time until we could get transportation to different homes. We had heard before we had gotten here how the country and the people were broken up, but we found business going on the same as though there had been no war, and the women walking along the streets, wearing tall skyscraper bonnets, fashionable at that period. I stepped into the "Occidental Clothing Store" on the corner of Illinois and Washington streets, and bought me a suit of clothes. I bought a gray suit as that was my fancy then, and paid $40.00 for it. I could get the same suit now for $5.00, and I thought then I was getting it cheap at $40.00.

After a time we left the city and went up into Hamilton county. I went out there with Capt. Dunn and remained there while we had thirty days furlough. We got off at Cicero and marched through the mud and went up to a place that was known as Boxville Town.[1] During my stay there I stopped with Dr. Collins.[2] His family treated me very fine. Those men who stayed at home and opposed the war and said that it was done "to free the niggers" said they did not intend to have any "niggers" come into Boxville Town to stop. They took Capt. Dunn to task about it and he said that he had brought me there. They swore they would run me out of town and he swore they would not; he said if they did, they would have a very warm time doing it. The boys all had quite a banquet when they returned home, and everybody gathered in to give them a great feast. There was a settlement of colored people there and throughout Hamilton county. While I was there I visited around and had a nice time. The thirty days were up and we had orders to go back to Indianapolis.

While I was in Boxville I took the measles and came very near passing out. For about five days and nights I suffered from a gathering in my throat, and could neither eat, sleep or drink. Mrs. Dr. Collins was such a fine lady and treated me just as if I had been one of the family. She was a lady that I can never forget. We had been living on hard tack, what was called sow belly, and beans, and when we went to Dr. Collins we had eggs, coffee, etc., and I was permitted to sit down to the table with the rest of the family. This was strange to me. It cost me while I was there $5.00 a week for board and doctor bill. This left me in debt about $20.00. The doctor kept an account of it. Now it was getting time for the regiment to move back to the front again. All the boys were going back. The colored boys said they were in a strange land and they were going back South as they wanted to go home. The fellow I "messed" with said he was going back. I told him that I was not going back. He asked me why and I asked the advice of some of the soldier boys and they said that if they were me they would not go back. I told them that I did not propose to go out of heaven into hell. They marched off and I stayed in Indianapolis, I loafed about a week looking for something to do.

This was in April '64. I went up Meridian street and hired to Judge Martindale[3] for $15.00 a month. All east of him at that time was owned by a colored man by the name of Freeman.[4] I stayed at Judge Martindale's three days. I stayed at home on the first Sabbath night and kept the children while they went to church. I thought I had served my time at keeping children—had served an apprenticeship at it. I had a friend of mine who came on Sunday to see me. He was not treated just as I thought he ought to be. I was told that I should see him in the wood house. I had my little room up stairs and in that little room I had a little carpet sack made out of black oilcloth, and in this little carpet sack I had my earthly possessions. I slipped it down stairs and sat it out in the wood house, and as the judge came down he asked "what that meant," and if that was my carpet sack, and when I replied that it was, he asked what I intended to do. I told him I was going to quit, and he asked me if I did not like it there. I said I had quit and he asked me what I quit for. I told him I did not have enough to do there. I would rather go somewhere else and get more money. He took me in his buggy and on the way he talked to me and told me I was very foolish for quitting, and that I was just the boy they wanted and that they were all pleased with me, but I told him that I must have more money. He said that I would run around and never do any good, and that I had better stay with him. The fact of the business was, it was too dull and lonely for me, after being in the army and I wanted to come down town, where it was more lively. I did not even ask him for pay for the work I had done.

I only had twenty cents in my pocket. I went to the Bates House[5] and got a job there at $18.00 a month as yard man. The first night I was there they had one black man there who had charge of all the china of the hotel; his name was Dorsey. He hired me to black 150 pairs of boots for 50¢; I did not commence this work until eleven o'clock in the night. As I was not accustomed to this work, it took me quite awhile to get through. At that time all the boarders would put their boots outside of the door and the bell boys would bring them down. About three o'clock in the morning I got through and the boys had all the boots carried away. The next morning the man paid me for the job; I then had 70¢ in money. The next day he wanted me to do the same job again. I asked him how much he would give me; he said he would give me 50¢ and I told him I would not do it for that. I told him I would do it for 75¢. He was standing up about thirty feet from the ground in a hallway between the help-house and the hotel. He told me not to get too smart or he would give me a thrashing. This aroused me and I told him that if he came down from where he was I would break his head with the shovel I had in my hand. This bluffed him out and that did away with my boot blacking for a spell.

The next day the landlord called me and said "yard man, I want you to come up higher." I went up in the hotel and he said that he wanted me to be porter upstairs. I felt that was rather a promotion for me. I was not there long until I was made head porter. It was right in the time of the closing of the war and money was plentiful. I made about $10.00 a week extra. I was there about six months and had saved up about $100.00, bought me two suits of clothes and a trunk. The president of the street railroad boarded there. He was the president of the first street railroad in Indianapolis. During the State Fair I wanted to go to it. I had orders not to, but I went any way. While I was working in the hotel I went up into a room one day to get a valise and there was a one-armed officer who was going down to take the bus to go to Cincinnati. He had dropped $75.00. I brought it down and gave it to him. He thanked me very much and gave me a dollar, the landlord doing the same.

76

One day I got into a dispute with the clerks who claimed that I had misplaced something and it could not be found. I said I had not, and the landlord had so much confidence in me that whatever I said was so.

I quit the hotel. I thought I wanted to be a barber and went across the street opposite the Bates House where there was a barber shop, and from what I could see from the hotel, I thought that it was a pretty good business and I wanted to learn. The proprietor of the shop did not take to me, but the foreman of the shop did and he recommended that I be given a job of porter. This I accepted and got along very nicely. I made as high as seven dollars a day there, and every opportunity I would get I would shave some one. I worked here and the boss became very reckless and lost his shop. Then, of course, he had to make a move. Others took the shop and this threw me out of a job. The new boss said they would go to Kokomo, Ind. I had not got to be much of a barber yet. They were all broke and I had the money, and they said if I would furnish the money, I could go along and finish my trade. They concluded they would not take me along. They would go without me, but would take my money. I told them that if I could not go, my money could not go. They said all right, I would go. We went to Kokomo; I think that was in January [1865], and opened up a barber shop. We got along very nicely until one day while I was in Indianapolis some one pawned me a pair of brass knucks for 50 cents. I let them drop one morning out of my coat pocket and forgot them. The chambermaid brought them down stairs to show them what a deadly weapon I had about me. I told them that they were not mine but they had been pawned to me. We stayed there until March when the shop down town was sold. I left Kokomo then, but the last Sunday I spent there seemed to be about as lonely a day as I ever spent in my life. All of them had left but myself. I said that if ever God would forgive me, I would never spend another day in Kokomo as long as I lived. I was the only colored man there.

This was in March '65. I came back to Indianapolis, and bought out a little barber shop on South West St., waiting table at the old Pyle House for my board. When I went down to wait table the first morning, and went into the dining room to get my first order, every one was whispering and I heard some one say "they shot him!" I asked some one what was the trouble and they said that Lincoln had been assassinated. That was a gloomy day in Indianapolis. The next day a great procession went through the funeral exercises. Some rejoiced and were glad that he was assassinated. Orders were issued that any one rejoicing in the death of Abraham Lincoln should be arrested. They arrested several parties. I closed my barber shop and came down and went to work on Illinois street. By this time I began to know something more about my trade. After that I went to work at the Spencer House. At this time the soldiers began to come home, and the prices ran high. I took in as high as $20.00 a day myself, the other barbers as high as $35.00. I knew that this could not last long, so I went over to the Sherman House and bought out a barber shop. The man misrepresented it. He said I had a lease on it as long as I wished, but I was not there but a short time until I found that I would have to give the room up. It was poorly furnished, but cost me $75.00.

This left me dead broke and engaged to be married. My affianced[6] was at her father's home in Howard county. I had to have some money soon, so I went down to Edinburg and hired to work there for $15.00 a week; I stayed there about two weeks. I went to Indianapolis on a visit and got arrested three times in one day for a bounty jumper. That was caused by the style in which I was dressed. I had on a $45.00 overcoat, $35.00 dress coat, a $10.00 vest, a $16.00 pair of pants, and a large watch chain thrown around my neck, fastened to a big brass watch, and they thought by my somewhat flashy dress that I was a bounty jumper; so they came and took me from the side of the young lady I was escorting. I went down to the train to go off and there I was stopped again.

In the meantime I had lost my barber shop in the Sherman House. I saw that business in Indianapolis would have to go down as the soldiers would soon all be away, not leaving much to do. I went to Greenfield. I knew it would not do for me to get married unless I had a position, and this was about four weeks from the time I was to be married. I rented a barber shop there. I had lost my money. I borrowed $2.00 to move my straps and reached there Thursday evening dead broke. I opened up the shop that evening and shaved a man and got 40¢ for the job. I bought bay rum and hair oil with this money. The furnishing of my shop consisted of one chair in an eight by ten room, with a $1.25 vinegar keg for a tank and a 15¢ wash pan and a dry goods box to set my keg on, also one bench, one sitting chair, one cup case and one looking glass. Thus I started into business.

At the time I came to Greenfield prejudice was very high, not only in Greenfield, but all over the State of Indiana. There were a great many places in Indiana where a colored man was [not] allowed to stop, for instance in such counties as Wayne, Randolph, Miami and others. If you were a new man coming into the community it was a question whether you could stay there or not. This was my fear in going to Greenfield. I was told that a colored man could not stop in Greenfield. A good part of the regiment with which I came to this state, lived around about here, in Knightstown, Greenfield and other places. A large number of Co. A of the 57th Indiana settled around here. The soldiers had plenty of money when they returned home and spent it with me freely. The dyeing of the hair, mustaches and whiskers was very fashionable at that time. I would often black a man's moustache and eyebrows, leaving his hair white. On one occasion I blacked a man's hair, eyebrows and whiskers. He was a regular blonde, and when he went home he was so thoroughly changed he was not known. I will not mention his name, as he is familiarly known to many of the older citizens.

Among the men who returned to their homes about this time were Milton Marsh, Jack Smith, H. H. Belville and Thos. Orr. A man by the name of Wm. Boyer advised me to go to Greenfield.[7] I would like to state that H. H. Belville is now a prominent real estate dealer in Indianapolis and has grown quite wealthy. He was at that time a tin peddler and was a great friend of mine. Having occasion to go through the country quite frequently and meeting a great many people, he always spoke a good word for me, which benefitted my business and broke down a great deal of prejudice. The prejudice in Hancock County at this time was pretty strong with some people. It was about re-construction days and the people all thought that an equal was to be made of the Negro.[8]

When I had been in Greenfield about six months, a lady friend came out to visit us, and on her departure for home my wife and I went to the depot with her. My wife being very light complexioned, as we were returning home, some men observing us said, "that is what the Republican party is doing for the people of this country—a nigger going down the street with a white woman." Being informed that it was my wife no further talk was made. Upon another occasion I went into a grocery store owned by Billy Woods. While I was there some men commenced talking about equal rights and social equality. Old man John Williams[9] said: "What do you think these Republicans are going to do? They want to make the nigger an equal with us white people." I said to Mr. Woods: "My God, is it possible that the Republican party is going to bring me down to the level of this man? I am the scared party, because I prefer my position to his." Such things as these were happening quite frequently.

Years before the war there was a barber in Greenfield by the name of J. McKinney, who was a favorite with a certain element of the town because he indulged in playing cards, and everything that made things lively, and would fight also if necessary. I was told by one John Jones who had lived in Greenfield a number of years, that I would not stay in that town. I told him I had not seen the place where I could not stay, and I thought I could stay there. He told me that a justice of the peace by the name of Raiden[10] came up to his place one day with a wheel barrow filled with law books and commenced to read and quote the statutes of the State of Indiana, and according to a certain statute no Negro was allowed in the town, and that he had to get out of the town as quickly as possible. Bill Sebastian[11] and the squire were great friends, and they both said that I could not stay in Greenfield. Fortunate for me, I had formed the acquaintance of Major A. K. Branham.[12] He told Mr. Sebastian and Squire Raiden that I was just the kind of man they needed, saying he knew I was alright and that it would be best for them to let me remain. I did not know that Major Branham had interested himself for me in this matter. Mr. Branham was one of my faithful customers and was called the "barber's pride," coming to me to be shaved two or three times a week.

I had an attack of the chills and fever, and one day I had been shaking with the chills, Mr. Sebastian came along and said to Mr. Branham: "Major, that 'nigger' is drunk now, and we had better run him out of town." Mr. Branham replied that I was not drunk but had the chills and fever. I had just gotten through shaving him. On another occasion it was said by the people that I must go. A man by the name of Sol Kobble[13] and others came to me and informed me that it was against the law for any Negro to stay in the State of Indiana or Hancock County. Dr. N. P. Howard, Sr., then in the prime of his life, fearless as a lion, in the meantime hired a colored boy to work for him, and Taylor Thomas[14] another. The people said this would not do. "We will run these 'niggers' out of town and that barber too." Dr. Howard informed us that he was ready to stand by us and he was going to see that we staid there. He said to our annoyers, if you pay your doctor bills and let these people alone, it will be better for you. I treated Squire Raiden and Mr. Sebastian so nicely that at last they came to my shop to get shaved and being pleased with my work, they became regular customers and good friends of mine. They concluded that Major Branham was right in having me stay there.

It was difficult for me to rent a house when I first came to Greenfield. At last I got an old house with no plaster on the walls, and holes in it that the birds could fly through. Mr Raiden came to see me and said I could move in one part of his house. All these things were engineered by my friends, unknown to me at the time.

Greenfield at that time was a town of about 600 inhabitants. It was a very muddy and dirty place and the walks were made of two planks. The people all knew each other. No one came to the village but was known by nearly all. When I went to Greenfield there was only one colored family[15] living there. They had been there about twenty years. Greenfield at this writing is one of the best towns in the state for colored people. They are treated very nicely. When you go there, you hate to leave the town, you are so well treated by the people. A great change has been brought about. If a colored man gets into any difficulties there now he will have as many friends as any other man, even though the trouble be between a white and a colored man. When I first went there, if a colored man just crooked his finger, the cry would be, "chase him out!"

One time we experienced a great deal of trouble in the Sunday school work; we were without a teacher. A minister by the name of Rev. Mr. [James F.] Sloan,[16] a very good man, said he would go down in the morning and teach his own school. He was informed by his congregation if he taught the "niggers" they would not require his services any longer. I told him that he was the kind of man God liked to have in his service. He dared to do the right and did what he could to help those needing the gospel preached to them and the heavenly food. He could do nothing better. He that dared to do right was the only man that could be a success in this life. After this trouble, he finally gave up his charge and another man took charge of the school. His name was Hardpence.[17] He was a very liberal and good man, an editor of a paper and did not care much for the opinion the people had of him, when he was conscious of the fact that he was doing right. He had a very nice school about two and one half miles from Greenfield at Mt. Lebanon. His school was doing nicely but when the members of his school heard he was teaching us they told him he could not teach us and them too. He informed them that he could not teach them, but that he would keep up our school. He, with Dr. O. M. Edwards, were great workers in our Sunday school.

The most serious trouble I had while in Greenfield was on account of a boy, who was working for me and a boy working in a butcher shop next door. On the night of the trouble there was an attempt made to waylay the young fellow who was working for me, but he kept so close to me on his way home that they could not get their hands upon him. Friday night I heard that they were threatening to whip him and my advice to him was that he must be careful and not be guilty of anything to bring on trouble, and then if trouble was thrust upon him, it was his duty to fight in self-defense only. His idea was to assail his enemies by throwing rocks at them. My suggestion was that the rock might miss and then they would get him. I advised him to fix up a "billy" and he did so.

In those days it was our custom to scrub the barber shop Wednesday and Friday nights. After we had finished Friday night, we received word that the enemy was laying for my boy and was going to stone him to death, having stones piled up in a corner of the fence, waiting for him to pass. We could have missed this fight by avoiding this route home, but as it seemed nothing would do but a fuss, we came to the conclusion not to postpone it any longer, but have it out, no matter what the results might be. We started home and our shop boy was walking between myself and one of the hands and the fellow who desired to quarrel with him came up and the two began to fight; the others in the meantime commenced throwing rocks, at which I took a hand in, to the extent of warning them to stop. I told the boys they must stop throwing rocks at the boy. They said they were throwing stones at a white boy. I told them they must stop throwing stones, no difference whether it was at a white or colored boy. The battle wound up by my boy getting the best of the fight, he running one way after the skirmish was over, and the other fellow another.

About that time the city meeting held at the City Hall had just adjourned, and the news of the melee having spread throughout the crowd, many were incensed that the colored boy got the best of the fight, and a fellow by the name of Jobe Tindall[18] swore that he could wipe out all of us. The county clerk, Erick Swope[19] and a Democrat, told him that was a pretty big declaration to make and informed him that I had a great many friends here.

Forbearance had at last ceased to be a virtue with me and I told him in a manner that he understood I meant what I said, that if it was not for pity's sake, I would paralyze him. The officers in the meantime coming up, stopped further disturbance. The excitement of the hour and the general town talk having reached the ears of my wife, she started down town bringing my revolver to help me fight the battle. I met her, however, and assured her that the trouble was all over for the present. The next day, Saturday, the excitement was still unabated, the street corners being crowded with people, discussing the event of the night before, our enemies charging that we had assailed them and commenced the attack. It was very soon intimated to me that I had better leave town. All kinds of threats were made, some of my loud-mouthed enemies declaring that they would like to have a hand in running me out. I decided, however, that I was not going to leave Greenfield, that I had committed no crime, and that being my home I was going to stay there and told them in so many words there were two things I knew I could do—I could either live there or die there and that the first man who touched me would be a dead man. About 10 o'clock in the day, some of my friends came to me with the information that I would have trouble that night, that the people were getting together to mob me, etc. This same Tindall it seemed, was leading the rest, in his frothy declarations of what he could do and what he would like to do and once more declaring he could whip me and all my friends, young Dr. E. B. Howard,[20] also a Democrat, took occasion to say he could do no such thing. They had misrepresented the matter and stated we had waylaid them. This made it show up bad on our side until the facts were known, and as soon as the people generally, found they had waylaid us for the purpose of stoning us, the sentiment turned considerably.

These events happened in the month of May [1866?] and this particular day was a very pretty one. The town was filled with people from the country and it was just such a day as when a man, full of ambition and life knowing he had committed no crime, would object to dying on. There was a picnic about three miles from town and I knew that the leader of the intended mob, Ben Rains, Jr.,[21] was going to be there. He being a Kentuckian, coming from a state where it was death for a colored man to strike a white man, I felt that unless he was checked and something done to hinder him, a number of people would be killed that night. In my imagination I could see a bloody fight. I felt that it would be a bloody one, because I knew I was determined to fight if necessary for my rights, liberty and protection, and my friends were just as ardent along the same line.

The leader of the mob owned a very fine and spirited horse which was to take him and his girl to the picnic. Just before he went Jobe Tindall came around the corner with the threat, that "we'll get them tonight."

Filled with gloomy anticipations of the outcome of the day, not knowing whether I would be living twenty-four hours from that time and valuing as never quite before, my rights as a citizen and free-holder and head of a family, which was very dear to me, some powerful influence drove me to utter the following prayer. The impulse to make it may have been the result of fear, of timidity, not for myself because I did not fear for myself, but for those who were dear to me, and a certain class of religious purists may claim that my prayer was an evil one, nevertheless, I asked the Lord with all the earnestness and sincerity it was possible for me to have, to do something to hinder this man. I said and I feel that the Lord heard every word that dropped from my mouth and was a willing listener to my prayer. I said: "Have his team run away that he may break some of the bones in his body, that he will not be enabled to lead this mob to-night, if it is your will, if not, if something is not done to stay him in his mad and wicked determination, there will be many people hurt to-night." Ever since that day I have known, and all the scoffers, skeptics, etc., in the world could not convince me otherwise, that the Lord does answer prayer. About two and one half hours after I had made my appeal to Jehovah, word came to the town that this man's team, the intended leader of the mob, had run off with him, broken the buggy to pieces, broken his wrists, dislocated his shoulders and nearly killed him, thus leaving the mob without a leader, and answering my prayer as directly and effectually as the parent answers the pleading of his child. The young lady with him was unharmed, the horse also.

Closing our shop at 11 o'clock, in the meantime having been re-enforced by friends, we gathered together, armed to the teeth, and waited for the onslaught which did not come, the night passing quietly without trouble.

Dr. E. B. Howard, Joseph Baldwin, John Windsor and Oscar Thomas[22] with others, numbering about forty, escorted us home. We were armed with all kinds of weapons—clubs, hatchets, some had knives and revolvers. The point where we were expecting to be attacked was just below the railroad in a common, near where I lived. It was about half past eleven; we could see the men slipping round about, looking to see if there were any chance to slip upon us and charge, but we were ready for the attack as one man. We knew we were safe for the present. I went home and brought in the ax and armed myself. The doors were barred, and we went upstairs where we could hear the people as they walked on the plank side-walks for three or four squares away, and often imagined they were coming to our house. I said to the men who were with me and to my wife that if it was necessary, we would die together, as I had done nothing to cause the trouble.

Friday morning the report was current, which made the sentiment run higher, that this boy was badly wounded and not expected to recover. Later in the day, however, it was learned that the report was put out for the purpose of prejudicing the whole town against us. We had learned that the boy was not at home as reported, but had been sent by his employer, Capt. E. P. Thayer,[23] down to the slaughter house and was rendering lard. This somewhat abated the excitement, but as soon as my nerves began to quiet somewhat and I became more composed, someone would whisper in my ear, "they are preparing to mob you to-night," and then all would assume gloominess once more.

In the middle of the week, the matter took a serious turn. It was said that Capt. E. P. Thayer was going to take up for his boy because I had taken up for mine. He and I were personal friends and I sent him word at once that whatever I had done, growing out of the unfortunate quarrel, between the boys, was not to start trouble or to keep it going, but to defend the right and myself. All I desired was to be left alone, and my statement that the first man who touched me would die was called forth because I realized that the time for palavering had passed. I further told Capt. Thayer that I had no desire to be in the trouble or to defend one boy more than another. I was drawn into it against my wishes entirely. I had nothing to do with it. It was purely the boys' fight. As the fight had been commenced, I simply tried to separate the boys, and because the colored boy had the best of the fight, his (the white boy's) friends thought the fight must be had out. Capt. Thayer said if such was the case, if I had nothing to do with it, he wanted nothing to do with it. I told him also that the people who kept it up continually were enemies of mine, and that the fair-minded people of Greenfield had nothing against me, as they knew I was not connected willingly with the affair.

The threatening clouds gradually passed away and sometime after, one of the fellows who had intended with others to attack me, asked if I meant what I said when I declared I would kill the first man who bothered me. I told him that I certainly did and did not say so to frighten anybody, or to appear boastful, but simply because my sense of manhood compelled me to say so, knowing that I had wronged nobody and had been guilty of a commital of no crime, or imposition upon my friends, neighbors and fellow-citizens.

I had always been a kind of adviser in the town. A man by the name of Isom Ray of Shelby County sent his son [Newton Ray], who was a Democrat and a lawyer to Greenfield. He was a very brilliant young man and very conscientious. He had been there a couple of years, and was engaged in making an abstract of the county. The abstract was valued at three or four thousand dollars and he had it nearly completed. He was a frequent visitor at my shop. He came to me one day and I said: "Newton, the fact of the matter is, you are smart and brilliant; you are neither fit for a Democrat nor a lawyer; you are too conscientious to be a lawyer, and there is only one way out of this." Well, he said, "what is it?" "There are two things for you to do; give up the law business and join the Republican party." He answered me that he did not know how he could do that, as his father was backing him in everything. I told him that this father would not object to his doing what was right. He told me he had just written his father a letter, speaking of the speech that had been delivered by Dan Voorhees,[24] and he was always a great admirer of Dan. Well, I told him, you can get out of that alright. Sit down, I said, and write your father that you are going to change your plans, that you are not satisfied with being a lawyer, and that the time had come when you must change and that you think it would be the best thing to become a minister. I continued to urge upon him he would make a very successful minister, and asked him to keep the matter under advisement.

While he was considering the matter, he had an engagement to speak at a temperance meeting about six miles out in the country. Some boys, mischievous fellows, tried to keep him from filling his engagement. They had gotten about a mile from town, and he found he had only six minutes time to get to this meeting, which was six miles away. The boys told him that it was too late now that he could not get there anyway. But he went, and although he was late, he addressed the meeting, was well received and had a good time. Some of the boys came to me and told me what a trick they had played on Newt. I told them that while they might still be living in Greenfield years afterward, he might be far away making a man of himself if he took my advice.

When Newt came back, I said: "Newt, the boys think they have a great joke on you. They thought they would keep you from filling your engagement. They could not do it, could they?" He answered he had given his word and would not break it. There, I said, that is what I have told you all the time. You are too conscientious for a lawyer and a Democrat. Inform your father of it. So he wrote his father, telling him that he intended selling his business if he could get $2,000 for it, and with this money he would take a theological course at some college. His father, after receiving his son's letter, folded up the letter he

87

had received from Dan Voorhees and put it in an envelope. On the back of the letter he wrote, "my son what do you think of this letter that you wrote, speaking so well of Dan Voorhees?"

I told him that the very best of men made mistakes and that he made a mistake if he kept on in the business he was in. A few weeks afterward he preached his trial sermon at Greenfield.[25] I went to hear him and pronounced him a success, and told him all he had to do was to train himself. He then went to the conference, received an appointment but did not stay at it long. He attended a New Jersey Theological school and educated himself for the ministry, and is now one of the ablest pulpit orators in the country. He is married and has a nice family. Whenever he comes to the city the first place he makes for is my shop. I have often twitted his father about sending his son to Greenfield a Democrat and a lawyer, while I sent him away a Republican, a minister and a Christian. On one occasion the elder Ray said to me that he had never undertaken anything but what he had accomplished. I said to him Brother Isom, there is one thing you failed in; you failed to make a Democrat and a lawyer out of your son Newton Ray. I know that you are prouder of your son now than you were before. He has done something for you and all his friends to be proud of.

One evening as I sat in my shop I heard three men talking. They seemed very much interested in their boys. One suggested that the carpenter's trade would be a good trade for his son to learn, another thought the painter's a good trade. The parents of the three boys finally concluded that they would have their sons learn the painter's trade. The men were Captain [Reuben A.] Riley, Morris Pierson[26] and Mr. Lipskin. It seemed strange to me to hear these white men talk of putting their boys out to learn trades, as where I came from white boys did not have to work. The boy who was most indulged and petted, and did the least was thought the most of. I wondered why three men took such an interest in their boys, as I thought to teach the white boys to work was out of the question. One of the boys who was to learn painter's trade was James Whitcomb Riley,[27] now the "Hoosier Poet," another Wm. Pierson, now Dr. Pierson of Morristown, and the other Harry Lipskin. They all learned their trade from a man by the name of Kiefer,[28] who could paint all kinds of pictures. He was thought quite an artist by the people of Greenfield. Some of the boys were more successful in their trade than the others. Young Riley seemed the most apt. He could draw anything and would take up his pencil and a piece of paper and make a perfect picture of anything he wanted to. The boys, when they were out of the shop [Keefer's], would come to my place of business to lounge and idle the time away. James Whitcomb used to come quite often. He seemed different than the other boys and did not choose his associates from among the boys, but the men, such as Dr. Milligan, Ed. Milligan[29] and others. The other boys would keep coming, and bother me more or less, while young Riley would come around, but seldom bothered me or got in the way. I said to him one day: "J. W.," I always called him that, "you can come around to the shop when you desire; I like to have you; you are not like the other boys." He gradually became a frequent visitor at my place.

As time went by Mr. Riley passed from boyhood to young manhood, he was frequently away from the town at long intervals, coming back periodically to visit us. We were always glad to welcome him. He had grown to be a pronounced local celebrity. My shop was a great place to catch the farmer dialect. There Mr. Riley received many of his first impressions and training in that direction. During the years that he had made my shop off and on a place of resort, etc., he had little by little mastered the broad farmer dialect prevalent at that time and discovered in the speech of most of the old settlers. Having a keen sense of the ridiculous and fine powers of delineation, he already gave abundant signs of the great gift that has since made his name a household word everywhere.

As I contemplate Mr. Riley now, view him in the full fruition and maturity of his genius, I can understand how little many of his neighbors and early associates realized they were harboring one of the world's famous singers in embryo, but for some reason or other, intuitively, I away back in those early years had a feeling and a belief that he was destined to write his name amongst the princely few and pluck a garland of immortelles for his deserving brow, yet it may be that even I did not dream how strong was to become his hold upon the admiration of the world. I believe I have called the attention of my readers previous[ly] to the fact that he was somewhat of a painter—a sign painter, etc., and I may add now that frequently I found him of service as a decorator of the shaving mugs that ornamented and did service in my modest institution, he receiving for his skill in that direction 35 cents per mug, for which there never was a time he did not seem duly grateful and appreciative. He was frequently the subject of the petty envy of his associates who were not blessed with an accomplishment that would begin to bring them so much money. Without any special understanding to that effect, it may be perhaps well enough for the purpose of history to state that during five years, in return for the many services rendered in the line of his trade, I kept him "shaven and shorn" without price or remuneration save as he paid me in the manner indicated above.

I nicknamed him Mr. Jones and we played at imagining that he was a rich farmer of eccentric ideas, and fixed impressions of his importance and standing as a tiller of the soil. I would frequently say to him: "Well, Mr. Jones, how does it happen that you are in town so late to-day," and he would reply in the dialect of the Hoosier farmer, accompanied with the peculiar nasal twang that have made his recitations famous—"Wal, I kum into teown to-day, intendin' to go right back as soon as possible, and what did they do but pop me on the jury first thing. I put up at the tavern and there was so much noise about I couldn't sleep, so I got up about 4 o'clock this mornin' and bought me a cegar—two fer five you know—they last longer. I kum over to git a shave; how much do you ask for a shave, George." I would say ten cents. "Now, that's too much; I'll give you five cents for a shave."

He had an imaginary son by the name of Will, and in reply to my question he would say: "That boy has gone to the dogs. He's no good; he's gone out West and is goin' to make a cowboy of hisself." He would speak discouragingly and I would say, "Well, Mr. Jones, that boy will take care of himself after all; he's a chip off the old block." "Yes, I guess he'll manage to take keer of hisself. That boy's as sharp as a steel trap; they can't fool him, when you kum to think about it; he'll keep buckle and tongue together; I understand he'll do well out thar; he'll keep his end up; he got to dealin' in fast hosses, and spends his money; he's gone to the dogs; I guess he's got that gray hoss yit—I spose you've seen him 'round town, he's a fast hoss—guess he'll trot it in 2:40; now that's purty fast for a hoss to go, eh George; I expect thar's a woman mixed up in it too; thar giner'ly is, yer know. But that boy kin spend money! He's spent all he's goin' to git frum me; I spose the ole woman gives him some—just like a woman—his mother, yer know. Any how, first thing yer know he's in town. I believe he's got a hoss entered in the Greenfield fair; I guess he'll take first money out there—just like him."

"Well, Mr. Jones, I understand you have lost your wife."

"Yes, George; lost her better'n a year ago—my fourth wife—and the wust was she died right in the middle of harvest, and she could beat anybody at punkin pie—finest the crow ever flew over."

"Mr. Jones, I understand now what takes you to town so often. I see you over there on State street; hear you are courting the rich widow on State street, is that so?"

"Now, George, who told yer so?"

"Well, I can see, I can see; she's pretty well off too."

"Well, George, yer know I don't keer anything 'bout her money; I've got plenty mysef, but I am land poor, land poor, George; taxes is eatin' me up."

"Yes, Mr. Jones, I understand you have plenty of money, lots of land, and money in the bank. You understand your business; you know what you mean."

"Yes, George, yer know I don't care anything 'bout her money, but she's worth $40,000, and it is all in her own name too, eh?"

After Mr. Riley had attracted the favorable notice and attention of one or two of the great periodicals, and had made a great hit in Boston and New York, and the Indianapolis Journal had taken him up and pointed with pride to the fact, and dubbed him the "Hoosier Poet," it was not difficult to find his old neighbors and associates on all sides, who in former years had sneered at him, spoken derisively of him and declared him no good, and rather ridiculed and discounted my fidelity to him upon the ground that I was wasting my friendship upon an individual who was unappreciative and would never amount to anything—ready to applaud and laud him to the skies. All at once they remembered that he was a "purty good fellow," that when he was a boy he was "purty smart," "that Greenfield had a right to be proud of him," "he is our poet, our Riley," would be chirped from a hundred mouths as periodically news would reach us of the achievements and of the fame he was fast gathering to himself. I cannot deny that at this time I was filled with a fine glow of satisfaction. I realized with pardonable exultation that I had made no mistake in my diagnosis of the uncouth, apparently worthless, lazy, lounging boy, as he appeared during the early years of my acquaintance with him.

Neither did I hesitate or fail to remind his now enthusiastic supporters and admirers and predicters of these things, frequently causing them to expostulate or attempt to explain and some times to bow their heads with shame, when they were compelled to acknowledge that had I listened to them on more than one occasion, instead of encouraging him, throwing a dollar here and a dollar there in his way, making him welcome in my humble business home, I would have driven him as I was compelled to drive, on divers occasions, others of the "bad boys" of the town from my shop. In reply to their "I told you so's," I did not fail to remind them that they did not have to tell ME so, for I first and always claimed that given an opportunity he would make his mark and be an honor not only to Greenfield but to all the great State of Indiana.

As an incident, valuable only as affording a contrast of the length and breadth of his fame as compared to what it is to-day, I recall a discussion that took place one day concerning his growing importance as a poet. There were all kinds of opinions expressed and declarations made. One man said that he was the greatest poet in the United States and had no equal, which declaration was met by perhaps as wild a one, and surely a more ridiculous one, by a young lawyer named McLow, now living in the west and enjoying a splendid practice. Said the young limbo of the law who by the way was quite witty, and concealed beneath his youthful visage was a vein of humor and a sense of the ridiculous, "I know one thing—I know that this man Riley is the greatest poet in Center Township,"[30] a truth that the years have amply verified and that now can be said with equal truth of many townships and many states. It would be, perhaps too much to say of Mr. Riley:

> That he has touched his harp,
> And nations heard entranced.

92

It must be admitted, and I enjoy a special and peculiar pleasure as I take pen to write, that he had garnered to himself a distinction greater than any previously or now accorded to Indiana's sons and daughters, regardless of a conservative, and it may be a biased, judgment that as yet, has denied him admission in America's select circle of singers, graced with the genius of the Longfellows, the Lowells, the Whittiers of the age which closed with the death of Holmes. That he is destined to ascend still higher the "mount of song" is a most rational supposition. Mr. Riley has, however, not escaped in his individual self, aside from the tribute freely and enthusiastically accorded him as a poet, reflections unpleasing to contemplate. Many of his oldest friends, neighbors, companions, and playmates of former days, who are with him, if not the bread of indigence, at least shared with him the shades of obscurity, complain of an evident spirit upon his part to no longer encourage their familiar friendliness.

As if he would emphasize the fact that fame and distinction had overtaken him, they profess to note a spirit of exclusiveness about him, and an evident desire to "flock alone" with himself despite the ties of other days, and the claims of friendship sanctioned by years of association. Once he was plain "Jim" Riley with the friendly nod, the genial smile, the hearty grasp of the hand in stock at all times, and for everyone. Now he is JAMES WHITCOMB RILEY, the "Hoosier Poet," the brilliant and sought after man of elegant letters, who has evidently forgotten the depths from whence he arose, and those who encouraged him in ascent. Without expressing an opinion pro or con, the reflections of Hamlet, "This is a mad world, Horatio," comes vividly to my mind.

When I first went there [Greenfield] I could do all my work [by] Saturday evening and be done by seven o'clock after which I would go to Indianapolis and spend the Sabbath day, returning to Greenfield Monday morning. It was now four weeks of the time I was to be married, so I called on my landlord and asked him if he would not credit me for two weeks' board as I was going to get married and needed the money. The first Saturday I was there I took in $6.00; that made me feel encouraged. I had a sign painted on a piece of canvass, which the boys one night took for a flag. They returned the sign and as I said nothing to them, they felt as though they owed me an apology.

Greenfield was then a town with about 700 inhabitants. One evening I got tired and some men sitting on a goods box whittling, said I had better leave the town while I had money to go. I told him that I thought I would make it all right there. A man by the name of Raines[31] barbered in the town who had been shot in Morgan's raid in the hand. When I went there I asked him if he had any objections to me starting up and he said no. I had this object in asking him: I knew that he had many friends who I felt would not stand for any one to come there and run in opposition to him, without his permission.

The wedding day had come, the 4th day of October in '65. I had saved out of my earnings, besides paying some debts, $12.00. This was to bear the wedding expenses. I paid $2.40 for the license, spent $6.00 for nick-nack, candies, nuts, etc., and finally, the late Rev. Moses Broyles,[32] pastor of the Second Baptist church, officiating, I was married to Miss Aurilla S. Harvey.[33] Having made arrangements for Mrs. Knox to remain a space in Indianapolis until I had succeeded in making suitable arrangements to receive her at Greenfield, judge of my feelings, when just as I was about to start for my country home, she expressed a desire for money with which to purchase calicoes and other needful articles for the home and family. As a matter of course, she was sweetly oblivious of my rent, and "Broke" condition, at that moment not having enough money at my disposal to jingle on a tombstone. I told her not to mind about that then, but let it go for a while. In about four weeks we moved to Greenfield. I had to pay about $8.00 a week for board, and we boarded with the only colored family[34] there. At that time there was a great deal of chills and fever in this country. Everybody was suffering with them. I took it, and an old man, when the fever was on me said "you had better run this fellow out of town, for he is drunk already."

It kept me moving to make ends meet. I did not have any credit, for no one would credit me. Some days—bad rainy ones—I would take in 35 to 40 cents. There was one man who did trust me for about $2.00 worth of groceries which I turned in to our boarding mistress, thus helping me considerably. Seeing that I would have to make a change, I arranged for my wife to go to her father's and stay until I could get a start. I went to the depot and bought her a ticket and giving her ten dollars I had but 25¢ left. Her father was well-to-do, owning about 200 acres worth about $75.00 an acre, money in the bank and plenty of stock around him.

I paid about $30.00 for some second hand furniture, buying it on time. I could buy that furniture and the old cook stove now for $2.00. Time passed on and my business increased and I employed help. I needed larger quarters, and had to move from my little room. We got a young man by the name of Gappin[35] to intercede and get me a place known as Gooding Corner.[36] I thought now that I had gained quite a victory. Everybody came in to congratulate me on my new quarters. One day I thought I would go out and buy a load of wood. I called a countryman and asked him if he would sell me a load of wood and he replied that he would not; reason: I was a Negro. And this, dear reader, this was Indiana, hardly thirty years ago. For downright narrow cussedness and cruel meanness I doubt whether the South even at that day, could have surpassed this. This man afterwards came to be my best friend. Everything went on nicely except when Saturday night came; then it was pretty rough. They sold whiskey by the quart and fellows would come down the street, knocking down signs and do[ing] other damage. We would put out the lights and hurry home as soon as possible. They would get in there of nights and I would have a hard time to keep order. Sometimes they would get to fighting in the shop and would want to whip a fellow because he could not walk a line.

Our shop finally became the headquarters for the professional men, the doctors, lawyers and merchants of the village, except on Saturdays, and then I had a rule that no one was to loaf in the shop on that day. It was in this room where I made my first attempt to learn to read and write. My first copy was set by a colored preacher who came through there by the name of Anderson. I began to study, and my wife would teach me. Sometimes, it would seem I could not make it and I would throw the book under the bed, but would get it out again, determined to learn. The "small boy" bothered me considerably. One evening about eight o'clock I was working away, when a ring-leader with about 100 boys behind him, formed into a kind of a V shape and commenced marching in to the shop, filling it up. I felt that something had

95

to be done or these boys would wreck my chances in Greenfield. I took hold of the leader and shouted in his ears if he ever attempted to come in there again I would break him in pieces; the boys marched out and I had no more trouble with them.

I went into the cigar business and bought [them] by the 1,000, and sold more than any other place in town. I also took steps to own a piece of property—a house and lot. The most exciting time I ever saw in that town was the time [1868] that [Horatio] Seymour and [Francis P.] Blair ran for president against Grant and [Henry] Wilson. On Saturday the Democrats had a big rally and it was estimated there were 25,000 people in town. I went into my shop at six in the morning and never came out any more until five in the evening.

We established a school in our town,[37] our first teacher being a man by the name of [John] Bailey. I would get my lessons and go down and recite. I would work away, laying my book on the stand to study it. First one and then another would come in and instruct me how to read and write. The school went on very nicely. In '70 and '71 we organized an M.[ethodist] E.[piscopal] church and secured a man to preach for us by the name of James. Before this we had a Sabbath school superintendent, a man by the name of Snow.[38] He was an Englishman and taught us to read in Sabbath school. The colored people thought a great deal of the old man. He had a good deal of opposition. He was one of those men who did not care what was said about him. When Teacher Bailey had taught two terms he was succeeded by a man named Gillum[39] who boarded at our house, so each night I would recite him my lessons.

The campaign [1876] came on and Mr. [Rutherford B.] Hayes was elected. This time I began to take a hand in politics myself and began to try to make speeches. I organized a literary society and this gave me a start in speaking. I was superintendent of a Sabbath school and three white boys volunteered to take part in the Christmas exercises. All but one backed out; his name was [William J.] Sparks.[40] He was a poor boy, but he had an education. His father had been rich but was broken up; like many boys he was somewhat "wild" at times. I told him that for standing by me in the Christmas entertainment that I would always stand by him. I urged him to be elected superintendent for the

Christian church Sabbath school and promised if he would make the race and keep straight I would get him elected city clerk.

This was in January and the election came on in the spring. I secured him his nomination and he was elected. After he was elected, there was no one to go his bond but Nelson Bradley, the banker, and myself. He filled that term out and was re-elected again. Then I told him that I would secure his nomination for mayor of the city.[41] That term I was instrumental in having several of the streets improved, graded and graveled. The Hancock Democrat came out and charged that I was running the city government and by my influence there was too much extravagance in the way of improving the streets. Mr. Sparks served out his term. I told him that I would secure his nomination and see that he was elected again. The Democratic paper came out and charged that I was running the Republican party and the city, and that Mr. Sparks was nominated, but he was only a figurehead. The election came on, and on the day of the election I went to all the workers and told them what they must do to meet success. The Democrats persuaded the citizens to bring out a ticket in opposition to the Republican ticket.[42] That ticket was to be led by Capt. R. A. Riley[43] the father of the Hoosier poet, James Whitcomb Riley. He and I were very warm personal friends. They thought if they could get him out that would bring about the defeat of my man.

I saw it was a Democratic trick to defeat the straightout Republican ticket. So they put out a straightout Democratic ticket headed by Israel Poulson, a wealthy lawyer worth about $30,000 or $40,000. They thought by this means they would bring defeat sure. This aroused all the Republican workers in the city and we came together and had a council. It was ordered that every man would go out to work on election day. We were to make no noise and to work quietly and about noon we calculated we would have them defeated. About noon they came running to me, wanting to bet $50.00 or $100.00 that we would be defeated. I had our majority figured out from fifty to seventy-five. My man was elected by seventy-five majority. By this time Mr. Sparks had accumulated some property and had made some money and gotten into pretty good shape, and marrying a banker's daughter he became very prominent in local politics.

I moved away from the city in '84, but happened back there about the time he received the nomination again. He sought my advice about it before he was nominated. I told him that in my opinion and in my judgment that if he was nominated he would be defeated. He asked me if I could not help him out and I told him, not being a resident of the city, it would not be proper for me to take any hand in their politics. This took place in '85. He was defeated and the Republicans went out of power and were out for many years. To go back—my first step in politics in Greenfield was brought without my seeking. While in the city of Indianapolis my friends made me candidate for the nomination as councilman of my ward. We only had four colored votes in the ward and I had to depend entirely on the white votes of the ward. I was nominated by one majority, but some of the Republicans thought that it would not do for a colored man to be nominated so they opened the polls again and called for more votes. They got two more votes and thus I was defeated. A white man by the name of John Spangle[44] was declared the nominee. After the election, all the county officers, all Democrats, came over as a committee to wait on me and to see how I was feeling. They said: "Now Knox, the Republican Party, while it wants you to vote for them, does not want you to hold office, and we would advise you to come over to the Democratic party." I informed them that the gentlemen on the election board did not constitute the Republican party nor its principles. That I was a Republican from principle and not from revenue and therefore I would have to decline their invitation. Among the number was Ephraim Marsh,[45] the county clerk. That was in 1879. I had been chosen as delegate from the State of Indiana to the National Colored Convention.[46]

The political event which preceded and led up to many exciting and stormy incidents in Greenfield's history are matters of record and I shall only refer to them as a prop and support to my memory. In the year of 1866 [sic] the Indiana Legislature passed the 15th amendment,[47] but they had a great time doing it. A great many of the Democrats left their seats and returned to their homes. We had a representative there by the name of John Addison[48] who was one of those who resigned his seat and came home. A mass meeting was called to find out whether the people endorsed his action in resigning or not. The night of the meeting the courthouse was crowded and he was asked to give his reasons for resigning his seat in the House. He commenced by making a speech, saying that Tom Hendricks[49] and Dan Voorhees and all the leading Democrats advised him to resign his seat. Mr. Addison said that he could not afford to vote for that "nigger thing" and he would not do it so he came home. "If you approve of my course, alright; it is all left with you." He was re-nominated.

United States Senator [Oliver P.] Morton[50] in a speech declared that if a representative resigned his seat for such a purpose his seat should be declared vacant. The obstropulous [sic] representatives managed to get back to their seats, however. It was necessary that Indiana should accept the 15th amendment in order that the great amendments should become laws. When the first election under the amendments came off, the Democrats of Greenfield announced that they would not vote at the same polls as the "nigger." A city election was on and we were told by some of the Republicans, Capt. A. L. Ogg[51] being one, that we should go in a body and vote. This was talked about in our council. I said no; it seemed to me that we should cast our votes individually and go on as if we had been voting all our lives, thus causing less excitement.

A man by the name of John Dobbins[52] used to declare that he would never vote beside a "nigger," but as I went up to vote, he was with me and said he considered it an honor to cast his vote by the side of George Knox. Everything passed off quietly. The time came on for the Congressional nomination. The Hon. David S. Gooding[53] received the nomination for Congressman [in 1870] against the Hon. Jere Wilson[54] of Connersville, if my memory serves me right. Mr. Gooding had been marshal of the District of Columbia and boasted of being an "Andy" Johnson Democrat. I well remember his opening speech. He spoke in the court-house yard just across from my shop. He arraigned the Republicans for being for the "nigger being turned loose upon the country" and asked that the Radicals be turned out. He said, "you people of Hancock county are being taxed to maintain these good-for-nothing, lazy niggers of the South out of your hard earnings. You are taxed for this purpose." This excited the people very much, and he went on to tell them that the "niggers" would all come north and they would be veritable pests, shouting in a loud voice that the

99

"nigger" had no rights which the white man was bound to respect.

My shop being right across from the court-house in the court-house square, the people could look right into it. When he was through speaking, the people would stick their heads in the door [of the shop], saying "these people should not be allowed to remain in our town and county" etc., but by the assistance of cool heads we were kept from having any bodily harm done us. When the excitement had quieted down somewhat, John Addison came in the shop and asked me how I liked the speech Mr. Gooding had made that afternoon at the court-house. I said it was a speech that could not be countenanced by anybody, as it was delivered only for the purpose of riding into power by arousing prejudice against a poor and defenseless people who had no way to protect themselves. I further said such a speech was not becoming to anyone.

Shortly after, Mr. Gooding came in the shop and said, "Well, Knox what did you think of my speech this afternoon?" I answered I did not like it. "Why didn't you like it?" "For the reason, Mr. Gooding, such speeches do harm, not only to me, but my whole race. You know the people do not understand these things you are charging against the Republican party, and you do it for the mere purpose of arousing their prejudice for your own selfish motives, therefore I do not like it."

Mr. Gooding's highest ambition was to go to Congress. He seemed to be in the bloom of life and every avenue seemed opened up before him. He could not turn but what the papers were speaking of him. He was considered a great leader. Finally he received the nomination to Congress. Mr. Wilson was elected by a very close vote.

After the election someone reported to Mr. Gooding that I had said he had asked me to vote for him. At that time he thought he had been defeated by about a three or four hundred majority. He came around to the shop to see me about the report and appeared very indignant. He said, "Knox, I understand you have been telling around town that I asked you to vote for me." I assured him that I had never said anything of the kind, saying "I believe everybody gave you credit for more sense than to ask me to vote for you." Well, he said, if you did not, that is all right. My reply was, "I did not, and never thought of voting for you, especially when I heard you say that you would ram all the 'niggers' down Mr. Wilson's throat; I thought I would just let you ram me down Mr. Wilson's throat, for Mr. Wilson was a man who supported and advocated the rights and freedom of the Negro." He said that is all right, but I did not want the idea to go out that I had asked you to vote for me.

In a few days the returns came in and we found that Mr. Gooding had been defeated for Congress by only a four majority. One day I went in the office of the Hancock Democrat and Mr. Gooding was there. He said to me, "Knox wouldn't you have been proud to have had a Congressman from your own town?" I replied, "I expect I might have been, and I had it in my power to elect you, but now I am proud that we have not got a Congressman from our town." "Why so?" "After the election was over, and you thought you had been defeated by three or four hundred majority, you came to my shop and talked as if it was ridiculous for anyone to insinuate that a 'nigger' had voted for you, therefore I am proud we have not got a Congressman from our town. Any man who thinks it would degrade him, should I vote for him, I could not be proud of him as a Congressman." The election was contested, and the Republicans being in the majority in the House, Mr. Wilson was seated. Congress allowed Mr. Gooding $3,000 for contesting his election.[55]

Two years after [in 1872] David S. Gooding and Mr. Wilson were re-nominated and the campaign was the bitterest I have ever experienced in my life. Mr. Gooding, during the war, had been a very radical Union man. He had made some very bitter speeches against the Democrats. On one occasion he had said that were it in his power "he would uncap hell and put all the Democrats in and then cap it up and let them burn." The old-line Democrats had neither forgotten nor forgiven what he had said, and many of them joined hands with the Republicans to defeat him.

Mr. Gooding was a powerful stump orator, a voice like a lion, and you could hear him for a mile nearly, while Mr. Wilson was a small, spare-made man, with a great head on his shoulders. He was, however, a very brilliant and able man. On one occasion when he got up to speak, a big German fellow said, "My God, who is that; who robbed the graveyard?" You can judge from this how he looked. From his experience in the former campaign Mr. Wilson learned he must meet the enemy with his own weapons. A Democratic friend of mine named [Morgan] Chandler[56] asked me to go over and hear the speaking. He said, "I am very sorry for your man Wilson because our man Gooding uses him up so bad." We went over and stood near the speakers. Judge Wilson opened the speeches, giving Gooding about 15 minutes to close in. When Wilson commenced his speech, he prefaced his remarks by saying, "In our first race for Congress I treated my opponent as a gentleman, and I expected I would receive such treatment from his hands, but I find that I did not and my experience teaches me that if I fight the devil, I must fight him with fire and use the same weapons that he uses." Mr. Wilson spoke for over an hour, completely annihilating his man. The Democrats then hustled around and got crowds together so that when Mr. Gooding made his last 15 minute speech, they could get some enthusiasm into the audience, and they were to cheer whether they felt enthusiastic or not. After the speaking was over, I asked Chandler what he thought of it. He said, "I acknowledge your man has done ours up bad today."

My first experience as a presidential voter was in the Seymour and Blair and Grant and Wilson campaign [of 1868]. During this time large delegations would come from the country and it was a rather exciting campaign. The next was the Grant and [Horace] Greeley campaign [of 1872]. During that time much was brought to bear in trying to influence such men as Ogg and others I cannot mention to leave the g.o.p.

Thos. A. Hendricks came to Greenfield on one occasion to make a speech. It was by persuasion that he came at all. Dan Voorhees said he would not work and went to the races. Finally they did get him to do a little work in the campaign. A conference was held by the Democrats and Greeley men. Mr. Hendricks spoke in the council and said he could stand everything but one thing and that was the "nigger." Capt. Ogg and I were friends and he told me of this one incident of the council. Greeley, as the world knows, was defeated by an overwhelming majority. It seemed there would be no resurrection of the Democratic party, but this party, knowing no death and acknowledging no defeat, rallied in 1876, the leader of their standard being [Samuel J.] Tilden and [Thomas A.] Hendricks, against the Republican candidates, [Rutherford B.] Hayes and [William A.] Wheeler. Our county being about 600 or 700 Democratic, this was another exciting time in my life. The campaign was a very hot one. Clubs were organized—Grant, Lincoln and other clubs by the Republicans and Tilden and Hendricks clubs by the Democrats and there was continual speaking during the campaign. Of course, this was at a time I did not take part in politics. I simply voted. I would not do much talking but did a kind of missionary work. The election was to take place in November, and there was some discussion as to who was to have the last rally day, the Democrats or Republicans. The Democrats, being strongest, got Saturday, giving the Republicans Monday, the last day before election. The Democrats had published that they would have the "favorite son," Thos. A. Hendricks, with them on that day, and scores of other prominent Democrats and local speakers.

Before sun-up the people began to come in. The clubs wore their uniforms, and by eight or nine o'clock the town was crowded, and at 11 o'clock the town was just alive. The crowd was estimated at 25,000 and you could hear nothing but "Hurrah for Tilden and Hendricks!" and occasionally "G_d d_m the Republicans and nigger lovers." The crowd began to get very rude and boistrous, especially around my shop. There were very many wagons, decorated with banners on which were "Clean the Radicals out," "Clean the black Republicans out," "White husbands or none." About 11 o'clock my shop began to fill up and a great crowd gathered outside the shops; they seemed to think there was a curiosity inside the shop. One man especially, (I never knew his name, but always wanted to know it, as I had made up my mind to whip him if it was the last thing I did in my life) came into my shop and got on my stove. I asked him to "please get off the stove" and he answered, "Don't give me any of your black sass." Had I touched him they would have torn my place to pieces. He also threw the water off the stove, and I asked him to get away from there. During all this excitement I had a friend named Gibbs[57] in the chair. He was a Democrat. He was getting shaved and whiskers blacked. He called to Paul Jones, who had been a soldier and did not fear anything, and said, "I want you to defend these men while I get shaved. I want to get out of here." Jones drove them back but they came in again. I happened to be looking at one of my barbers, and I saw one fellow standing in back of him in the act of striking him. I said, hold on there! This same fellow kicked the dye stand over; I asked him not to do it. He took my razor and commenced cutting the straps with it.

The town was full of people. They were speaking at the court-house, on the corners, speaking everywhere. They were ranting against the Republican party, charging they had turned these "nig-gers" upon them and promised them equality. This added fuel to the already great excitement. One German fellow standing next to my window cursed the Republicans and Abolitionists for about two hours. He was a tailor and worked right next door to me. His name was Charlie Fisher.[58] When the excitement was the highest, after the wagons had made their rounds, women would put their heads in the shop and say, "Hurrah for Hendricks, Seymour and Blair!" They would say to the men [customers] in the shop, "I would not let those men shave me." During all the excitement I did not dare to leave my building; my face would have brought death. I sent word to the mar-shal to help quiet the people in my shop. He was a Republican and he asked the people to leave my place alone; they kicked him out, saying, "Get out of here; we are running this she-bang today." The excite-ment right south of me was running still higher. The Republican boys were in uniform, white shirts and blue pants. The Democrats said if you come out with your uniforms on we will take them off you.

The boys had revolvers and went into the postoffice. One of the marshals of the day, whose name I do not care to mention, rushed up on horseback and shouted to the crowd, "Go for them!" The day was long and tiresome. We were crowded and could not work to any ad-vantage. About 12 o'clock the excitement was very great. One Irish-man with a face like a full moon who had been a digger up about Pal-estine [Indiana], wanted to break in the shop to: "clean the niggers out." Four or five men held him back, however. The sheriff of Han-cock county, a noble man and a Democrat by the name of William Wilkins,[59] was told by some one that a mob was trying to tear me out of the shop. He came down, crowding his way into the shop and ad-dressed the crowd as follows: "I am sheriff of Hancock county, as good a Democrat as any of you, but these men are attending to their business and I command you, in the name of the law, to disperse and leave them in peace; I want you to vacate this barber shop." This brought temporary relief.

104

I had gone through the army, passed through exciting times, had experienced the quick terror of the midnight whisper, "the enemy is upon us," but even on the battle field of Mission Ridge, that bloody spot, where men were being killed in platoons all around me, heads and legs torn off, cannon and minnie balls flying as thick as hail, at no time did I suffer in feelings, as on that awful day. I felt I had no protection; the Republicans had nothing to say. The fellow who in the morning had rode [sic] my stove, came back about 1 o'clock. He had been in the south part of town, and entering the house of a woman sick in bed, carried on ridiculously and insulted her. He came to my door and called one of my customers out asking him what his politics were. Being answered Republican he at once knocked the man down and managed to get away. The law-abiding people were powerless. All you could hear was, "Hurrah for Hendricks, Seymour and Blair! Clean the G_d d_m niggers out!" The day before, the Democratic committee went to the saloon-keepers and pled with them not to sell any whiskey on this day. They would not hear the committee.

A strange colored man who had come to town, not knowing what was going on, was set upon by the mob. A man by the name of Billy Craig,[60] a Democrat who wished to do no harm to any one, undertook to get him away from the hands of the mob. The mob then turned upon him, declaring "anyone trying to protect a nigger should be killed." However, after much trouble and anxiety the strange colored man was got away. This day was one upon which I longed for the sun to set. About three o'clock the bands began to play, the wagons moved on and procession after procession from Jackson Township, Sugar Creek Township, Brandywine Township, Vernon Township, and Buck Creek Township began to take their departure.

About half past three when the crowd had thinned out considerably, one of my barbers, who was very light and would not be taken for a colored man, slipped out to get something to eat. My wife thinking there was something wrong, brought me my dinner; she being very fair, could not be told quickly from a white woman. During the evening, not being much of a crowd any more, a fellow followed a man by the name of Shel Osborn[61] and called him a "Republican s_n of a b_tch." Not being about to stand that, he turned around and gave the fellow one of the worse beatings I suppose he had ever had. This was about six o'clock in the evening. The people had mainly gone home except a few stragglers. Another man came by the shop and stood by my door cursing and swearing. I told him we had been treated to all we could stand today. I further urged him to be careful how he talked, as I would not take it off of him any longer. When he saw he could get no reinforcements he sneaked off.

The following Monday the Republicans were to have their demonstration. They did not think they could bring out as large a crowd as the Democrats had. As the sun began to rise, the people commenced to come in from all directions. The Democrats got their crowd from all the adjoining counties. We hurried and opened the shop expecting to have another rushing day's business, not the same experience as we had on Saturday. One of the largest delegations came in from Knightstown, Henry County. In that county the Democrats did not have a word to say. When the crowd had come in, I saw some of the same people who had been in town making disturbance on Saturday. They began again to curse the Republicans as they had on the previous Saturday, and one little fellow, whom I felt very good towards because he had done no harm on Saturday, but only hallooed hurrah for Hendricks, began to halloo around today. I said to him, when he began to halloo around, you are mistaken; this is a new crowd today. He had gotten about five feet from the door-sill cursing the Republicans, when one of the Henry County Republicans struck him in the nose and he came rushing back into the shop saying "you told the truth, but I did not believe it, but now I know it." He ran through one door and out the other. That was the last I ever saw of him.

The big German fellow who had cursed us on Saturday commenced the same thing on this day, and another big German fellow from Knightstown, who thought a Democrat should not have a word to say in anything, struck him on the nose and face and knocked him down. His friends then carried him in the meat shop and stood in the door, with meat knives and cleavers in their hands to protect him from any further injury.

A committee of Knightstown Republicans who saw what results would follow if the saloons were kept open that day, gave orders to the saloon keepers to close up. They refused to do so; the committee took the law in their own hands and compelled them to close as the

106

Democrats should have done. On Monday instead of undergoing what we had undergone on the previous Saturday, things moved along nicely. Many colored people took part in the procession in wagons and on horseback. A great change had taken place. The day before the same race of people were threatening our lives, while on this day we were taking part in the parade as American citizens and as God would have it. This endeared me more than ever to the Republican party.

There was great excitement on election day. As there was no one in particular selected beforehand to swear in the colored voters, I did it. Being a business man, this action made me many enemies. I had sworn in one vote when the county clerk came to me and said, "I have a writ for your arrest." I said, "alright; read it." It proved to be a mere attempt at scare. I went right on swearing in my men. The next morning the news came that the Republicans had won. The Democrats said fraud had been used in every part of the country and later when they saw that Hayes and Wheeler's majority was dwindling away they became frantic in the hope they might procure the election of Tilden and Hendricks. The Republicans were feeling rather blue, but about 2 o'clock in the afternoon the news was confirmed that Hayes and Wheeler were elected. The Democrats had been rejoicing, but they now went home and the Republicans rejoiced. Every train that came in for a week after, we would go down and hear the news about the election and wait for the papers to get the full returns.

I was very much interested in the election. Some said that I was taking too much interest in politics; it would not be good for my business; I would lose my trade, but I kept right on. This election was contested, but eight beating seven always. Hayes and Wheeler were declared elected. Primary conventions had been held and nominations made for the city and county election in 1878. Several men were running for nomination for the same office. The man for sheriff was named Cook, a Democrat, and the candidate running for the nomination for county auditor was Henry Wright.[62] Mr. Wright by some means was unpopular in the county and everything was being done to defeat him for the nomination. He felt somewhat uneasy. The Democrats would sometimes come into my shop and hold their little councils and caucuses. I would be working away apparently paying no attention to what they would say. Ephraim Marsh always said I knew the shaping of the county politics as well as anyone in the county. He said to Mr. Wright "if you want to know what you must do, see Knox."

One morning he came to me and asked if I had any news that would do him any good. I said if you will come back to my shop at six o'clock in the evening, I think I will have the news you want. He was a strong Democrat and a customer of mine and I always desired to help those who helped me, regardless of their politics. One of the principles of my life has always been to hold old and add new friends. In the evening he came back and I said, "Mr. Wright, you have a hard fight before you and the idea is to defeat you to-morrow before ten o'clock. The plan is to send a man to each precinct in the county with the report that you have withdrawn from the contest and that you are not a candidate for nomination." He asked me how he should meet it. I advised him to take all his brothers, he had four or five, and personal friends and send them out to every leading Democrat and to every precinct in the county, arm them with authority saying that you are a candidate for nomination and when the other men came up, demand they show their authority, and thus throttle the lie they intend to tell. He took my advice and was nominated by a very close fight.

John V. Cook, a very enthusiastic Democrat and a personal friend of mine, came to Hancock from Marion County purposely to be elected as sheriff of Hancock County. He bought a large farm in that county, and spent about $1200 trying to get the nomination. He came into my shop after the day's work was all over and was waiting for the returns. He was telling people in the shop what a good Democrat he was and that he had been a Democrat for thirty-three years. He was a Democrat and nothing else. I made the remark to him: "Mr. Cook, you have been a Democrat for thirty-three years, but the Democrats to-day will take more Democracy out of you than you have had in you these thirty-three years." He asked why so; I said "they are going to defeat you; you are defeated now." When the returns came in he was defeated by a very large majority. He was the sorest and sickest man I ever saw. He cursed the Democrats from one end of the county to the other and said they were the biggest liars he ever heard of. He left Hancock County and went to Henry County,[63] one of the strongest Republican counties of the state and turned to be[ing] a Republican.

So my prophecy that he would have more Democracy taken out of him in that day than he had had in thirty-three years was true.

I had been working in literary work,[64] and by this time I had begun to speak quite well, and I did some campaign work, doing all I could to promote the interests of the Republican party. My work was to arouse and keep the colored voters together. At the same time I did not make enemies among the white voters by the cultivation of certain humane principles which I trust to always practice. Many a poor white man in distress had been provided with clothes and shoes through my efforts. As the campaign went on, just the evening before the election, Lon Ford, a friend of mine, came to me with this message: "Henry Wright sent me over to see you and ask you if you were going to vote for him or if you were going to work against him," saying further, if I did not he would never step in my shop again. This threat was too much. I at once sent word to Mr. Wright that being a Republican on principle, that he could count on me doing what I could to bring about his defeat. The next day was election and I saw all the men I could and saw some who were going to vote for Wright. I told them they should not try to defeat Walker[65] and persuaded them to vote for him.

One Dr. Howard[66] had a colored man working for him and I said to him, you want to let your man vote just as he pleases. Do not interfere with him. Let him vote as he pleases because if you do not, you will lose a great many votes by it. Afterwards he came to me and said he had voted his colored man. I said for this I am going to try and change other votes. I went around to some of the men who intended to vote for Wright and I said to them if they were Republicans they must vote for Mr. Walker, because he was a man everybody could support. I said whenever a man tries to hinder me from voting as an American citizen I won't be hindered. I said we must try and defeat Wright. After the votes were counted it was found that Henry Wright was elected by only one vote.[67] This ended the campaign.

Recalling the National Negro Convention of 1879,[68] I went there determined as best I could to represent the wishes of my people. The convention was a very exciting one. It was a time when all the Ne-

109

groes of the South were very much depressed and were looking for some place to go. This meeting was supposed to, and it was hoped would, mark out a way or designate a locality where the oppressed members of the race might find a habitation and enjoy as they should enjoy, being American citizens, life, liberty and the pursuit of happiness. During the convention, while making a speech in defense of the rights of our race, and expressing my views as I felt them, some Southern gentleman present became very indignant at my remarks and shouted from the gallery, "take him out! take him out!" etc.[69]

On my return to Greenfield, I found great excitement existing throughout the town and county, owing to the report that thousands of colored people were on the way North and West and a great many of them would stop in Indiana,[70] etc., and so on. It was given out that they were to be brought here, simply to vote the Republican ticket and carry the state for that party. It was charged by my political enemies in Hancock County that my ideas in attending the Negro Convention was for the purpose of voting down the wishes of the white people who were opposed to them. It was reported also that I had introduced a resolution there to that effect and that the Democratic paper published in the city where the convention was held, styled Capt. A. L. Ogg, John W. Jones[71] and myself as the bosses of emigration. Our official titles were: Jones, Secretary of State; Ogg, Secretary of War; Knox, Secretary of Treasury.[72] One of the street ballads chanted by the urchins of the town contained this verse:

> Four and twenty Negroes
> All in a block,
> Waiting at the depot
> For Jones and Knox.[73]

This, as a matter of course, put us in a bad light temporarily, before the citizens of the county, especially that portion that belonged to the Democratic party and it may be said, an occasional member of the Republican party. Time has demonstrated, however, the wildness of these rumors, and while it is not to be denied that a great many of those who came North during the exodus, located not only in Hancock County, Greenfield, but in different portions of the State, they

110

were also some of Indiana's most prosperous citizens and have added much to the wealth of the State.

But to return to my narrative. One evening about four o'clock a dispatch came to Greenfield that there were seven car loads of colored people en route to Hancock County. The four o'clock train arrived with one car load. I shall not forget as long as I live, the sensation the news made in the city and the querulous and anxious and frequently condemnatory looks that were leveled at me from all sides. As I looked up the street I noticed a strange colored man coming with a large envelope in his hand. It is well enough to state here that I had been denying all the time that I had anything to do with the exodus. This colored man came up and handed me the envelope and asked if my name was Knox, following his interrogation with the remark that he had "twenty-seven head."[74] I asked "twenty-seven head of what," and he said twenty-seven of his people, which answer caused a murmur of surprise to run through the crowd of spectators who had gathered about my place of business. I took the envelope and saw it was addressed to John Jones. I said to him, "they are not billed to me; however, I will go with you and see that you come out alright." This set the spectators wild. The excitement was reaching fever heat. I went to the depot and was greeted with a crowd of all kinds of colored people, in all kinds of habiliments of all ages and conditions. The couplet from the nursery rhyme, so familiar to us all, is an apt illustration:

> Some dressed in rags, some in bags,
> and some in velvet gowns.

The next thing was what to do with them. I must confess that while my zeal was unabated, and while I was doing a Christian and humane duty, and knew I was [right] in clinging to my own, and felt that they had made no mistake in getting away from the conditions that had become so oppressive to them in the South; nevertheless, for a moment or two I was at my wits' ends. I could feel I was the target of observation and quiet comment on the part of the citizens of the town, and was conscious of the presence of a rising perspiration on my brow, to say nothing of an occasional trickle down my back. Nevertheless, a reserved determination and stubborn resolution that up to this time

111

had never deserted me in life, enabled me to face the situation with respectable equanimity.

A shooting match that had taken place that day had called a great many farmers from the surrounding townships together. When the news reached them that the depot was thronged with Negro emigrants, come for the purpose of overrunning Hancock County, etc., a great number of them came down and, being dressed in coon-skin caps, clothes of leather, etc., and accompanied with dogs, powder horns, guns, and everything else, some of the simple-minded colored people feared that they had left the South only to be thrown into the hands of an unmerciful band of Northern ku-klux. I told them not to be alarmed, that they were surrounded by, if picturesque and queer looking hunters, at least harmless as far as they were concerned and that they had no desire to frighten them. The first night we kept them in the depot and secured their supper from a store-keeper in the town, one Oliver Moore, an active young man with a kindly inclined heart, who donated the same, and for it, be it said to the eternal shame of those who connived at and engaged in it, his store was shortly after burned.[75]

The next day we found quarters for them in a big empty building, filling it upstairs and down and in this way we kept them until we secured homes for them. Donations were made by Republicans and an occasional Democrat whose humanitarian principles were stronger than his partisanship. Friends came to me and were very solicitous, especially my Democratic "friends," that I should have nothing to do with them, that it would hurt my business, etc., and that I would make enemies for myself. Whether their zeal for my business was greater than their zeal for party, I will not undertake to say. I will leave that for my readers to judge. But I felt then, as I have never failed to feel since, and hope never will, that before I would go back on my countrymen, members of my own race, in their destitution and desperation and sorrow, I would beg bread upon the streets.

A few days after the stirring incidents recorded above, one evening near the hour of twilight, while my wife was busy preparing tea with the remainder of my little family playing about my feet, a man with a sick child in his arms hallooed in from the street. I went out and asked him what he wanted. He said he was hunting a place to stay. He was accompanied with his family, wife and seven children. It was rainy and cold and I bade him come in, knowing at the same time the moment his presence was noised about town, I would be subjected to the usual amount of comment and blame.

The Hancock Democrat came out and boldly charged me with being the boss of emigration, saying I had received "another invoice." Editorially, it urged its patrons and readers, that a man who would do what I was doing with a desire to pauperize the county, should not be patronized, claiming that I was bringing into the county the poor, lazy "niggers" for the purpose of taxing the white people to take care of them and that they (the whites) should withdraw their patronage from me.

I kept on, however, attending to my business, and my friends on the other side rallied to my support. As if to emphasize the feeling that was being fostered against me from Democratic sources, another shop doing business was known as the Democratic barber shop.[76] So anxiously, apparently, were some of my political enemies that I should be compelled to close up business, that daily pilgrimages were made to my shop for the purpose of peering through my windows, no doubt accompanied with the wonder when I was going to move out. Yet I would be neglectful of the truth did I fail to state, during the years that recorded my residence in Hancock County, some of my warmest and most faithful friends were members of the Democratic party.

There is an old saying that it makes a great difference whose ox gets gored, and as I recall the events associated with my residence in Hancock County there is an occasional reminiscence which crowds its way to the surface that reminds me of the truth of this axiom—one in particular that has a bearing upon the matter.

There was a man living in Greenfield, very popular in the county and a Democrat, whose nomination for the second term of sheriff I had virtually secured, but before receiving his nomination a charge of drunkenness had been made against him by members of his party, who desired the nomination of some one else. Finally the investigation narrowed down to the agreement that a committee, in a sort of confidential way, should wait upon me and ascertain if I knew anything from observation that would corroborate the charges of intoxication against

113

the would-be candidate. They came to my place of business and the spokesman asked me what I knew about Wm. Thomas'[77] drinking habits. My reply was that I had seen Mr. Thomas for two years and over, at late hours of night, when if individuals had mean dispositions or indulged in mean habits, they would crop out, but I had never seen the man drunk whose habits the committee were investigating. I said it was very probable he would take his "dram" occasionally, but as for seeing him drunk or believing him to drink to any excess, that was not my experience.

The committee took my word and upon the strength of it, the man charged with being a "drinker" was nominated and re-elected. Now for the application: Remembering that I had done him a great favor. When the exodus movement materialized and I found myself directly or indirectly associated with it, he was the first man to start the cry against me and advise the people not to patronize my place of business. His idea was that his action would add to his popularity throughout the county and thus enable him to eventually become the county clerk, for which position he had ambitions. In order, however, not to treat him unfairly or take snap judgment on him I inquired of Messrs. Ephraim Marsh and Morgan Chandler as to what they knew about the charge that ex-Sheriff Thomas had been busy in circulating and endeavoring to harm me from a business standpoint, in the estimation of the community.

With an evident desire not to commit themselves, nevertheless, Mr. Marsh stated he had heard something of it. My reply was, that if it should prove to be a fact, Mr. Thomas could never receive the nomination for clerk of Hancock County. However, he (Thomas) did come out for the nomination for clerk [in 1882]. In my individual capacity, I waited upon Ephraim Marsh, the then Clerk of the county and a Democrat, suggested to him that he allow the use of Chas. Downing's[78] name, a deputy clerk in his office, for the purpose of nomination for clerk instead of Mr. Thomas. While Mr. Marsh seemed to take kindly to the proposition, diplomatically he felt it would not do for him to appear upon the surface as urging the nomination of Mr. Downing; inasmuch as the latter gentleman had been his deputy for eight years, the enemies of Mr. Downing and the friends of Mr. Thomas might make the argument that to make Mr.

114

Downing clerk would amount to keeping Mr. Marsh in office, as he would virtually be clerk.

There was some force in his argument. Nevertheless, I asked Mr. Downing to make the race, knowing he was very popular with the Republicans as well as the Democrats, and I assured him for this reason also, that he could be nominated. He finally consented to place himself in the hands of his friends. On the evening of the day that the primary election for nomination came off, about supper time, I met Mr. Downing and Mr. Marsh with their heads both hanging down, as though they bore bad tidings. Asking the news, I was informed that Thomas had beaten Downing, carrying Center Township, Brandy-wine Township, Jackson Township, etc. It seems a report had been started and worked for all it was worth, by certain friends of Mr. Thomas, Wm. McBaine,[79] Steve Dickinson[80] and others, to the effect that Mr. Downing had concluded not to make the race, and the report going uncontradicted as a matter of course, it was hurtful to that gentleman's chances. I at once urged Mr. Marsh and Mr. Downing with all earnestness at my command to counsel with their friends and send them to every township and voting precinct in the county to counteract this report that had been started by Mr. Downing's enemies. "Do this," was my parting injunction, and "to-morrow when the convention assembles, Charlie Downing will be nominated on the first or second ballot."

Saturday morning, bright and early, Thomas and his friends were up and about, no doubt confident of the easy victory they were going to have over Mr. Downing after the convention assembled. Thomas was a man you could hear laugh blocks and blocks away, and on this particular morning he seemed to be in overflowing glee. A friend of his passing me said, "there goes the nominee for clerk of Hancock County." I still insisted that he would be beaten on the first or second ballot and not only that, his defeat would kill him so dead that we would not hear him laugh for two months. By this time the local excitement had reached high water mark. It proved to be a most exciting and interesting county convention. The forces of Thomas were defiant and almost insolent in their belief that Downing would be quickly and easily vanquished when it came to the final test. To make what might be a long story short, Mr. Downing was nominated on the second bal-

115

lot and I was mistaken, for Mr. Thomas did not laugh for six months. Defeated in convention, the object of Mr. Thomas now was to defeat his opponent for election.

Stanton J. Peelle[81] at that time [in 1882] was a candidate upon the Republican ticket for Congress, "Billy" English,[82] son of General Hancock's running mate for the White House being his opponent. Mr. Peelle had stumped the county, he and Mr. English, making the subject matter of their campaign mainly "trace chains," as being a farm commodity of more or less interest to the farmer, as their price might be effected either up or down by the tariff.[83] When Mr. English entered the county to make his campaign, he took into his confidence as his right-hand lieutenant a young man by the name of Erick Swope,[84] and for some reason this aroused the ire of the late James J. Walsh,[85] then a prominent young man of the county and afterwards a member of the legislature. It seemed here was my opportunity, so I took secret advantage of the situation and persuaded Walsh to work against English in favor of Peelle and Downing. On Saturday before the election Mr. Peelle, who was in the county, came into my place of business and stated in a confidential manner that he was going to carry Shelby and Hancock counties.

Jaunty Tauge,[86] a well-known character of the time and the town, asked me how much I thought Mr. Peelle would carry the county. My reply was that he would not carry it at all, my argument being that on the presidential year, the county was reliably 600 majority, but on the off year, it was just as reliably 500 Democratic majority. Besides there were other reasons, but upon the other hand, there were arguments in favor of Mr. Peelle, namely, the peculiar sort of campaign conducted by Mr. English in Hancock County. A saloon campaign might do in Indianapolis, but hardly for Hancock County, as I understood it. I told Mr. Peelle he would reduce the Democratic majority to somewhere in the neighborhood of 440. He talked so confident of his election that on election day a great many of his friends who otherwise would have been zealous workers in his behalf, simply voted and left the polls. It was plain to me that if something was not done, he would be defeated; so I stopped my business for the day and worked for him, the young Irishman, Walsh, and myself working together. Walsh's attitude in this campaign puzzled the members of his own party as well as those

116

of ours. In fact, "Jim," as he was familiarly called, was trading English in favor of Downing whenever he could. Capt. Ogg was one of the judges on the election board. He was worried lest Walsh was deceiving me and using his influence against our man. I finally had to tell him that whenever he saw me nod my head it was a sign for him not to challenge that vote.

When the returns were finally in, it was seen that Mr. Peelle had carried Shelby County and had reduced the majority in Hancock to 443, Mr. Downing being elected clerk by about 133 majority. It may be well enough for me to say here at this stage of my remembrance, that my first object in taking such an interest in Mr. Downing's election, was that Mr. [William S.] Wood[87] who had educated and adopted him, had been a great friend and had helped me when I could not help myself, Mr. Downing being, as was then known, one of the "New York Boys" sent out by some philanthropic society of that city to different localities in the West. Then Mr. Downing had also married a daughter of another great friend of mine, Mr. Arthur Williams.[88]

Wm. Wood at one time owned a great deal of property. About the time I started in business in Greenfield, he started in the grocery business and went from that into the hardware business. He accumulated property very fast and finally went into the banking business. He built a fine building for the purpose and had three of the wealthiest men in the county, Philander Boyd,[89] John Simmons,[90] and Israel Poston[91] associated with him. After the bank was open and going nicely, and he apparently coining money, I said to my wife one day, feeling quite discouraged from contrasting my success with that of Mr. Wood, that I was a "dead failure." Somewhat surprised, she asked me why, what I meant. I replied, "Wm. Wood and I started in business together; although he had $6.00 while I did not have a cent but the $2.00 which I borrowed from him and the capital represented in my little shop. Today he is worth $30,000 and I am not worth $2000 all told, which makes me feel that as a businessman I am a dead failure." My wife replied, "you are all right, keep going ahead; if you keep going ahead, no matter how slow it may seem, you certainly will not go back."

Shortly afterward Mr. Wood met with business reverses and while his mind was clouded and depressed through his misfortunes, he com-

icide one day in the depot at Indianapolis by taking mor-
fter his estate had been settled up, debts paid etc., he was
still worth $2000, but the unfortunate man had passed be-
yond the possibility of enjoying the satisfaction of that knowledge. I
then said to my wife that I was not so bad off after all; I was worth
somewhere in the neighborhood of $2000 and still alive, while my
friend and benefactor, although worth $2000 above his liabilities, was
dead.

During the [James A.] Garfield campaign of 1880 I took an active
part and stumped the county for the party. On one occasion Col. A.
A. Black,[93] Lafayette Reynolds[94] and myself were sent by the committee to Blue River township to speak. We had different speeches, all
converging to the same point, the glory and greatness of the Republican Party. The arrangement was this: Col. Black was to lead off on
"Order No. 40,"[95] Reynolds on "The Tow Path to the White
House," while the subject of my address was "The Prosperity that
would be brought about by keeping the Republican Party in the
White House." Just about the time Col. Black was about half way
through, attention seemed to be directed toward the back part of the
house where I was sitting. Presently the crowd commenced to shout,
"Knox! Knox!" and they kept it up so incessantly that the Col. had to
bring his speech to a close. I took the floor and soon had the meeting
feeling good and running over with laughter.

I told the boys on our way back home that the interruption of Col.
Black reminded me of the incident that happened when I was present
at a mass meeting in Indianapolis. It was the year [1880] that Gov.
[Albert G.] Porter[96] was a candidate against Frank Landers,[97] the
Democratic nominee. The colored people of the Capitol City were
having a mass meeting and I happened in the city that night and wan-
dered with the crowd to the Second Colored Baptist Church, and being espied by the chairman of the meeting was asked to make a few remarks. Jas. T. V. Hill[98] obtained the floor after I had finished and
made quite a good commencement of his address, when a tall, stately
looking colored man was observed entering the church. It did not take
the crowd long to realize that they were honored by the presence of
Frederick Douglass,[99] who like myself had happened in the city and

118

had been persuaded by the local magnates to make a short visit to the mass meeting. At once the great crowd assembled, shouted, "Douglass! Douglass! Douglass!" but for some reason or other Hill seemed disposed to pay no attention to the wishes of the meeting but to go on with his speech.

It was useless, however, as the temper of the meeting demanded that he take his seat and give way to Mr. Douglass. "The Sage of Anacostia," with that modesty which is never absent from the truly great, and that was peculiarly characteristic of Mr. Douglass, insisted that he be permitted to enjoy the pleasure of a looker-on and incidentally the eloquence of the young man who had the floor, but to no avail. Pandemonium reigned until he faced the audience and favored them with a five minute talk.

Election day [in 1880] finally came around and found me at the polls swearing in votes. An effort was made to interrupt my work by a posse of Democrats who came rushing up to me, declaring they had a warrant for my arrest. It, however, proved to be a harmless bluff and I went right on with my work. After the polls had closed and while the results were as yet unknown, the Methodist preacher and myself, until waiting downtown somewhere in the neighborhood of 12 o'clock, resolved to go home and learn the results on the following morning. I was so worn out and exhausted that I soon dropped into a heavy slumber, only to be awakened about two o'clock in the morning by the music of a band and yells and shouts that seemed to come from thousands of throats. The noise grew very distinct and I soon perceived that the crowd was coming toward my home. The editor of the Hancock Democrat,[100] being a close neighbor of mine, I first thought that it was the jubilating members of his party coming to apprise him of a Democratic victory. I awakened my wife and informed her that we were beaten. I remarked, Republicans did not make noise like that, but I soon changed my mind when I caught the words of a song they were singing, "We'll Hang Jeff Davis on a Sour Apple Tree," etc. This convinced me that the crowd approaching was a Republican one, as never to my knowledge, had a Democratic crowd, especially on the occasion of a victory, indulged in singing that immortal hymn, "John Brown's Body lies Mouldering in the Grave."

Led by the band and fully 1,000 strong, they reached my humble

119

residence and halted. One man in the crowd shouted, "Knox, we concluded to bring the news of [James A.] Garfield's election to you first!" I ran upstairs, dressing as I went, and opening the door, stepped out on the verandah. The crowd shouted "speech." Before responding to the invitation of my happy friends, Capt A. L. Ogg, who had been selected as the spokesman for the crowd, pressed to the front and spoke in part as follows:

"Col. Knox:—I have been selected by this delegation of your neighbors to deliver you the news of the victory—the great victory that the Republican Party has won to-day. It has carried New York, Michigan, Indiana and a part of the Southern states. It is an occasion worthy the jollification and shouts of all men who love and believe in the continuity of free institutions and whose proudest hopes and highest political aims in life are to follow the standards of that party, whose leaders, dead and living, and whose principles embody and contain within themselves, all that places American citizenship above that of any other nation, and that guarantee to all men, irrespective of race, color, present or past condition, the privileges of life, liberty and the pursuit of happiness. We know that you will join with us in this moment of thankfulness and satisfaction."

Like Artemus Ward, I felt too full for utterance to say anything of a feeling almost akin to timidity which seemed to paralyze my tongue. Bowing to the crowd, however, thanking them for the honor and compliment of their visit, I contented myself and evidently pleased my hearers in saying:

"I perceive from the noise you are making that you have glad tidings, that the telegraphic wire has brought you news of good cheer, that you—that we—have met the enemy and they are ours. Without speaking with authority, intuitively I feel that the Republican Party has, by this day's work, planted her banners on the pine bluffs of Maine to the golden gates of California, from the great lakes of Michigan, those inland seas that represent in their size their breadth and depth, the majesty of our common country, to the cinnamon groves and sandy bottoms of the South. We have redeemed Indiana and placed her once more in the ranks of those states whose chief glory among the pages of history will be, that in the hour of their country's

120

peril they were true to that country. You have vindicated the silent honor of the 250,000 boys in blue whose bones are bleaching in the Sunny South, whose unmarked graves, billows one half of our country from ocean to ocean. You have honored our great war governor, Oliver P. Morton, and have proven how true and how eloquent a prophet was Lincoln when he declared that the men who gave their lives at Antietam, Appomattox and the Wilderness gave them freely, that this government of the people, for the people, by the people should not perish from the earth. You have further declared by the glorious result of your political fealty, as recorded amongst the achievements of this day's work, that you are opposed to that spirit of mal-legislation that would induce the Congress of our nation to spend thousands of dollars to investigate why American citizens, even though many of them were former slaves and descendants of slaves, should be interrupted or checked in their desire to migrate to any portion of our common land their interests or inclinations may urge them to."

"In conclusion, fellow citizens, you have branded with the stamp of your condemnation the action and the voice of Daniel W. Voorhees, the Democratic senator of this State, who in his zeal to serve his party rather than right, has dared with all the power of his eloquent tongue, of his matchless gift of persuasion as an orator, to brand American citizens migrating from one state to another, as enemies of the public peace and as unworthy the protection due them as upright men and women. Would I make too large a draught upon my imagination did I say to you, in conclusion, that I believe that in this day's work, the Sumners, the Lincolns, the John Browns, the Lovejoys, all of that throng of glorious citizens of the New Jerusalem, are with us in spirit at this very moment and partakers of the pleasure of this great jubilee?"

It is a real pleasure to record at this juncture, that among the many warm friends of the opposite political faith, whose kindly personal offices to me and mine during the years of my sojourn in Greenfield, must always remain a white stone in memory, there is none more deserving of recall than William M. Mitchell, for many years the able and brilliant editor of the Hancock Democrat. Despite whatever attitude he felt called upon to take to serve his party, his kind treatment of

121

me was never warped by my color, or the conditions from which I emerged to find in Greenfield a haven and a home. Such men are the salt of the earth—"Sages with wisdom's garland wreathed."[101]

In 1870 I interested myself in the organization of a Sunday school. On the occasion of our opening Sabbath, we had two members, which consisted of one scholar and the teacher, superintendent, librarian, secretary, sexton and treasurer, all in one, which office I filled. This condition of affairs would have been discouraging to a great many people, but I rather relished it, out of a predisposition to take hold of undeveloped affairs and build them up. The school flourished like a green bay tree. It became the talk of the town and little by little the resort on Sabbath days. All the colored people of the city, one by one, became members of it—every young and old person and every child. Among the teachers were Dr. O. M. Edwards[102] and the Hon. Wm. Sparks at that time mayor of the city.

The school antedated the church, as up to this time the colored portion of the community had not been favored with a separate place of worship. Two years after the organization of the Sunday school, preliminary steps were taken toward the organization of a church, our first pastor being Rev. J. A. James, sent us by the Lexington, M.[ethodist] E.[piscopal] Conference.[103] Shortly after the organization of the church a revival was started, which continued four or five weeks. The late Rev. Marshall W. Taylor,[104] then in the full meridian of his great power, perhaps the most eloquent Afro-American in the pulpit of this country, was present to assist. The people of Greenfield, irrespective of race, had never listened to one more eloquent before. The result was that the house was packed every night to the window tops on the outside to listen to the gospel as it dropped from the lips of the eloquent divine. Many joined the church, I being one of the number. One cold day, the earth being covered with snow and ice, in company with Miss Martha Hunt,[105] I received the sacrament of baptism in what was known as the "Brandywine,"[106] which at that time was at high water and ice-cold. The Rev. Dr. [Andrew] Bryant officiated. It seemed that the whole town had turned out; the banks and roadside as far as the eye could reach nearly, were lined with a moving mass of humanity.

122

There is no doubt that this day marked one of the controlling incidents in my life, as I then considered and still consider it. The church continued to move on nicely and Rev. Mr. James was succeeded by Rev. Geo. Hudson, he remaining with us one year. Shortly after, Presiding Elder [W. C.] Echols came to us to hold his first quarterly meeting. The presiding elder, however, was a disappointment, as his preaching did not begin to reach the expectations of him. Rev. Geo. W. Zeigler was next sent us and during his time [1881] we concluded and did hold the first camp meeting, which was a success, spiritually and financially; the Revs. Dr. Hammond[107] and S. S. Johnson assisting us. The receipts were in the neighborhood of $400.00, which paid the pastor and the presiding elder well. Previous to the meeting, Mr. [Philander] Boyd, the proprietor of the grounds, was warned that if he permitted us to have the camp meeting, that the woods would run with blood. A guarantee from me that there would be no trouble on the grounds was sufficient. The camp meeting became an assured fact. We had use for three tents and the meeting was conducted so nicely and quietly that the whites immediately took a fancy to it. The attendance the first Sabbath was 1,500, followed by 3,000 the next.[108]

Realizing that nothing could be conducted properly without system and organization, whether matters of business or religion, I had the ground thoroughly policed, or fenced in by officers, having employed 30 good men and true to attend to this feature. Some one asking jocously [sic] who was to be chief of police, I replied at once that I was. Each Sabbath we collected ten cents a head at the gate. A notorious character about the town was one Jim Wilson, who making his appearance at the gate on Sabbath morning during the meeting, one of my police hesitated to let him enter. Being appealed to in the matter, my instructions were that we could not refuse him entrance, as it was the business of the church to permit everyone to gather about the shrine. I said of course, let him come in, but gave orders that at the first intimation he made to disturb the meeting, to arrest him. "Jim" was feeling pretty good and he soon convinced us by shouting "amen," that he was out for a little fun. He was arrested, taken to jail, tried Monday morning and fined $16.00, which no doubt at that time he considered a pretty big price for saying amen once.

Our preacher the following year being the Rev. Moses Franklin.

White and colored people alike were anxious that we have another camp meeting, so in September [1882] we opened our second annual meeting. On this occasion we had service for five tents, and renting the ground out for eating stands, etc., we easily paid expenses and in the end the meeting was very profitable. Dr. Hammond, one of the most eloquent Negro divines in America, assisted us at this meeting, and preached the first Sunday to 2,500 people. The offices of Superintendent, Chief of Police and Treasurer were filled by myself, while Mr. Calvin Gilliam became my secretary. On the second Sabbath 4,000 people attended the meeting.

Conference having sent us a man by the name of Simmons the next year, we did not keep him, as not being satisfactory in any respect. Asking me for money to return home, I consented on the condition that he did not return, as the people did not want him. Our third annual camp meeting was held in September of that year [1883]. Dr. Hammond proving such a drawing card that we again secured his services. On the first Sabbath he preached to 3,000 people, and on the last to 5,000. At these meetings I do not think there were over 100 colored people in attendance. Services began promptly at 6 o'clock in the morning, succeeded by 10 o'clock and 2 o'clock services, from 1,000 to 2,000 people attending the night services.

At our fourth annual camp meeting [in 1884] we had ten or twelve tenters on the ground, several whites tenting with us. The occasion proved a very pleasant one. Elder Hammond, who was to take charge of the meeting but was detained at Greencastle on the first Sabbath, sent Rev. Jesse Mundy[109] to fill his appointment. When the people found out that Dr. Hammond was not to be with us, they were very much disappointed, some of them going so far as to charge me with fraud by advertising a man to be present when I knew that such would not be the case. I at once called a council of war composed of myself and the six or seven ministers on the ground and stated the situation to them—how Elder Hammond had disappointed me and that the people were mainly out of patience and some of them quite angry, concluding by saying something had to be done, as I felt perhaps unduly sensitive that my integrity was in the balance.

It was arranged that Rev. Vaughn[110] should take charge of the meeting, that is, conduct the worship of the meeting, but I reserved to myself the privilege of effecting the plan which was, that we would have a class meeting at two o'clock in the afternoon, at three o'clock Rev. Henry Stein[111] would preach, followed by Rev. Vaughn at seven, my parting injunction being, "If you men [have] ever sung or preached in your life, you must do it to-day." About 10:45 I mounted the platform and facing the angry mass of people who in no gentle tones were proclaiming that I had wronged them, talked to them about fifteen minutes, making such a plea as I had never been called upon to make before, reading letters and dispatches to convince them I had made the contract in good faith and I was not to blame, that Dr. Hammond for some reason or other had disappointed us. In lieu of his presence, I reminded them that we had some eight or ten able men on the ground who would sing and preach to them, concluding with the promise that when the day was finished and they were not satisfied, I would take my stand at the gate and would return to everyone the money he had paid to come in. That seemed to pacify them. They began to feel better. When the last sermon was preached they all admitted with one voice that they were more than satisfied.

Monday morning bright and early Dr. Hammond arrived on the ground and at once commenced a very pleasant time. At this meeting there were seventy-three converts, the whites and colored all kneeling at the same bench. There were six thousand people on the ground. On the second Sabbath, at which time we had carried the meeting over, it took six people to sell tickets, two of them, B. A. Roberts and my eldest son, William, acting in that capacity. The receipts for the day were so large that I hesitated about keeping the money with me in the woods and finally persuaded the banker to open the bank and place the money away for safe keeping. Altogether this camp meeting lasted three weeks. All the meetings in the county, of whatever description, and all the ministers of the other race dismissed their meetings and attended this. We were plentifully supplied with jubilee singers, and in fact had a regular old-fashioned Methodist camp meeting. On the last Sabbath evening, different converts were given charges to preach in the different churches.

The following year [in 1885] we held our fifth annual camp meeting. This was also very successful, ten or twelve families camping on the ground during the meeting. Dr. Hammond was again on hand.

125

The first Sabbath we had 4,000 people on the ground and the next 6,000. On this occasion we had a little opposition for the first time. Mrs. Woodworth,[112] the well-known trance revivalist, was engaged in a meeting at Willow Branch about nineteen miles away. This as a matter of course affected our attendance somewhat but not enough to be noticed particularly. We had come to the conclusion to continue this meeting into the third Sabbath, provided we could secure the service of Mrs. Woodworth, who was creating a great deal of excitement and curiosity on account of her peculiar modes of conducting a meeting. It was decided to make an effort to secure her services. Mrs. Kate Applegate and myself were selected to effect the arrangements. This lady, Mrs. Applegate, was one of the teachers of our High School in Greenfield and a person of great piety and consecration in matters of the church.

We started on our trip Monday morning about 4:30. It was the general opinion that we would be unsuccessful in our quest, but I roused hope to the contrary by stating that I never went after a person that I did not get. When we reached Willow Branch it was about 9:30 and I found myself in the midst of friends and acquaintances, although I had never been in this part of the country before. When asked what my mission was, I replied that I had come after Mrs. Woodworth to go to Greenfield. Their answer was that they thought I could not secure her. I answered that I had come after her and must have her.

First I waited upon her husband, detailing my mission. He said his wife was tired and he did not think she would go. I requested an audience with himself and wife alone, which being granted she said she did not know how she could go as she had made arrangements with Dr. Troy to rest a week, after which she had other engagements to fill. I said to her, "The excitement you have aroused and the reputation you have made for yourself, we can have on the ground, if you will be present with us, eight or ten thousand people. Of course that means a thousand dollars; of course, you are not preaching for money, yet you have to pay your expenses." She said: "Yes, that was so; she was not preaching for money," and to accelerate matters I at once made a commercial proposition to her, i.e.: That I would give her half of the gross gate receipts. Then she commenced to study. I gave her ten minutes to decide and before the time was up, she consented to go. We started

126

and arrived at Greenfield at 12 o'clock. When it was noised about that Mrs. Woodworth was on the grounds, it was not long before the people were coming from every direction. I arranged that no one should see her that afternoon and she should have it to rest in. The multitude was much disappointed. However, I promised that she would preach at seven o'clock that evening which she did to some 4,000 people.

On Wednesday she had several in a trance, men fell, white and black, mainly white, as though they had been shocked, she even had the Methodist minister in the town and several others at the mourners' bench praying for more power from high. The meeting was crowded day and night; people would go into trances and lie for three or four hours unconscious. Occasionally she herself would go off in a trance; friends would take her up and carry her to her tent. When Sunday came the crowd was not as large as we anticipated, but in the afternoon the tent which held 4,000 was crowded. She preached a powerful sermon and Dr. Hammond followed with one of his moving prayers, and the people began to fall in every direction, Mrs. Woodworth making the statement that they were stricken down by the power of God. This meeting was a great success spiritually as well as financially.

In 1886[113] we held our 6th annual camp meeting [in Lawrence, Indiana]. Dr. Hammond not being with us, Elder Sweres, somewhat a noted preacher in his day, of the A.[frican] M.[ethodist] E.[piscopal] church was selected to conduct it. We got along nicely and had a pleasant season, but no accessions to the church as Sweres was not as able a man in that direction as Dr. Hammond, and while the crowd was not so large, on the last Sabbath we had from four to five thousand people.

We reached Lawrence[114] on Thursday. Friday we erected our tents. Saturday we opened our meeting. In making up my police force I approached a reputable citizen of Lawrence and requested if he could direct me to a good man to serve as a policeman. He replied he knew of one person who would make a good officer, but he was so tough and such a dangerous man, who would fight, that he hesitated to recommend him. He had knocked one or two men in the head and was noted for general cussedness. I replied that was the man I wanted. The fellow suggested to me was a bar-tender. He said if I would hire him he would work for me. I had about ten policemen. As the word had gone out it would be impossible for me to go on with the camp meeting, I was determined to do so and with the best of order.

A few miles from Lawrence a camp meeting was being conducted by the whites but which was broken up, so it would be understood that my zeal and desire not to be treated in the same manner was very great. My instructions to Henry Stein [*sic*] were to go and open the meeting with song and prayer. He did so and then called the people together. As I surveyed the crowd, I noticed that a great many of the men present kept their hats on and were smoking cigars, etc. I saw that trouble was brewing; in the meantime it was getting dark and the light from the lamps was quite dim. A colored man by the name of Brew was one of my officers but it was soon apparent to me that he could not handle the people put in his charge. I had furnished my officers with stars and I looked about but was unable to distinguish them from the crowd, as instead of wearing the insignia of their authority on the outside of their coats, they had pinned them on the inside and buttoned their coats. I had promised them $2.00 a day for their services but when I found that they had their coats buttoned, I told them they were cowards and not the kind of officers I wanted. I wanted men who were not afraid to show their colors and if they wanted to act for me, they must show their stars. The hint was sufficient. Within ten minutes stars were glittering in the lamp light and quietude and serenity reigned upon the grounds.

Saturday night it rained very hard and the grounds were very muddy. The seats were so wet, there was so much water and mud that we could not hold our meeting in the grove, so I waited on the president of the fair grounds and secured the hall, which had to be seated and a platform built in it. By this time it was half past ten when the people began to come. About five hundred people were present at the morning meeting and we had perfect order. In fact the citizens of the town were surprised that such good order was kept. At the evening meeting, however, it began to look as though our powers to keep order were about tested. The young ladies were very rude, more so than the young men. I had to wait upon two or three of them and insist that they keep still. They were having a great time, eating peanuts and candy, chewing gum, etc. One of them asked me "what I was going to do about it" and I replied that I would be compelled to show her if she did not keep quiet. On the outside were some fellows inclined to be rough. I waited upon them with my officers and insisted that they must keep order. Two of them rushed back into the dark, away from the lights and drew their revolvers, which glistened as the shadow of the lights fell upon them. I spoke very loud addressing my officer, with the intention of making myself heard by the ruffians in the dark and said I intended to have order or I would fill Marion County jail so full with them that they would stick out of the windows. This had the effect; things grew quiet and the services went on. Everyone was well pleased but more surprised than pleased that we had such good order on the ground. Some said no wonder we had order, as we had all the saloon-keepers and rowdies on the police force.

The second Sunday was our big day. I sent to Greenfield for one of my reliable officers, who had been with me during my camp meetings there. On Saturday evening preceding the second Sabbath I called my staff around me and gave them final instructions, which were: 1st, we must have order on the morrow at all hazards; 2nd, they were not to make any arrests unless compelled to do so. I had been told that a great many ruffians were to be present to run things their own way. I reminded them that my reputation as a successful camp meeting manager was at stake and that they had to be careful or the meeting would be broken up, and concluded by insisting that if they did their duty, there would be no trouble. By ten o'clock we had a pretty good crowd on the grounds. About this hour I noticed a couple of fellows acting roughly. I took an officer and went to them at once. I informed them that their actions would not be tolerated and that we had ten officers backed by the law.

In a subsequent conversation with my officer, my instructions to him were that if he saw anyone acting rough, he was to go to him and to endeavor to quiet him; failing, he was to, if necessary, call to his assistance every officer on the grounds to make the arrest. George Newhouse, who had a stand on the grounds, served notice on the disturbing factions, that they might as well come to the conclusion that order would be had on the ground. He told them that he knew me, that he had been with me in camp meetings before, and that I would do just as I said I would.

129

I overheard one man say, he believed the "niggers" were going to take Lawrence Township and he was going to leave before he would stand for it. I saw he was getting ready to go, so I walked toward the gate when the people were going in. I pretended that I did not hear anything he had said and insisted on him not going away which he concluded to do.

Taking it for all in all, our meeting passed off very nicely from beginning to end, but when it had finally closed, and all the people were on the way home, I felt as if a great responsibility had been taken off of my shoulders as it had been freely predicted I would make a failure at this place. The influence of the meeting was good and the citizens generally declared that it was the best thing that had ever happened in Lawrence.

The next morning we returned to Greenfield. It might be well to state that the expenses of this camp meeting exceeded all the returns, about $75.00. Financially, therefore, it was not a success. This wound up my camp meeting experience as a manager.

PART THREE

Foremost Black Citizen of Indiana:
INDIANAPOLIS, 1884-1894

IN 1884 IN A CONVERSATION WITH MR. MESSICK, A MEMBER of the firm of Messick, Cones & Co., Indianapolis, Ind., I expressed a desire to open a business in that city, and requested him that if he saw an opening at any time to apprise me. He shortly afterwards apprised me of an opening on Meridian Street, between Washington and Pearl streets. This was in the month of February, 1884.

On the day of the unveiling of Governor Morton's monument,[1] I suggested to my wife that I go to Indianapolis as I had received information of a good location there and was anxious to investigate the matter. She readily endorsed the proposition. Once in Indianapolis, I was present at the unveiling of the monument, dedicated to the great war Governor, Oliver P. Morton, and after those ceremonies were over, I made some inquiries in regard to the room and location suggested to me by Mr. Messick. I was informed by the parties in charge that the room would not be rented for a barber shop and that Mr. Conduitt,[2] then, as now, one of the leading wholesale merchants of the city and property owner[s], did not want to rent it for such a purpose. I was, however, not deterred by this first set-back, as it is somewhat of a characteristic of mine not to take anything for granted but to see for myself. I made it my business to call upon him and was met by a Mr. [John N.] Scott, his legal council [sic], who informed Mr. Conduitt that there was a colored man who desired to see him about renting the room for a barber shop. He said he did not want to see me, as he did not want to rent his room for such a purpose.

Mr. Scott rather insisted "that he had better see him as he is a pretty good-looking fellow." He said alright, let him come in, and asking me to take a seat, I told him my business, and that I had come for the purpose of renting his room for a barber shop. He reiterated that he did not want to rent his room for a barber shop. I said: "Suppose I should run a barber shop and conduct it with the same business precision and care that you would a dry goods or grocery store, you would not object to me having it then, would you?" He told me that would be a difficult thing to do and I replied I could do it and could give references as to my manner of doing business, and named a number of businessmen in Greenfield that he could communicate with as to the creditability of my word and my manner of conducting business.

I felt somewhat flattered at his reply, which was to the effect that he did not desire any references as my face was a sufficient recommend[ation] to him. The room, he said, would rent for $150 a month as it was, but he would cut it about half in two and that would make the rent about $66.66. My readers will understand that this sounded pretty big to a fellow who had been paying but $15 a month for rent; however, I realized that it is sometimes true, nothing ventured, nothing won, and I had a sort of intuitive belief that I was making no mistake. I at once stated to Mr. Conduitt that the idea of cutting the room in two was satisfactory to me and that I would be willing to pay the last named sum, $66.66. He took my address and said he would inform me shortly if my proposition would be accepted. I returned to my home and to my surprise within two days received a letter from Mr. Conduitt accepting my proposition.

I at once, as was my custom, took council [sic] with my wife concerning it, and noticed very quickly that while for sometime she had expressed a desire and willingness to leave Greenfield, that when the test came, when the opportunity was presented, she did not seem so anxious. She said she did not know what to say. I finally closed the conference by declaring that as she had urged me to the step she must stand by me, as I was going. I also, before taking the final step, advised somewhat with a few reliable, staunch friends in the city of Greenfield, among them, James Morgan,[3] Andy Hart,[4] John W. Jones, James A. New[5] and several others, whom I cannot at present recall. In the opinion of some it was quite a venture for me, their argument being that inasmuch as I had been successful in Greenfield, had come up through that great tribulation and in the face of many impediments, that I should hesitate before moving. James Morgan, a man in whom I had great confidence and reliance, as far as judgment was concerned, and who had been one of my warmest friends and most sincere backers, said he would hate to see me go away, but thought perhaps it would be best, as it was evident to him that I had outgrown the town. Others tried to discourage me by saying I would break up there—move to Indianapolis, make a great display but no money. I reminded them that I noticed boss barbers in Indianapolis, who did not work themselves, had their horses and buggies, wore gold watches, dressed fine and could make a living, and said it would be peculiar if I could go there and work and not make a living while others who did not work, made a living.

One of my barbers said to me, you think you have got too big for this town. I replied that I had outgrown the town. I would go to Indianapolis and when I got trimmed down to the size of this town I would come back again but if I did not get trimmed down I would never come back. I still held my shop in Greenfield, and coming to Indianapolis closed my contract, although many said I would fail. Some said I would come back to Greenfield walking. My answer to all these doleful predictions was that I never blamed a man for failing, but I did for not trying.

Not desiring to take too many chances, and if possible find the safe side, I took in as a partner with me in my Indianapolis venture, one William Bibbs, an old and well-known barber in the city and who at that time owned one of the best barber shops. On the first day of March we opened up. I was a country barber, coming right in the city, not knowing the customs of doing business there, etc. Our first Saturday's receipts were about $16, and when we ran the books over at the end of the week, we found that the week's receipts amounted to $40; the next week we ran up to $50, and the next $65. That was in March, and in September, I had increased the business until it ran up to $190 a week.

During the time we were fixing up the room for business we had considerable work for the plumber. Being from a country town, I had had very little, if any experience with that class of tradesmen. Some advised me to close a contract, others not to make a contract with the plumber. I chose the latter course, J. Giles Smith, a well-known plumber of this city, being engaged. Judge as to my surprise when after his work was finished and I expected a bill somewhere in the neighborhood of $150 or thereabouts, he brought in one for $565. This was my first lesson and experience with plumbers and I had promised Mr. Bibbs, that if there was any work to be done in the future, I would always close a contract and would know before hand what their work would amount to.

Mr. Bibbs demurred at the bill and declared he would not pay it. My reply was that as I was a new man in town and we were a new firm, it would not do for us to commence by refusing to pay our bills,

135

and that we had better pay this, which we did. I attended closely to my business, working side by side with my barbers from Monday morning until Sunday noon. I had six barbers and at that time I was satisfied with that number as I had always believed that was as many as I would require.

This was in the spring of 1885, and the Bates House[6] Barber Shop being about to change hands, Mr. [Louis] Reibold, the proprietor of the hotel, let it be known that he desired a fine barber shop in the house. One day about this time I went into the First National Bank to ask E. F. Claypool[7] if I could not get a room he had had built South of me, as my shop was no longer large enough and I desired to run seven or eight chairs. A year before this, Mr. Claypool had refused to talk with me, but after he had seen my methods of doing business he was willing to talk with me on the subject. He told me [he] had something better than that room and he would let me know about it next day. Next day he told me he desired me to take the Bates House Barber Shop. I told him that was quite an undertaking for me and asked him how much rent he wanted for it. His answer was $125 a month. I said I had been in the habit of paying $8, $10 and $15 for barber shop rent and that I would let him know the next day about the matter. Seeing him at the time suggested, I formally accepted his proposition. He suggested to me that perhaps I would have to spend in the neighborhood of $2,400, and rather insisted that that amount be spent upon the room to beautify and get it into shape, calling my attention to the proposition made by another barber in the city to spend that amount. I replied I thought I could do that very easily.

He then said that he had another proposition to make me, namely: That I take Mr. Carter, the old and then proprietor of the shop, in as a partner, Mr. Claypool suggesting that Mr. Carter had money and that would make it easy for me. I made no objections to the plan and readily agreed to enter into partnership with Mr. Carter, upon the condition that he would not get in my way in making the shop what it should be, as everybody was predicting that I should fail. By this time the news had circulated that the country barber was to take the Bates House Barber Shop and that Mr. Carter, an old and well-known and honorable citizen, was to go in with him. Some one suggested [to] Mr. Claypool that we were a couple of old "fogies" from the country and that we would not put in a barber shop. Mr. Claypool informed them that he was from the country too, and that would be no objection.

The lease was drawn up for five years and we at once turned our attention to our plumber for the purpose of drawing up our plans for the future shop. Several persons advised me to go to Cincinnati and other places to look at some fine barber shops. I informed them that I had not been to these places, but I had a barber shop in my mind that I intended to put in the Bates. The plans were drawn up in about two hours and contracts signed. The consideration of the contract was for $4,000. I had worked very hard and had been standing so continuously on my feet that my ankles gave out, but I never stopped. In the meantime I held on to my Meridian Street shop.

On the first day of March, 1885, Mr. Bibbs and myself dissolved partnership [in the Meridian Street shop] and I substituted him by a well-known barber of the day by the name of Beach. Prior to this, Mr. Beach had opened a shop on S. Illinois Street in March, 1884, the same day I opened my Meridian Street shop. The prediction was that I would fail, being a country barber, and he would succeed, but it was quite the reverse, for in about six months he failed while I did not.

I cannot look back with pleasure upon the reception accorded me by the barbers of the city. When I would enter their shops, out of a friendly spirit with the purpose of forming acquaintance they frequently would not speak to me nor ask me to take a seat, in fact, had no time apparently for a country barber. Fred Brandt, a well-known character in his day, a white barber, was then in his glory; Charles Lanier, who had since spent time in Washington as the private messenger of President Harrison and his successor, President Cleveland, with Albert Farley, Henry Moore, Heckler and others[8] were the prominent leading barbers at that time, yet I felt if they did not look upon me or give me the consideration due an interloper even, they certainly had very little time to spend in cultivating friendly acquaintance with the barber from the village of Greenfield who had dared to come to their city and launch out in the manner he did. I mentally resolved to myself that I would wring respect from them and make them treat me with that consideration and courtesy due me as an upright citizen and straightforward tradesman.

It has been a kind of impulse of my life to compel men to respect me whenever they display a predilection not to do so. Most of the barbers of Indianapolis of that day are gone—have dropped out of the ranks of business; the very localities where their shops were located and run for years, are forgotten, and they themselves in several instances; it is hard to recall their names—some are scattered in the far West, some are dead and some have sunk into innocuous desuetude as far as business is concerned and have no following or trade, while perhaps one or two of them survive.

I can record with a pardonable pride that the country barber of Greenfield, aided primarily and first by his own thrift, his own courage, and his own industry, his own determination to achieve success, supplemented with the friendship, the assistance, the co-operation and the patronage of the best people of the city of Indianapolis, gave to that city the finest shaving institution it ever had, and to this day is reckoned as second to but one other such institution[9] in the whole world, in the matter only of money represented in it.

Long before the old barbers had broken up and scattered they had learned, whether they meant it or not, to seem to respect Mr. Knox, the country barber, to be willing to permit or allow him to stay on the earth, and in numerous instances have not been ashamed to seek his suggestions and advice and to copy his system and mode of conducting business.

After I had finally settled down in the city, I began to make inquiries concerning the whereabouts of Joseph Cameron. He and I were old acquaintances, dating back to the years '65 and '66, while I lived in Greenfield and he in Knightstown. We had become, in the course of years, very intimate friends. On one occasion, telling him of my intention of going to Indianapolis for the purpose of going into business, he stated he did not think it was the best thing I could do. "The city, you see, is full of barber shops and if you go there, the chances are that you cannot make it pay." We were standing near a telegraph pole, which seemed unusually high, and I, bending my eyes on the top, he observed me and asked what I was looking at. I replied that I could not see a barber shop up there. He then asked me what I meant. I told him that in my new business venture I was going to commence at the top, saying to him, "these barber shops that you speak of are all on the

138

ground." He then understood that I meant to open a barber shop superior to any in the city. I also further reminded him, in a jocular way, that because he came from Knightstown and failed in the music business in Indianapolis, it was no reason why I should not make an attempt to go into the barber business.

After I had been here quite a while and was commencing to do business, I employed a barber, very popular at that day in the city, known as "Dude" Brown. He was especially proficient as a cutter of ladies' bangs, which at that time were becoming "all the rage." Being fine looking, polite and affable, a neat and tasty dresser, he had, as a matter of course, a great following. I gave him employment and being a "country barber," the city barbers took every opportunity they could to ridicule me. A gentleman entering one of the shops where Brown had formerly been employed, and asking where he was, received the following description of my shop and how to find me: "You go down Meridian street about four doors from the corner on the east side of the street, and there in a room 21 x 21, you will find Brown working for a barber just from the country." The gentleman following directions finally found my place of business, and coming in, asked if there was a man there who had opened a barber shop, who came from a little country town. I spoke up very readily, and said: "Yes, I am the man." He then said that he did not want to see me but wanted a man by the name of Brown who was working for the country barber. I told him I had a man, and also said in conclusion that although I was a country barber, I was glad I was in town.

Returning to the Bates House venture, we commenced in February preparing and getting ready and were to open on the first day of April 1885, but we did not open until the 18th of April the same year. We threw our doors open on the 18th and the shop being brand new, furnished and arranged beyond anything ever before attempted in Indianapolis, it as a matter of course created a great local sensation. It was the talk of the town. The daily papers made extended and complimentary notes of it and throngs of people, men, women and children, were attracted thereto and came in groups to inspect the country barber's new place of business. The barbers of the city hastened to predict we would fail. They said in about six months the shine would be off and we would have a great shop upon our hands but no business. I replied

139

to them when occasion required it, to the effect that the shine on our shop was like the colored man's blacking—the more it was rubbed the worse it would shine.

Up to this time, neither I nor my family, particularly speaking had taken any part in the social and church worlds of the community. I had been attending Simpson Chapel M. E. church[10] and finally joined it. I attended closely to business to the evident dislike of the "croakers" who insisted upon starting all kinds of absurd rumors and reports about our business, among other things claiming that Mr. Carter was the moneyed man of the firm, was paying all the expenses, and that we were bound to fail. About two weeks after we had been opened, it rained one day in the neighborhood of two hours very hard, and there was not during the time a customer in the shop, but in all the years that have passed since then, I record with gratification that not thirty minutes have gone by but what there was a customer, one or more, in the shop.

About two years after the opening of the shop Mr. Carter, my partner, died, and when this sad event in our business life occurred, the gossippers commenced again. All kinds of wild predictions, some ridiculous and very funny, the concensus of which were, now that Mr. Carter had been taken off, he being the man who held the moneybags, that the shop would either go to the wall or pass into the hands of some aspiring white man. I said nothing, but "sawed wood." The gossippers even went so far, while Mr. Carter still lingered in life and was prone upon his death-bed, to visit his house and warn his family that I would surely rob them and that they ought to make some arrangement while it was time, to prevent me from taking their property from them. Mr. Carter's attention being called to these things, he said to his wife that he would cheerfully trust all he had on earth in my hands. He knew that I had dealt honestly and justly with him, that I had opportunities to rob him of hundreds of dollars, but did not do it.

On Mr. Carter's demise, his wife was appointed administratrix. She appeared to be apprehensive for fear she would have trouble. I called upon her and in about two hours we had the business settled amicably, to the mutual satisfaction of all parties concerned, between us. Mrs. Carter's comment being that the man she expected to have the most trouble with turned out to be the easiest to handle. I offered

140

her and she accepted $2000 for her interest in the business. She would like to have continued in the business, but I insisted that in the end of two years I did not intend to have a partner; my reason for this step being that it put me in a position to dictate and arrange my affairs as affecting the shop as I saw fit. Although the first cost of the shop was $4,000, I had made up my mind not to stop here, but to place on it some extensive improvements. Since the day, April 18, 1885, when we opened our place of business, then by far the finest that Indianapolis had ever seen, at an expense of $4,000, I have spent upon it in beautifying, re-arranging, re-fitting with modern appliances, etc., $10,000. The barber shop proper, distinct from the ladies' department,[11] gives employment to twenty-seven people. In my barber business alone in the city of Indianapolis I give employment to forty people.

In 1888 I was chosen from Simpson Chapel as a delegate to the conference which convened in Cincinnati, Ohio. I was, by this conference, elected a lay delegate to the general conference held in New York City during the month of May, the same year. This being the highest position accorded the laity of the church, I, as a matter of course, found myself confronted by numerous aspirants for the place. After what the politicians call a "heated contest" my star triumphed and the greatest honor that had up to this time overtaken me, in my relations with the church, was secured. A lay delegate's position, besides being one of honor and distinction, is also sought after for other reasons, which tend to enhance its value. Among these reasons, not the least is the fact that the great church pays all the expenses of the delegates to its general conference; mileage, hotel bills, etc., contracted during a space of thirty days, are all met and paid by the mother church.

Never having visited New York prior to this time, I was instructed by those in authority that I would be met at the Union Station by Col. [Eli F.] Ritter,[12] a well-known warrior of the church and a lawyer of almost national repute, who would take me, as it were, under his wing and travel with me. Promptly on the day and at the hour of their departure, I bade a temporary farewell to the cares of business and associations of home, and sure enough, was joined at the station by the gentleman designated as my companion. He met me with that cordiality due a brother in the church and we traveled together over the Panhandle, taking our first meal, dinner, in the beautiful city of Richmond, Ind. Continuing our journey, which from beginning to end was a most pleasurable one, we supplied the "inner man" next at Pittsburgh, Pa. By this time a great many preachers and delegates had been picked up at the different stations along the line. As I entered the dining room, I endeavored to make myself feel, and [to] conduct myself in a manner as would be expected from the whitest man in the delegation. The only incident that transpired to disturb my mental equipoise and remind me that I was not a white man was the action of a colored waiter, who, when he saw me entering with the other gentlemen composing the delegation, was evidently flusterated and surprised, jumping back and giving me a look which indicated that he was laboring under the illusion I was entering the wrong place. I, as a matter of course, noticed his dilemma, was amused somewhat at it, but paid no more attention to him than I would have a wooden Indian, nor as much, but went right on and took my seat. Outside of this harmless and quite natural incident, my stay in Pennsylvania's second city, that because of her many blast furnaces, etc., some writer has spoken of as "hell with its lid off," was very pleasant. The journey in other respects was a very pleasant one, as we swept by with almost lightning speed the villages and towns, the lofty mountain peaks and picturesque scenery that dotted the course of our journey. I neglected to mention that the turning of many curves and the rolling and rocking of the train made me sea sick, if such a condition can be obtained on land. Out of sympathy for my condition and in his capacity as guide and general advisor on the trip, Col. Ritter decided that when we reached Pittsburgh we would from that point take a sleeper.

I requested the Col[onel] to engage berths for two and I went back in the sleeper. I approached the colored porter and made known my desire for a berth. His reply was quickly given "We are full, sah." Not giving up my quest, however, I met the conductor and making known my wishes to him, his reply was that he had but two berths at his disposal and they were already secured for two gentlemen, and as it turned out, Col. Ritter was the gentleman who had secured them, for himself and me. This being my first experience in a sleeper and having an upper berth, it seemed that I must be thrown out and that the cars would certainly go down the embankment. Gradually, however, I yielded to the insinuations of Morpheus, was soon in the "land of Nod" and when I awoke, found myself in the city of Philadelphia, the historic "city of brotherly love." Remaining there for about thirty minutes, we pulled out for New York.

It was during this trip, from Philadelphia to New York that I met a colored gentleman, also a traveler, from St. Louis to Gotham. He lived in New York City, and very kindly, it seemed to me, volunteered to show me how to reach my stopping place, as that had already been engaged in advance, saying that if I gave myself up to a hackman, he might be disposed to haul me around and around in a circle to make it appear that he had taken me a great distance and charge me in the end two or three prices for the same. I thanked my colored friend for his solicitation, and I bade my traveling companion, Col. Ritter good-bye with the promise to meet him again at the Metropolitan Opera House, the place selected to hold the conference. I then took the elevated cars, and this was something new and astonishing to me, riding up on a level with the third story and over telegraph poles. Reaching Thirty-seventh street, I got off and went to my quarters, The Sumner House. He found the hotel crowded, hence was given a room not overly comfortable. Dr. Hammond and I were given rooms together, while Rev. Daniel Jones and [Thomas R.] Fletcher[13] occupied rooms separate.

The remark was frequently made to me, before leaving my own city, Indianapolis, that I might be a big man at home but I would not be heard of to any great extent in New York City. After I had been a temporary resident of the big town for about 21 days, I began to feel and realize that the prediction was about true. On the 22nd day, when the time had arrived to elect Bishops, the question came up as to extending the time allotted to preachers to remain in control of a charge, in other words to extend the time from three years to five.[14] I had several pronounced views upon this question, which I desired to place before the conference and had made several efforts to obtain the floor but all in vain. Dr. Buckley,[15] who sat just in front of me, the great scholar and polemist, a Christian gentleman whose fame is world wide, was blessed in this particular in that he could catch the eye of the chair at most any time. When I made my second attempt to be heard, I was disappointed again and went down in the midst of forty or fifty others.

143

At my third trial, Dr. Swindells,[16] of Philadelphia, moved out in front of me and by so doing caught the eye of the chair, who at once recognized him thus according him the floor. But, he having moved out from his seat too far, a point was raised that the chair's recognition of Dr. Swindells was not deserved by that gentleman, for the reason that to obtain recognition he had moved too far away from his order. The chair held, however, that the point was not well taken upon the ground that the rule only obtained during the debate of "The Woman Question";[17] namely, that every member must be recognized directly from his seat.

I felt somewhat discouraged but Dr. Buckley, knowing of my desire and evidently being sympathetically inclined toward me, urged me to try again. I did so, and Bishop Mallalieu[18] being in the chair, and I having the honor of a former acquaintance with the reverend prelate, paid me the grace of recognizing me.

I began my speech by saying that I had "sat in this conference floor for 22 long days, heavily laden down with a speech, but not alone in that respect, as it seemed to me, by no means." Addressing myself directly to the question of discussion before the conference, I proclaimed myself in favor of extending the period of a charge from three years to five years, first prefacing this statement with the rather startling declaration that I was really in favor of no limit at all, but feeling that the conference would not look with favor upon this extreme view, I wished to put myself on record as favoring the five year limit.

Warming up to my subject, as the first scare of the moment vanished, standing there, as I was, in the midst of the most polished and cultured body of thinkers and debaters, that perhaps the world had ever seen assembled together under one roof, I said, it has been stated on this floor that five years was too long for a minister in the M. E. Church to stay in one place, and I reminded them that there was pending before them two reports, which should appeal to their most patient and mature intelligence before being summarily disposed of, the majority report suggesting four years as the limit of a charge, the minority five.

Continuing, I said, "I stood there and wished to have it recorded in the history of the proceedings of this august gathering that I was in favor of the minority report of five years, instead of four. I am conscientious and sincere, Mr. Chairman and Members of the Conference, in my advocacy of the minority report because I believe that its reception and adoption would be for the best interests of the church and if you will allow me, I will take New York City as a precedent, where Methodism is comparatively dead."

When I reached this place in my speech, winding up the sentence with that remark, I noticed very quickly that I had created a sensation. For a bare instant, it seemed that my friends, those who believed with me, caught their breaths, while those upon the other side, opposed to me laughed a species of derisive laugh, as though by this means they might hoot me and shame me "out of court." Whether they believed it or not, they seemed to convey the impression by their demeanor and ejaculations, that I had bitten off more than I could chew, which, however, let it be said without charge of egotism, was not one of my apprehensions. Sure of my position as I understood it, conscientious and earnest in its advocacy as it was possible for a man to be, I was no more awed by the saldes[?] and guffaws of laughter of the men upon the other side, and the silence of my friends, nor the presence of that august body, the hall on this occasion being filled with 6,000 people, than I would have been had I been in my own city, a participator in an ordinary debate conducted by one of the church literaries, so numerous at that time in the "City of Concentric Circles."

My second breath had come to me, I had the floor, and in the language of the New York Tribune[19] of next morning, "I pulled down my vest" and started in with renewed determination and vigor to be heard, and prove the justice and wisdom of the premises I had laid down. Many voices shouted "Go to the front; Come, forward so every body can see and hear you," to all of which invitations I replied that I felt I could be seen and heard from where I was. As I had made the statement that Methodism in New York was comparatively dead, I girded myself up for a final and convincing effort, for I felt that it would be expected of me to corroborate myself. Addressing the chair once more, I said, "Mr. Chairman and Members of the General Conference, I am told that in this city of a million and a half inhabitants, an investigation but verifies the statement, this city which the world and the nation had been wont to look upon as the fountain-head of Methodism, this great Commercial metropolis of the Western Hemisphere,

145

the home of the millionaire and philanthropist in their most numerous and powerful conditions, in this great metropolis adjacent to that other metropolis across the stream, known as the "City of Churches," whose spires by the hundred, I was going to say, point heavenward, mute advocates of the Kingdom of God upon earth, in this great city let me repeat, Mr. Chairman and Members of the General Conference, a world within itself and that to-day has centered upon it the eye of civilized universal Christendom, because of the meeting of this great body; in this city again let me say, that should team with the votaries of Methodism, the great church of the great masses of the world, what is the fact? While numerically speaking, the Methodist Church should count a membership and reckoning of at least 100 and 150 thousand, the statistics tell us that she can place her hands upon but 15 thousands. Comment is unnecessary and yet how natural is the impulse to comment upon this startling fact.

"Were I to be accorded this floor from now until the close of this session to-day, were I gifted with the aggregated eloquence, the aggregated erudition, the aggregated power of disquisition and argument of all the members composing this great body, from its venerated head down, I would even then be unable to produce a more pungent fact than is contained in the five figures that tell us of the numerical strength of Methodism in the city of New York. Now this being the case, and it is the case, for figures cannot lie, what is the reason of it, and the cause? Is there a reason; are there reasons? Is there a cause; are there causes? Is it because the fibre that constitutes the moral tendencies of the citizens of New York, the rank and file of the multitudes that swarm in this great caravansary of human nature, is different and unlike that which is found in the composition of men and women elsewhere, seeking for the light of the church and the maintenance of her spiritual devotion?"

This question answers itself in the negative, for human nature is alike the world over. The fault, therefore, Mr. Chairman and Members of the General Conference, is not to be looked for in the people of New York, but in the administration of our church and the laws that cripple and hedge about its usefulness. I cannot help but feel that in a city like New York, and in all of our larger cities, the too often changing of the itineracy is inimicable to the welfare of the church. About the time a minister becomes acquainted with his work and his charge, he has to leave. But I am told that there is no one in all of our great church able to hold one charge longer than three years, and as I look over this conference, I find myself awed in the presence of the accumulated and aggregated wisdom and intelligence of our great church, as I peer into the faces of the men sent here on this occasion, I cannot help but feel that the statement is not a reliable one, and that we have not one, but many men able to hold one charge not only five years, but as is the custom in the Presbyterian, the Catholic, Episcopal, Baptist and other Christian sects of the world, ten, fifteen, twenty and twenty-five years or during a life time, or good behavior, if necessary. In a city like this we should at least be able to point to 50,000 zealous, active, reliable members of our church, (a voice interrupted the speaker saying, "yes, a hundred thousand") and the speaker repeated, yes, a hundred thousand would not be too many.

I said "Mr. Chairman and Members of the Conference, it has been stated this morning on this floor that the church has been moving too fast but Mr. Chairman, in my limited vision, as I see and understand things, I cannot believe that the church, any more than the individual, when in pursuit of, and in behalf of the good and the necessary, can move too fast. This is a progressive age. Standing in sharp contrast to many of the ages that have preceded it in the history of our church. In 1844, for instance, men, influential and powerful in the councils of the church met in this city and in the conference then said, as men say today, that the church was moving too fast. They said it was taking steps which were in advance, and were advocating things which were ahead of the present age. They were then advocating these principles. They said the old mother church could not submit to one thing that was wrong. While one half of the conference was looking through the Bible from Genesis to Revelation, to find one passage of scripture so that they might declare slavery a divine institution, I could even then feel the shackles and fetters, which bound me as a slave, slipping away from my hands and feet. (Applause.) That class who desired the great body, which held their conference here forty-four years ago, to agree that slavery was a divine institution; and put itself on record as favoring that monstrous declaration, I apprehend had they been living today would be with this class who claim we are now moving too fast, in our desire to take such steps to break down another barrier in the forward march and glory of the Church. By these principles of the great mother church, by not stooping to that which was wrong, compromising no place, but hewing to the line of right, I have been enabled to stand here in this great conference body and advocate the rights of the whole mother church. It is not a question whether Elder Jones, etc., can hold a charge three years. The church must be greater than that. She must look to the interests of the church and not to the welfare of the individual. It makes men do better work, it makes them study harder, it puts them upon their merits, but when a minister knows he can only stay three years, he only prepares for that amount of work. Men with the ability and talent of a [Thomas DeWitt] Talmage or a [Charles H.] Spurgeon are hindered by this time limit. When Mr. [Henry Ward] Beecher found that the "time limit" hindered him, he became the head of the Congregational church. When Dr. Talmage found that it hindered him, he sought other fields. At one time the church thought fit to remove Dr. [John Philip] Newman,[20] but he saw fit to stay and staid. I am told that the church prospered during his administration. When we bring men in the church who have not the ability to hold the people together, here is where the injury comes in. The time is at hand when ability must speak and must take prestige if we expect the church to increase in its power. It will not effect small cities so much as it will larger cities, like New York, Philadelphia, Washington and hundreds of others. It effects them not by the hundred, but by the thousands. We move in a church where jealousies must be wiped out, and we must stand out Christ-like, if we wish to reach all classes. Let man not be protected by law, but by ability, and when he comes to his charge he will prepare to stay as long as the people want him. This does not license a man to stay in charge any longer. We will remove a man quicker in the five year limit if he does not prove satisfactory, than under the three year rule. In many cases where the members of the church are dissatisfied with their pastor, they will say: "well, he has only another year, they would ask that he be removed before the time expired. We must let Christ come in and He will do most for the cause of the church, and we will do that which is demanded of us as Christian people. In the olden days, when the man disobeyed the Lord, the Lord put him out of the way."

148

In the very midst of my speech, the people were so enthusiastic over some of the remarks made, that Dr. Hammond, who was sitting near me, said, "don't forget your thought in the midst of this enthusiasm." I replied to him that every thought stood out like a diamond; I had just to pick them off. When I was through speaking he grasped my hand and said, "Bro. Knox, you have done more this morning than you have any idea of." As the conference adjourned, I looked up to the galleries and even from the fourth and fifth galleries, handkerchiefs were waved at me, newspaper men began taking their notes, and as I went down the street, people who were far away from me in the conference hall, recognizing me only by my shirt front, came up to me and congratulated me on my speech. On entering the hotel, I heard one man say he liked my speech very much. Another told him that he liked the thought but was not so well pleased with the delivery of the speech to which the other man replied, that it was not the delivery but the thought that he cared about.

Prior to my speech the vote on Bishops had been taken and at the close of my talk, the teller came in and announced that the results of the vote would be read before the conference. The candidates were Fitzgerald,[21] Goodsell,[22] Dr. Newman, Dr. Hamilton[23] and others. A great deal was done to defeat Dr. Newman but the night before the colored delegates held a caucus, where they resolved to throw the solid vote to Newman and cast their votes for anyone else except the candidates which were expected to be elected, therefore we voted for any one who was not in the race. In the midst of our meeting, Bro. Shinkle[24] of Cincinnati came running across the floor, and said, "Knox, what do you mean? What do you mean?" I replied, "Newman to-day or never." He asked me if I did not know Newman was not loyal to the church? "Loyal to the church" is not the question, said I. "I know one thing, he is loyal to my race."[25] When Grant was President in 1866 [sic], when the church property of the South was to be confiscated by the rebels of the South, Dr. Newman went to the President and had a restraining order issued, and Dr. Newman came as minister of the President of the United States, went to New Orleans, and preached to the colored people, when it was almost a crime to do so, and suffered many hardships. I said he did not come from the low depths, but from the high places and went down to the lowly to help lift up a downtrodden race. That is why I am for him, uncompromisingly. When Dr. Newman was elected, I felt we had won a great victory. Dr. Newman from that day to this has never been proven to be anything otherwise than what I said—loyal to the church as well as to the race.

I received two telegrams from home, one from a friend, and one from my wife, urging me to return home immediately, as my interests, politically, were at stake. Knowing that I had been requested by several influential persons to make the race for the nomination for representative [in the state legislature][26] I returned home as I was informed that if I were on the ground, there would be no doubt but that I would be nominated. When I arrived in Indianapolis, I found my political affairs in confusion. I met several of my friends with whom I talked the situation over and found things pointing favorably to my nomination. Feeling confident of my success, I did not make much of an effort to secure the nomination. When the convention was called, however, I found my opposition very strong, it being caused mainly on account of my being supported by one Col. A. A. Jones.[27] When the roll was called for the first ballot, there were about twenty-five candidates for the nomination. In the midst of these were some colored candidates, Wm. Walden,[28] G. W. Cheatham,[29] W. Allison Sweeney[30] and myself.[31] Mr. Cheatham carried his own ward, which was about eighteen votes, W. Allison Sweeney receiving seven votes, and I eighty-four, which seemed a very flattering number to me, as I had made no personal canvass. William Walden received 240 votes. At the first ballot there was no nomination. I then withdrew my name from the contest as did also Mr. Sweeney. It was necessary to have a colored man on the ticket, and Mr. Walden received the nomination. As interest in the campaign was manifested, I rolled up my sleeves, so to speak, and went into the campaign for the success of the party and its candidates. In spite of our efforts, the Republicans were defeated.

After this campaign I re-entered with my usual zest into my business, putting in every hour of the day in order to make it a success. In 1890, the late Hon. W. D. McCoy,[32] being ambitious and desirous of representing the county, came to me and requested me not to enter the race, as he desired to make the race for representative. I replied to him

150

that as my business required such close attention, I would not enter the race, but would give him my support and would do the best I could for him. He received the nomination, and the campaign which followed was a very interesting and exciting one. However, he, with the other Republican candidates on the ticket, were defeated. In April, 1891, Mr. McCoy made an application for the ministry to Liberia, Africa. He was endorsed on every hand by the leading citizens. I myself took quite a hand in this matter, as I was desirous of him securing it. One day, having all along been urging his appointment, I met Mr. Dan Ransdell[33] and spoke with him concerning Mr. McCoy's appointment. He told me that he had no chance to get to talk with the President, but I reminded him of the fact that he and President Harrison, having been life-long friends, he knew him as no other man knew him, had been in the President's regiment and a commissioned officer under him, and that he, if anyone, could gain admittance to the President and his influence along this line would be of benefit to Mr. McCoy. I also told him that it was expedient that this appointment be made at once, as the colored people of the state demanded this appointment as a recognition of their efforts in supporting the Republican party. Mr. Ransdell assured me he would see about it, as he was going to Washington the next week. Within about ten days from this time, word was received from Washington that Mr. McCoy's appointment was confirmed.

Mr. and Mrs. McCoy[34] invited my wife and I to accompany them on their trip to Mr. McCoy's mission as far as New York City, and to visit the cities of Washington, Philadelphia, and New York which invitation we accepted. We left on a Saturday evening for Washington. Many people gathered in and about the depot to bid farewell to their fellow-citizen who was much esteemed as a teacher and educator. As our train pulled out of the station, we could see the people gazing at him for the last time, and Mr. McCoy was moved to tears. He told us that it affected him more than anything he had passed through. In a few moments we were out of sight. We traveled over the B. & O. Railroad. During our trip we saw many beautiful sights and beautiful scenery, especially when we passed through Virginia, as we went around the hills and knobs, looking down into the valleys and we even imagined we could see the graves of those who had fallen in defense of

151

the Union, and those who had fallen who were against the Union. We commented on different topics and finally drew near to the Nation's Capital. In the language of Parson Brownlow[35] of Tennessee, the nearer we drew to the city, I could feel a peculiar sensation coming over me.

This was my first visit to the capitol. We stayed here about ten days, visiting the principal points of interest in the city—the Congressional Hall, the Public Library, the Smithsonian Institute, the Washington Monument 555 feet high, and other places. We visited the Metropolitan church,[36] built by the A.M.E. Connection at a cost of about $150,000. We attended a meeting of the literary society, which discussed Burns and Macauley. We, being with Mr. McCoy, the minister and Consul General to Liberia, were shown many favors and courtesies. Mr. McCoy and myself were called upon to make speeches. While in Washington, Mr. McCoy spent much of his time in the state department, taking instructions concerning his position. We had the pleasure of forming the acquaintance of Dr. St. Clair[37] while here, who proved to be a very congenial gentleman. It seemed rather strange to us that while down stairs in the state Department, Mr. McCoy was known as the minister to Liberia, and up stairs, as the Consul General, these being the two offices filled by him.

We left Washington for Philadelphia, where we stayed two days, visiting the mint, stood in Independence Hall, saw the old Liberty Bell and other interesting objects. Leaving Philadelphia, we went to New York City, stopping at the Sumner House, on W. Thirty-Seventh street. We stayed in New York nearly a week, visited Dr. Talmage's church,[38] and heard the great divine preach. On one day, we went down to the "City of Berlin," the vessel on which Mr. and Mrs. McCoy were to sail. We saw the different departments of the ship, visiting the ladies' and gent's parlors, dining rooms, bar rooms and store rooms. After looking over the ship, I thought to myself, if I had my business all arranged, I would pay a visit to my native country with Mr. and Mrs. McCoy. The next day was the 16th of March and my wife and I started for Indianapolis, Mr. and Mrs. McCoy accompanying us to Newark. Taking Mr. McCoy by the hand for the last time, I expressed the hope that we would meet again and that his trip would be a pleasant and successful one. He replied also he hoped we would meet again, and also said "whichever way I go whether I live or die, it will make a majority," referring to the ministers who had survived their term and who had died in Liberia. Bidding Mr. and Mrs. McCoy farewell, we left for Indianapolis. It seemed to us so very cold and everything was as still as death, as we passed around the curves and looked into the icy waters and the sides of the hills, the weather being as cold as we had had in the middle of January. The next day we reached Ohio, and it seemed we had gone into a latitude much warmer, passing seemingly from the frigid into the temperate zone. We landed home safely being absent about seventeen days, and glad to see old friends once more. Arriving home, I once more plunged into the old routine of business.

Before Mr. McCoy had left Indiana, in 1890, Mr. Cooper,[39] the then proprietor of this publication [*The Freeman*], gave me a mortgage on the Indianapolis Freeman, the amount of which was to be paid in thirty days.

When I made the loan to Mr. Cooper, he said he would pay the note in ten days. I suggested that the note be made out payable in thirty days, thus giving him sufficient time to meet the payment. This note went on for eighteen months, but as I did not particularly need the money, I did not force collection. While sitting in my place of business one day, Mr. Reibold, the proprietor of the Bates House, called me, saying he wished to ask me a question. He asked me what I knew of the paying qualities of Mr. Cooper. I replied, I knew nothing of him except through my own dealings with him. I said I did not desire to say anything that would injure him, but previous to this time, about eighteen months ago, I made him a loan which he had promised to pay in thirty days, but up to that time had not made a settlement. I desired to know why Mr. Reibold asked me that question, and he replied that Mr. Sweeney and Mr. Cooper had come to him and presented things very favorably to him of the financial condition of the Freeman, requesting a loan of $300. I replied that if that was the reason he asked me the question, I would say nothing concerning the matter, leaving him to be his own judge as to whether he should make the desired loan or not. Shortly after this time, Mr. Cooper called to see me, stating that he wished to see me privately. After we had gone down stairs to my private office, Mr. Cooper began to speak in his

153

usual vein, speaking of my splendid business ability, how much credit I deserved for what I had done, what a fine looking fellow I was, etc., I following up his talk with saying I knew he was giving me "taffy" but that a man ate "taffy" when he least expected to and at the same time relished it. He hastened to assure me that he did not indulge in flattery, and what he said he meant, and in this case was simply stating facts. He then came to the business he wished to speak to me about, requesting an additional loan. I informed him that as he had not kept his promise in the first instance, I did not care to make him a further loan. I called his attention to the fact that he was an energetic young man, full of business and that the future before him was bright, but he must learn one thing—and that was to be punctual in keeping promises he had made. I suggested that if he had kept the promises he made me, that I now would have full confidence in him, and would let him have what he desired. We gain the confidence of others by keeping our promises. I told him that when a man fails to keep his promise his friends do not care to trust him further. "Whenever you learn that trait of character" I said, "to keep your word, your promises, there is no power on earth to keep you down, as you are a great hustler and have splendid business ability." A man who always pays his debts, not only for the reason that he may be accommodated in the future, but because it is right, will always get along. A person who will adopt this method of doing business will always be successful.

As is well known Mr. Cooper is a smooth talker[40] and he assured me that the matter had been overlooked, but that it was almost impossible at that time for him to do what he desired relative to this matter. I assured him, however, that I could make no further advancement. In about a week from this time, Mr. Sweeney and Mr. Cooper came to see me and after passing the time of day, Mr. Sweeney being the spokesman, began to tell of their methods of doing business and spoke in glowing terms of my future, giving me to understand that as I was looked upon as a lover of race enterprise, the "great" Negro philanthropist, they desired my assistance at this juncture in order to keep the Indianapolis Freeman going. I told Mr. Sweeney that I did not see how it would be proper for me to advance money for running The Freeman, but Mr. Sweeney spoke with the assurance that if the Indianapolis Freeman failed, which it was almost sure to do if I did not

154

help them, it would be a disgrace to Indianapolis, to myself and the race generally, which were additional reasons why I should lend them money. He could not understand why I should hesitate to aid them at this critical period.

I told Mr. Sweeney I could advance them no money, and told him I had previously advanced Mr. Cooper money, which had not been repaid, whereas Mr. Sweeney was greatly surprised and appeared quite indignant that Mr. Cooper had not told him of this transaction, assuring me that he would not have asked me for any money for The Freeman had he known of this. For Mr. Sweeney's benefit I repeated the conversation I had had with Mr. Cooper. Mr. Sweeney then took Mr. Cooper to task, as a father would a child, telling him he should not so have misled him as to get him in this predicament, and that the advice I had given Mr. Cooper, he had also given him time and time again. "You will always be a failure," said Mr. Sweeney "unless you take the advice given you by Mr. Knox." Mr. Cooper in his smooth way tried to clear matters, and Mr. Sweeney, indignant at Mr. Cooper's treatment of him, said he did not blame Mr. Knox for refusing to lend him money, thus trying to throw off any suspicions I might entertain that the plan was one concocted between them. Mr. Sweeney then withdrew in disgust.

Mr. McCoy was at this time preparing to leave for his post in Liberia. One Saturday morning as I was at my place of business, two gentlemen who had been there before, stepped in, looking more like Shylocks and money-lenders swooping down upon me than money borrowers. My customers glanced from them to me, and from the manner in which these men appeared as they came in and from the way in which they asked to see me privately, no doubt concluded I was heavily obligated to these gentlemen. If I had not known the gentlemen, I probably would have looked out to see a fine turnout, with coachman and footman attending. If I had not known them I would have thought they were some gentlemen from Wall street, or Eastern capitalists who had come to foreclose a mortgage on me.

When we reached my private office, Mr. Sweeney, (the reader has no doubt identified these gentlemen), again the spokesman, as usual spoke of my being a great man and considered such by the people of the country, to which I replied "that I could not be known all over the country. I was simply a barber, even though I had reached the zenith in my profession," but Mr. Sweeney assured me that because of my energy and push I had become a National Character. He continued that this time they had come on a mission, and they knew I could accommodate them. They had a large pay roll to meet and which had to be met immediately and they only required the use of my name. So saying, they handed me a promissory note, already signed by Mr. Cooper and Mr. McCoy, and all they required was the use of my name but the way the note was worded, I was simply to become the responsible party for the note, while Mr. McCoy became the indorser, the amount of which was $250. I told them I could not sign the note, but said to them if they brought a note from Mr. McCoy for thirty or sixty days, I would indorse it for Mr. McCoy. I thought by this I would get entirely out of the matter.

The gentlemen left and I had just begun to breathe more freely, imagining myself out of the matter, when I happened to look into the hotel office and saw Messrs. Sweeney, Cooper and McCoy together. "They think they have me to myself and I will not have the courage to say I would not sign the note," said I to myself, "but I will not sign it unless it suits me." It was nearly 8 o'clock and they were desirous of having money to pay off The Freeman's employees, who were waiting for their return. I told them even if I did sign the note they could not get any money, as all the banks were closed, but they said if I would sign the note they would have no trouble in getting the money. I then and there refused to sign it and told Mr. McCoy that as he was going away, the responsibility would fall on me anyway when collection was to be made. I told Mr. McCoy that no doubt Mr. Sweeney and Mr. Cooper had done a great deal for him through their paper in a political way, while he was making his race for the legislature and for the appointment as minister to Liberia and that he could afford to take some chances, reminding him that politicians feeling the knife in them must bear it and not say a word. With these remarks I left them.

Mr. McCoy had gone to his Mission in Liberia. I had resumed my usual duties, and in the meantime putting in my extra moments with my studies, etc., attending the literaries of the city, making political and ward speeches. Mr. Cooper, after a lapse of considerable time, called to see me one day. After retiring to my private office, he spoke

156

of the mortgage I held on The Freeman being still unpaid, and informed me of there being another mortgage for $350 against the publication. I told him I knew nothing of that, but did know one thing: That was, I held the first mortgage. If the creditors were ready to pay me my claim, I told Mr. Cooper, I would accept their proposition. As I understood it, I held first mortgage, therefore my claim took precedence to all other claims.

In a few days I received a note from a lawyer of the city, stating that he held a mortgage of $350 against The Freeman, which he was going to foreclose. In reply to the same, I stated that I had no objection and called his attention to the fact that I held the first mortgage. He then came to see me, and said the firm which he was representing desired their accounts settled at once, and they would enter suit. I told him they could settle my claim, which was first due, and if they did this, I, of course, would have no objection if they entered suit. We did not reach any agreement, so he went away. Suit was finally brought and judgment for the amount due [from] The Freeman was received.[41] As my claim took first precedence, Mr. Cooper came to me with a plea that if I would stay the judgment for six months he would be enabled to make payment. I first told him I was not inclined to do so, that all I cared for was to have my claim settled. He said to me that he had no way to lift the obligation, and I seemed to be the only person to whom he could turn for aid, and he, as on other occasions, delivered his usual amount of compliments and flattery. Finally I decided that I would stay the judgment. Mr. Cooper struggled on with The Freeman, and he being one of the "ten greatest Negroes in America,"[42] felt he had some cause for pride, and it was a great enterprise, one that was worth not less than $10,000 and [I] did not desire to stand by and see it go to the wall.

In March, 1892, was the time to elect the lay delegates to the General Conference, which was to meet in Omaha, Neb. My friends were pushing my claims as a delegate to the General Conference, but while I was absent in New York, the meeting of the quarterly conference being held during my absence, my opposers took advantage of the same. It was thought that I would have been elected a lay delegate to the electoral college, which was to meet at Simpson Chapel, Indianapolis, had not the presiding elder decided that the pastor had no vote in the quarterly conference. It was decided that a "hold over" session of the quarterly conference be held, which meeting occurred about a week after my return to the city. The conference convened at the residence of Mr. Thos. Rogister[43] on Howard street. Not knowing of the bitter fight that was being made against me, I did not muster my forces as I should have done, and was defeated, the presiding elder holding the same ruling, that the pastor in charge had no vote in the quarterly conference. I made a strong talk, wherein I took issue with the presiding elder, stating that the pastor was a member of the quarterly conference, and therefore should have a right to cast his vote. I told him if it was not for the trouble and time it would take, I would carry the matter to the annual conference. John T. Leggett[44] was the delegate elected to the annual conference.

I did not care much about this defeat, at least did not say anything concerning it, as I held another position, making me a delegate-at-large[45] to the National Republican Convention which was to convene in Minneapolis the 7th of June, 1892. I was feeling very good at the flattering vote I received for this position, having carried the convention of 1150 strong unanimously. I thought it was very complimentary to me, as it gave me a position, never before held by a colored man this side of the Mason and Dixon line.[46] But as Mr. Leggett had been successful against me as a delegate to the annual conference, he began to boast around that he had defeated the great "I am," and had won a great victory. At the same time he was desirous of being elected a lay delegate to the General Conference, a position which I also desired to have at the time. As Mr. Leggett had been elected a delegate to the annual conference, I thought I would not interfere, but hearing of the boasts he had made, that he would walk over my carcass, etc., I said then I was going to be elected a lay delegate to the General Conference. According to the old adage, "To get the strength from tea, you must boil it in hot water," and in this case, I was put in hot water and decided to show my strength. Mr. Leggett was of the opinion that as I had been defeated as a delegate at the quarterly conference, I would not be eligible as a candidate at the annual conference, but I informed him that that did not concern my being a delegate to the conference, as all that was required of me was to be a member in good standing of the M.E. church for two consecutive years. He, however, declared not.

I began to lay my plans for election, conferring with different parties who were in position to know about the matter. I visited and conferred with Presiding Elder Rollins,[47] Presiding Elder Sissle,[48] Dr. E. W. S. Hammond, L. M. Hagood[49] and other influential members. Things passed on quietly and when the annual conference met I had several of the delegates stopping at our house, among whom was Bishop Walden.[50] One morning I awoke about 3 o'clock and I heard some one in the next room speaking loudly and enthusiastically, I caught the remark that he had heard that I had been defeated as a lay delegate at the quarterly conference, which would prevent me from being a candidate for the lay delegate's convention at the General Conference. Afterward I found that it was Dr. Peters[51] of Cincinnati, and he informed me positively that, he was sorry, but I could not be a candidate. I informed him that the law of the church held that a member of good standing for two consecutive years of the church was eligible as a candidate. He took issue with me and stated that I would not be eligible. The point was to get a decision from the chair. One day I went to Bishop Walden's study and asked his opinion of the law relative to this matter. He told me that I would be an eligible candidate.

The convention was called to order on a Wednesday. I went to Presiding Elder Rollins and requested him to raise the question as to who was eligible for candidates as lay delegates to the General Conference. This caused a decision from the Bishop, which resulted in my favor. The next day was the one selected for the election of delegates. Mr. Leggett had secured the influence of Jas. T. V. Hill,[52] a colored lawyer of this city, who was to make an appeal for him. Mr. Hill decided that they would make their point this way; that I was not a fair representative of my race, that I refused to shave colored people in my barber shop, etc. They waged the war unceasingly and buttonholed every delegate, I following closely afterward. My friends were with me all through the fight. I also secured the cooperation of Dr. Brannon of North Vernon.

I met Mr. Hill down town the day before the election and he told me that the field was clear for his man, Leggett, and he would now let Mr. Leggett go for himself the balance of the way. I said no, I want to carry this war into Africa if need be. I am going to defeat you, and I want to see you go down before my eyes. "If you leave your man

159

now," I said, "and he is defeated, you will say it was because you did not stay with him to the end, and therefore I desire your presence."

After the convention had been called to order, and the chairman had been selected, the meeting was ready to proceed to business. Three candidates were nominated, Dr. Peters, a gentleman from Kentucky and myself.

The Rev. Collins[53] of Indiana put Mr. Leggett in nomination making a very telling speech, speaking of his good qualities, how he was a man who stood by his race, a man of influence in the church and Sabbath school, etc. After Mr. Collins had spoken, my man placed me in nomination, speaking of the different times and ways I had represented my race, of how I stood in general conference and debated the question of extending the time limit from three to five years and other things. When Mr. Collins finished speaking, I felt rather discouraged but after my man had finished his talk I began to feel better. The delegates and members of the conference desired to hear the candidates speak and we were called upon to take the platform. Mr. Peters responded first, and following, Mr. Leggett spoke. Mr. Leggett brought a direct attack upon me, and stated that I could not represent the race when I had refused to shave a colored man in my place of business and even went so far as to advise Dr. Morgan[54] that it was best for him not even to treat colored people's corns and wait upon colored people, as it would hurt his business.

By the time Mr. Leggett had finished his speech I was "hotter" than a lime kiln. Then I began my speech by saying: "Mr. Chairman and delegates of the Electoral College—At the beginning I did not think I would undertake to make the race for lay delegate to the General Conference, but owing to circumstances and some rumors that have been put forth, it is necessary for me to make this race. In 1888, I was a lay delegate to the General Conference held in New York, which gave me some experience in that direction and which will enable me to do more for the church in this conference than before. I will show you whether I am worthy of your confidence to be again elected to the General Conference and must pay my respects to Mr. Leggett, a gentleman who is a candidate against me. This gentleman in your presence has attempted to place me in a false light. There comes a time when the truth must be spoken, and although this is not a fit place to

160

make the remarks I am going to make, yet I know, under the circumstances, I will be excused. I want to say to you that the charges he makes against me are not true and whoever reported them is a lie." At this juncture Mr. Leggett jumped to his feet and said I better be careful, as Mr. Thornton[55] had made these remarks. I replied that I did not care, Mr. Thornton or anyone else who made the remarks were liars.

"I understood in the beginning when I fight the devil I must fight him with fire, and this is one time I must fight him, for the charges are purely manufactured for the purpose of bringing about my defeat. He says I am not loyal to my race—I am not the proper man to represent this conference, and why is it that he makes these charges? Simply for his selfish interest."

"In 1884 when I came from Greenfield to this city, I could have entered any church, yet I chose this one, as I felt and knew I could do more good in it than elsewhere, and it was the church of my choice. In your hearing Mr. Leggett has said I have done nothing for the church. The good book says: 'A man is known by his works, and the tree is known by the fruit it bears.' "

"If you will follow me now from Antioch Baptist church to Simpson Chapel where the annual conference is now in session, and will look at the addition that was put there, if you will look at the beautifully decorated walls, the beautiful paper tinged with gold, if you will look at the joists, tipped with brass and glistening like gold; if you will look at the floor covered with beautiful carpets; look at the beautiful Bohemian chandeliers, at the beautiful seats as they are arranged and look back at the pulpit where you will see a white dove suspended in the air by means of an invisible wire, seeing in imagination our Savior being baptized in the river Jordan by John the Baptist and hearing a voice crying from the heaven: 'This is my beloved son, in whom I am well pleased, hear ye him.' When you look at the beauty, the grandeur of this church I will say to you, Mr. Chairman, this work was brought about through me."

"When I was in New York the work was to be carried on, but the officers longed for my return as they found it impossible to carry on the work without me. I hurried home mainly on that account. Rev. Miller,[56] the pastor in charge, will bear me out in these statements. The reason I make these statements is to prove to you that I have done

161

something for my church. This very moment I stand responsible for a debt of $500, contracted in order to make the church in a fit condition so the annual conference could be held there. Yet I am told in your presence that I am not fit to represent the church in conference. It is the truth when I say that I have nothing but its work and its interest at heart. The lay delegation is not like the ministerial delegation. They have to look after their own as well as the interests of the church, while a layman must look direct at the interests of the church. The whole conference which met in New York in 1888 gave me the credit of being the prime mover in causing the extension of the itineracy of the church from three to five years, and this has already been such a benefit to the church that it will be only a matter of time when the limit will be removed entirely."

"And, Mr. Chairman, I wish to state that when a certain part of the church presented resolutions suggesting the change of the name of the Freedmen's Aid Society to the Southern Education Society, I was one who made a bitter fight against it. They wanted to change the name so that the southern white people might derive aid from the society, and not have it known that they were receiving help as the Negro was. In my defense I stated that it would be an injury and an insult to those philanthropic persons who had given millions of dollars for the cause of education of the freedmen of the South if they changed this name. The name was not changed.[57] During the New York General Conference I was placed on several important committees, the boundary committee, the church extension committee, the advisory committee and Freedmen's Aid committee, and I always did my work faithfully in order that the interests of the church would be advanced. Still, I am told I am not a fit man to represent the church. I leave the matter to be decided by you, and [if] you think I am not a fit representative, I request that you do not vote for me."

After the speeches were all made, ballots were prepared and the first ballot was taken. On the first ballot Dr. Peters was elected, and on the second ballot I was elected. I then felt very thankful to the friends who had assisted me in this fight, and felt that it was quite a victory I had gained. During my whole life I felt grateful for any assistance given me, and to this fact I think much of my success is due. I received many congratulations, and the ministerial delegation seemed quite pleased that I had been elected. The Indianapolis News ran my cut in its columns, giving a short biographical sketch of my life, etc.

It was now about four weeks until the meeting of the General Conference. I was taken quite sick and feared I would not be able to attend either the General Conference or the Republican National Convention which was held in Minneapolis. However, my physician said that if I kept to my room and remained quiet, that in about three weeks I would be alright. Having confidence in his ability, I obeyed his instructions and at the end of three weeks I was able to leave my room. During my illness I prepared myself for the conference, receiving many circulars and letters regarding both the General Conference and the Convention, concerning things which they desired me to give my attention to.

The time had come for me to go to the conference which met in Omaha. Owing to the distance to be traveled, we necessarily had to start about two days before in order to be there at the opening of the conference. My wife accompanied me. We took a sleeper to Chicago and while there stopped at the Sherman House. During our stay in Chicago we profitably employed our time by viewing places of interest in that city. By this time delegates from different parts of the United States were centering here. Everything seemed crowded with delegates, and while we were going through Indiana and Illinois, delegates were getting on the train at different stations who put in their time by discussing different topics concerning the church work, etc. We left Chicago for Omaha, arriving there on Saturday about 11 o'clock.

We were met at the depot by the reception committee. Many of the delegates had received cards from the Garfield Hotel. When I received one, I said to myself this must be the place set aside for the delegates. When I reached the hotel I found things about as I had expected. The place was newly built and newly fitted up. We were given a very nice room. The linens indicated that they had never been to a laundry. When I looked around I found also that we had no heat. As the delegates began to come in, they were directed to go to the Garfield Hotel. By some mistake the secretary had sent cards to some of the white delegates and when they arrived [at the Garfield Hotel] they were directed to go somewhere else. The affair caused some suspicion

163

and an investigation was made, and we found that these quarters were for some of the lesser lights. When fifty to sixty guests had arrived, the place was rather crowded. One long room did service for the office. I took it upon myself to make an investigation and found that the hotel had been made temporarily for the delegates. It seemed there had been a kind of speculation scheme gotten up. The company thought that running a hotel for thirty or sixty days with about sixty guests at $2.00 a day might prove profitable. The weather turned quite cold, it being in the month of May, and some of the delegates became ill. The Liberian delegates were used to such a warm climate, and being without fire, it seemed quite natural that they should take ill. I myself would have suffered also if I had not taken the precaution of bringing quinine with me.

On Monday morning the conference was to meet. I said that if I was to remain in this hotel, I would be compelled to bring the matter before the conference. The conference allowed us $2.00 a day and I thought we could use that as we saw fit. The proprietors thought if some of the kickers went away the balance would be satisfied. My wife and I then took quarters at 2225 Chicago Street, with a Mr. Ovall,[58] one of the best families of the city. Others at the hotel made complaint and finally the Bishop came to investigate the matter. The conference knew nothing of the circumstances until their attention was called to it. The scheme was gotten up by a Mr. White and Dr. Ricketts[59] to make money, but which proved to be quite unsatisfactory. Quite a number moved out of the Garfield Hotel. It seemed that someone had reported that the delegates were to be boarded free, and the people of Omaha were unwilling to take them in, but when they heard that they could make $1.00 to $2.00 per day there were lots of places where comfortable places could be had.

On the Saturday night before the opening of the conference the lay delegates held a separate conference to map out the course to be pursued during the general conference and to decide whether the lay delegates would be divided from the ministerial delegates. A great deal of feeling was aroused over the matter and much discussion followed. It was finally decided that if we so desired we could unite with the ministerial delegation; some did and others did not. I was opposed to the

164

separation, holding that it would cause two distinct conferences if we were to separate and during the time allotted us we could not transact all the business that was to be attended to. I thought also that it would be placing these delegations where the ministerial would be the higher congress and the lay delegation would be the lower house.

We met in Boyd's Opera House, but afterwards found out that preparations were being made to hold the meetings in the Exposition Building. While I was making my appeal opposing the separation of the delegations, ministerial and lay, I noticed a gentleman in the audience who said "you are right." I afterward found this gentleman to be the distinguished Dr. Grandison,[60] then of North Carolina. The conference at last convened and settled down to business and everything went along smoothly. When the committees were appointed I found that I was placed upon two committees. The delegate receiving the highest number of votes was known as the leader. This honor fell to L. M. Hagood. In our delegation were Drs. Hagood, Peters, Hammond and myself. When I found I was only on two committees, which was not as many as I desired, I took our leader to task about it. Were I placed on several more committees I could have made a choice of the committees' meetings I desired to attend, as frequently several committees would meet on the same afternoon, therefore I could attend the session where I thought I could do the most good and which would be the most interesting to me. I told Dr. Hagood I did not come for the purpose of walking the streets of Omaha, but had come to do some work for the church. After [the] conference had been in session about a week, a talk had been made about electing bishops, and the general conference officers were to be elected. I spoke to several of the prominent men of the convention concerning the election of bishops and as they knew that I had nothing but the interests of the church at heart, they spoke quite freely to me.

The Southern delegates wanted to call a conference of the colored delegates for the purpose of settling on some man for bishop of the colored people. The delegates from the North were not as numerous as those from the South. One of the characteristics of the Southern delegates is to stand for their candidate. I spoke to Dr. Hammond and told him that Dr. Albert desired to be elected bishop,[61] and if he was, there would be a vacancy in the editorial chair of the Southwestern [Christian Advocate] which position paid about $1700 a year. A selection for the bishop was made and Dr. Albert was their choice.

While on my way from New York [in 1888], I met one of the gentlemen from Omaha, at Harrisburgh, Pa., who had been there to secure the next meeting of the general conference for his city. I asked if he knew what an undertaking it was. He said he thought the people of the city knew how to handle them. Everything did not work as smoothly, however, as was desired, and the conference decided that hereafter it would make its own arrangements to entertain delegates. The committee had to appropriate several thousand dollars toward paying the expenses of the conference.

When Friday and Saturday came, members of the different churches of the city were looking around for some suitable person to fill their pulpits on Sunday. I was frequently approached to fill pulpits, as it was thought I was a minister. When I was accosted, I would often say, that all the duties of a minister I could perform was that of eating chicken. I always offered to find some good speaker for them when I was requested.

Finally the day for electing bishops came. The night before I went down to the hotel and spoke to several of the leading officers, and told them I desired to see Dr. Hammond elected to the editorial chair of the Southwestern, as Dr. Albert desired to be elected bishop.[62] I assured them that Dr. Hammond would prove satisfactory to the conference. I had previously spoken to Dr. Hammond and asked if he would accept the position. He replied that he would, but had no thought of being elected as the Southern delegation was opposed to him. I said, "Do not allow this to have any influence upon you." When Dr. Albert was put in nomination, different delegates jumped up to second him, in all kinds of styles. When Dr. Hammond's time came, Bishop Joyce[63] asked him who was to place him in nomination, the Dr. replied, "Bro. Knox." Bishop Joyce told him he knew I would be equal to the emergency. I had secured Dr. Gouger,[64] of Philadelphia, to second the nomination.

I at last caught the eye of the chair, and being recognized, at once put Dr. Hammond in nomination. I said: "Mr. Chairman, I have risen for the purpose of putting a man in nomination for the editorial chair of the Southwestern Christian Advocate who is a universal favorite, and whose pen is as balmy and soothing as the dew that falls in the month of May, a man whose influence will be felt in all that is for the best interests of the church, a man who will do equally well for the Creole, the Indian, the Caucasian, as well as his own race, and if elected to the position for which I shall nominate him, he will prove to the church that he is a man worthy of the position. His influence shall be felt and known from the golden gates of California, and go sweeping across the country and will not stop until it reaches the piney bluffs of Maine. Neither will it stop there. It will extend from the chilly lakes of Michigan to the flowery groves of Florida. This man, Mr. Chairman, whom I place in nomination for the editorship of the Southwestern Christian Advocate, is Dr. E. W. S. Hammond of the Lexington Conference."

Then Dr. Gouger of the Baltimore Conference, seconded the nomination. In the midst of the confusion and excitement, which followed the placing of Dr. Hammond in nomination, people cried, "vote, vote," and a vote was taken, and in about fifteen minutes the word was passed down the line that Dr. Hammond was elected by a majority of sixteen. I felt I had won quite a victory, not only for myself but for the church, and during the next few minutes congratulations were rolling in from all directions. The newspaper men wished to get my nomination speech. Dr. Hammond was completely surrounded by friends, receiving congratulations, and being asked where he would have his office, he replied, "anywhere I take my hat off," and taking out his subscription book, immediately commenced to solicit subscriptions for the Southwestern Christian Advocate. The secretary wanted to elect an editor of one of the German Advocates, as the editor, who was about to retire, had been in charge of the same for fifty years, and wished to resign in favor of his son, Theodore Nash.[65] After one of his German friends had placed him in nomination with a very eloquent speech, I tried again to catch the eye of the chair, and being successful, I rose to second the nomination. Several persons sitting near asked why I desired to second his nomination, as I was no German. In seconding the nomination I said "that I was asked why I seconded Mr. Nash's nomination. I know I am no German, but I do know one thing; my principles are like those of the old mother church, who knows no creed, no sect, no race and no nationality. Therefore, Mr. Chairman, I rise for the purpose of seconding the nomination of Theodore Nash for editor of the German Christian Advocate. Why should I not second his nomination? He is an exemplary young man, and under the training and guidance of his father who has wielded his pen for over half a century in behalf of the church and who now retires at the ripe old age of eighty-two years, will take up the work where his father leaves off. It makes me feel enthusiastic to know that the father can lay down his pen and that his son is qualified to take it up. Therefore I second the nomination of Theodore Nash and from what I have heard of him, I know I make no mistake in so doing."

Then came the election of other general officers. Drs. Spencer and Carnett[66] were to be elected secretaries. Dr. Spencer asked me to second his nomination. At this juncture, a ruling had been passed allowing no speech making as a preface to placing in or seconding the nomination of anyone. Some one had said that Dr. Spencer was an active man and would jump on a buck board to get over the country in order to attend to his duties, if necessary. I said, "as no speech-making is allowed, it is said that it requires an active man to jump on his buckboard, the train or carriage, and in no place are the services of active men needed as in the church, and I take pleasure in seconding the nomination of Dr. Spencer for secretary of Church Extension." Dr. Spencer was elected by a large majority and Dr. Carnett was also elected.

I found that my action in seconding the nomination of Theodore Nash won for me many friends among the Germans and other members of the conference. In the afternoon when the Omaha Bee came out, it had this remark to make in the way of sarcasm for me: " 'Dr.' Knox of the Lexington Conference, in placing Dr. E. W. S. Hammond in nomination, grew so eloquent that we think a portion of his speech hung in the clouds and never came down."[67]

Dr. Hammond had been presiding elder in the Ohio district and now that he was editor of the Advocate, someone else was required for that position. Bishop Walden took dinner with my wife and me one day, and the matter of appointing a new presiding elder came up. He asked me who I thought would be a good man for the place. I suggested Rev. M. S. Johnson of Cincinnati who was a very energetic worker, as a good man for the place. The Bishop appointed Dr. Johnson as presiding elder of the Ohio district, and the bishop has not had any cause for regret for making this appointment.

The conference was coming to a close. About this time I received a letter from Mrs. Lillian Thomas,[68] of Indianapolis, stating that I had better return at once, as The Freeman was going under, and in a financial strait, and it would need my immediate attention. I wrote back that I would be home on a certain day, and I thought the matter would keep until that time. At the suggestion of Mr. Sweeney, Mrs. Thomas sent me a telegram, stating that the paper had failed, and that I had better come at once. While I attended the conference in New York I was called away before the work was completed and I desired to see the closing of this conference, so I decided to remain. At the close of the conference we at once started for home. Many delegates and ministers were on the same train.

Bishop Foster[69] came and took a seat near me and told me that when I reached home, he desired me to agitate union, that being his particular hobby. He said that our people wanted office, and it was right for them to do so, but as long as the whites were in the majority their officers would be elected; but if we were to have one gigantic union of our church, North and South, and meet every four years, for the purpose of electing officers and Bishops, having colored officers to do the business of the colored churches, then we would have two sets of general officers and Bishops, which would give us an equal share.

I replied, "Bishop, I see your intentions are good and I understand what your ideas are. You know that the great split in the Methodist church was caused by the whites of the South leaving the church when the Negro was declared free and allowed in this church, and the South would not subscribe to any church or creed which advocated the freedom of the Negro. Now, these people left the church on these grounds, and your idea is, if you can get the Negro to go separately, the doors can again be opened to those who left the church. That is one thing I oppose. They went out because freedom of the Negro was advocated, and if they desire to again receive the protection and benefit of the Mother Church, let them come with the Negro in it. We are your children and you cannot get rid of us in that way. I know you think it would be for the best, but I shall never endorse your idea of a great gigantic union, with that end in view."

169

The next day we arrived in Chicago, and reached Indianapolis the following morning, (Sunday). On my return I found The Freeman had failed to come out the past week. It had been printed but it was not sent out. This was about the 1st of June [1892] and I was making preparations to attend the National Republican Convention, to be held at Minneapolis, and of which I was a delegate.

On the Sunday that I returned home I attended services at Simpson Chapel after an absence of about thirty days in attendance at the conference. On Monday morning the first thing to do was to ascertain the exact condition of The Freeman. I saw Mr. Cooper at The Freeman office, 91½ East Court street, and we talked over matters concerning the paper and I told Mr. Cooper that I did not care to take hold of the paper myself, as I had no experience whatever in newspaper business, and I thought it would be the best thing not to continue its publication. I suggested that it be sold, and let some one else take hold of it. Mr. Cooper spoke up and said it was a very valuable piece of property, and that the plant was worth $5,000, and that it would never do to let it fail. He thought that I should put it upon its feet again. Here Mr. Sweeney spoke up and corroborated Mr. Cooper's statement, and said for the sake of the race, it would not do to discontinue the publication of The Freeman, as I had it in my power to revive it. I said that as one issue had already been missed that would necessarily damage the interests of the paper. Mr. Cooper thought not, and said that even though the paper had not come out, daily receipts had amounted to $39.00 to $40.00, and previously, the receipts were from $50.00, $60.00 and $75.00. He took down his cash book and showed me where some weeks receipts amounted to $100.00, varying sometimes less and sometimes more, and prospects seemed very bright; I really could not understand how the paper could fail under such circumstances. Mr. Cooper seemed to think that because obligations which had not been met, demanding immediate settlement, was what caused his failure, and that as I had always held a personal mortgage on it, and secured another one, the best thing I could do was to take hold of it. I finally consented to put it on its feet again. We went across to my attorney's office, and I counseled with him regarding the matter. I told Mr. Cooper that I would take the paper, but should he want it back any

170

time, he could have it at the price it cost me, no matter what the income had been in the meantime. He had put so much time and expense upon it that it seemed but right he should be the proprietor of it and if he did not want to take the whole responsibility of the paper, I would probably take him in as a partner.

The papers were drawn up and everything was arranged so that no mistakes or misunderstandings would occur. To make things doubly secure, Mr. Cooper gave me a mortgage on all of his personal property and The Freeman. After this we went to the press rooms, where lay about 12,000 papers which should have been sent out the previous Saturday. I agreed to retain Mr. Cooper on The Freeman as business manager and Mr. Sweeney as editor. Sell's Bros circus was in town that day, and Mr. Cooper told me that owing to the paper not getting out the last week, he was financially embarrassed and asked me if I had some cash. I replied I had some and gave him and Mr. Sweeney between them $5.00. The parade was passing through the streets and the two gentlemen went to see it and seemed as anxious as two country boys to go to the show in the afternoon. I could not understand how these men, under the circumstances, could go to the circus, as I could not, and could have bought out The Freeman.

After the two gentlemen had left me, I went to The Freeman office, and found Mrs. Lillian Thomas, who during Cooper's regime had been correspondent editor, sitting in the cold room, the fire having been shut off, seemingly awaiting her fate. I told her I expected to give her employment in the same capacity Mr. Cooper had employed her. The next day I made arrangements with Mr. Fulmer to do our press work, and went to see the Bowen-Merrill Co. to make arrangements with them to furnish the paper. Mr. Cooper went with me, and Mr. Bobbs,[70] a member of the firm, requested me to take a seat in their office. I had not the time so we hastily concluded our arrangements, and this much was accomplished. In leaving the store, Mr. Cooper remarked that he had spent hundreds of dollars with that firm and they had never requested him to take a seat. I took this remark as a bit of "taffy." Sometimes you can touch a man's weakest spot by flattery and I did not know but what he was taking advantage of my weakness, as men are as susceptible to flattery as women in some cases. June the 11th [1892] was the day set for The Freeman to make its debut to

171

the race under the new management. Mr. W. D. Driver was one of the reporters of the [Indianapolis] *News* staff, and [he] took occasion to give me a nice write-up as the new proprietor of The Freeman, in that journal.

The National Republican Convention was to meet on the 7th of June in Minneapolis, and during the time I was making arrangements for continuing the publication of The Freeman I was also preparing for this convention. I was invited by the president of the Columbia Club,[71] Mr. Gordon,[72] to accompany the club, which was to have a special train of seven coaches. I accepted his invitation. Word came to me that some objections were raised to my going with the club and taking a berth on the Pullman car by a member of the club. I went to Mr. Gordon and told him that as I was going to pay my way anyhow, and was to be accompanied by my son, if there were any objections, I would prefer taking another route. Mr. Gordon informed me that if the complaining member did not like the idea of me accompanying them he could remain at home. I could not but give honor to Mr. Gordon who frankly expressed his disapproval of the remarks made by the club man, and I honored him for his broad principles and the stand he took for the right.

We left on Saturday morning, the club marching to the depot. We stopped at different points along the road, and great crowds welcomed and cheered the Columbia Club. We reached LaFayette [Indiana] about 12:00 o'clock, and Mr. Williams, a newspaperman of that city met us with a dispatch that James G. Blaine[73] had resigned the Secretaryship of State, and the President had accepted the resignation. This threw quite a gloom over the party and everyone expressed his idea of the effect the resignation of Mr. Blaine would have upon the nomination of Mr. Harrison.[74] It was thought by some that it would bring about the defeat of Mr. Harrison. As we pulled out of LaFayette Mr. Hervey Bates, Sr.,[75] took a seat near me, and asked what I thought would be the result of the influence of Mr. Blaine's resignation upon the nomination of General Harrison. I said: "As we see it now, it seems the effect will be damaging, but in a few days a reaction will set in, and the country will see it as another of Mr. Blaine's shrewd political tricks, to remain under the cloak of the President until just a few hours before the nomination. He thinks he will be nominated in a whoop, but that will not be. When the first smoke clears away the delegates will begin to see why he made this move, and you will see that Harrison will be nominated on the first ballot. There is no hope for Mr. Blaine, for in 1888 he expected to stay in Europe and have his name brought before the convention and nominated whether or no. As that scheme did not work, he is taking this course. While Mr. Blaine is a statesman, and has been a great service to his party and country, he can never receive the nomination. Mr. Harrison will surely be nominated. This is my judgment."

We passed through Illinois, and found ourselves out at Davenport, Ia. Somewhere on the road we were met by a dining car, in which we were to take our dinner. This was about 6 o'clock. We filed in one by one into the dining car and ate our dinners. We carried the dining car about seventy-five miles when it was dropped. About 12 o'clock we reached a town in Iowa, and a great crowd of people stood around the train. They had understood that we were a Blaine delegation and had come for the purpose of giving us a reception. This threw another gloom over the party, as everything seemed for Blaine. After a few moment's silence, the people appeared to be looking for something to be said by our party. I stood upon the platform and made a little speech in favor of Mr. Harrison. I said:

"Fellow Citizens:—This is not a James G. Blaine Club, and neither is it for Blaine. We are Indianapolitans, composed of the Columbia Club, one of the largest and most effective Republican clubs in the state, who are ardent supporters of Mr. Harrison, and as delegates from Indiana we intend to present his name to the convention to be nominated. We know that he is good not only for the merchant, for the banker, the laboring man, but he is good for the man who goes down into the mines. He fills the dinner baskets, makes the country prosperous, makes the smoke go curling to the blue skies from every factory, and the renomination and reelection of President Harrison means a continuing of the prosperous condition, not only of the Republican party but also of the Democratic party and this great Nation of ours. Therefore, fellow citizens of Iowa we intend to see to it that Mr. Harrison will be the nominee of this National convention which assembles on the 7th at Minneapolis."

At the close of my remarks, there came three rousing cheers from

Harrison, which split the very darkness of the night. By this time the train was pulling out.

On Sunday morning we traveled through Minnesota, and about 11 o'clock we reached Minneapolis, where we were met at the depot by R. R. Shiel[76] and several other Indianapolitans. The Club formed in line, and Mr. Gordon, president of the club, said that I should have the distinct honor of leading the club through the streets of Minneapolis. The club made a fine appearance with their linen dusters and white hats, and as we marched down the street, led by a Minneapolis band, we attracted a good deal of attention. People thronged every street and corner. A Committee on Reception escorted us to the West House, which were the headquarters of the Indiana delegation. We landed there in the midst of cheers and shouts of welcome.

The business houses and different buildings were decorated with flags, and altogether presented quite a festive appearance. As we marched to the Exposition Building, we went through an arch, which was composed of barrels, and away from the arch proper was a representation of a mill, one of the great industries of the state of Minnesota.

Upon arriving at the West House, we reported immediately at headquarters. Every man seemed to know his duty and was put to work. The Indiana delegation went to work with sleeves rolled up, and the best foot forward for Indiana's favorite son and the Nation's pride. We intended to make President Harrison the nominee of this convention. It seemed that the Indiana men, who first arrived on the scene, were somewhat discouraged as the Blaine men had the advantage of the situation, but when the Columbia Club came in with its seven car loads of Harrison enthusiasts, and banners flying, the Blaine men were not so sanguine, and Harrison men took possession and retained it.

The magnificent West Hotel was crowded with visitors and delegates. The hotel seemed to attract the most attention. The cry in Chicago had been "What's the matter with Harrison? He's all right"; but now it had changed to: "We've had him once; we want him again."

We were kept constantly busy. Once I found myself in the midst of a crowd of gentlemen who were talking the situation over, and a gentleman came to me, introducing himself, asking if I was not Mr.

174

Knox, of Indiana. Receiving an answer in the affirmative, he said he wanted my attention a moment, as the artist desired to make a sketch of me. I did so, and soon the artist was using his pencil, drawing a sketch of me which was to appear in the Chicago Herald.

Delegates were coming in from all directions. The Michigan delegation came, and the California delegation, with their tin umbrellas, made a fine display. Some delegations for Blaine came in, and those for Harrison were rolling in. This added more interest to the scene. Sunday evening delegations from Texas and South and North Carolina arrived and went to their respective headquarters. The South Carolina, Mississippi, Alabama and Georgia delegations had headquarters at the Brunswick Hotel.

In the evening the Indiana delegation held a meeting and it was decided then what steps it would take. Col. Richard W. Thompson[77] was the chairman of our delegation, and the views of the delegates were given. R. R. Shiel and Mr. Dearborn[78] made some good talks. Our line of work was well laid out. Different suggestions as to how the fight would be made were offered. It was decided that I should, as much as possible, give my attention to the Southern delegates, among whom it had been given out that Harrison was not favorable to colored people. I met Col. Murrell,[79] of The New Jersey Trumpet, and he gave me to understand that he was for Harrison, but I afterwards learned that he was not.

We also found out something that was never before known in the history of National conventions, namely: The administration had a candidate and the National Committee had a candidate. Hence, administration and National Committee headquarters were established. I had never known of such a thing as the National Committee and Administration having candidates, fighting each other, and members of the same party, as was done under the leadership of Clarkson,[80] Platt[81] and Fassett.[82]

On Monday morning we had orders to meet at Indiana headquarters for the purpose of arranging our business. Among the Southern delegates, N. W. Cuney[83] of Texas, was the center of attraction, being a delegate for Harrison. I had formed the acquaintance of some of the leading Southerners, among whom were Judge Gibbs[84] of Arkansas; General Smalls[85] of South Carolina; ex-Congressman Miller[86] of

175

arolina; N. W. Cuney of Texas. Frederick Douglass was there
﹍ an important part, as was B. K. Bruce.[87] Mr. Pinchback[88] was
there, but was opposed to Harrison.

John M. Langston,[89] on his way to the convention, stopped in Chicago and made a speech opposing Harrison. It was stated also among the delegates that Harrison was opposed to the Negro. I said, that in 1890 Mr. Langston, while making an address on the Emancipation in Indianapolis,[90] spoke in glowing terms of Harrison. I had been appointed a committee of one, by the Committee of Arrangements, to speak to Mr. Langston requesting him not to make a political address because the members of the race were choosing their own political affiliations and should a political address be made, the Democrats would say it was merely a boom for Harrison. After waiting upon Mr. Langston, he informed me that he would not make a political address. In his speech Mr. Langston said that "He thanked God that he had been privileged to speak to the citizens of Indianapolis, which city had furnished a Morton, a Richard Thompson, and best of all had furnished Benjamin Harrison, the President of the United States, who is one of the grandest and noblest men who ever lived." In his speech he also said that no one had done more for the race than President Harrison. He said he had given appointments that had never before been given the Negro, citing Jas. M. Townsend,[91] John R. Lynch[92] and Senator Bruce's appointments. He also said that, in speaking of the good qualities of President Harrison, he was not talking politics, and that as a soldier and general in the late war, President Harrison had done much to bring about the freedom which to-day the race enjoyed.

These are some of the nice things he said about President Harrison, and because, said I, he was not appointed to the Judgeship in the Court of Appeals[93] he takes an opportunity to get revenge and defeat Mr. Harrison for the nomination. I told some of the delegates that I believed Mr. Langston's utterances in Indianapolis were his opinions and were sincere. Of course, Mr. Harrison could not give every man an office, and even though he did deviate somewhat from the precedent established by previous presidents—appointing to office only those who had been of assistance—he had nevertheless done more good for the race. Mr. Harrison's was one of the purest administrations. He has caused prosperity all over the land, in the homes of the Republican as well as the Democrat. He preserved the American flag from insult and made our nation one that was to be respected by all foreign countries. Someone asked me what office I held, supposing me to be holding some fat office under Mr. Harrison's administration. I replied that I held none, but it was a pleasure to do business under such a clean and prosperous administration. As I was the only colored delegate from the Northern states, the papers took occasion to say that G. L. Knox was one of the attractions in the lobbies of the West House, with his white hat, his white hair appearing from under it, and his sombre face.

When Mr. Gowdy[94] heard someone remark that Mr. Harrison did not favor the colored man, he would always introduce me to him, saying if Harrison had not been true to my race he would not have selected me as a delegate-at-large from his state.

On Tuesday everything was moving along nicely and all working like beavers; the Harrison men as well as the Blaine and Alger[95] men. By this time I had gotten very well acquainted with all the delegates from every part of the United States. When it came to different arguments that Harrison was not a friend of the colored man, I always made this statement, that while Mr. Harrison was in the United States Senate, he was in favor of a bill which would give every man the right to vote and have that vote counted, while Mr. Blaine left his chair in the House to make a speech against the Force bill.[96] Mr. Harrison was in favor of the Force bill, while Mr. Blaine was opposed to it.[97]

In making this argument I gave the Southerners to understand that this was the reason they should not oppose Mr. Harrison, as he was in favor of giving every man his rights, regardless of complexion or previous condition of servitude. If you will notice the Cincinnati Enquirer, you will see it favors Mr. Blaine in preference to Mr. Harrison. It knows that Mr. Harrison is the strongest candidate. Mr. Harrison has shown at every step since he has been president that he is in favor of the Force bill, which was defeated by some of the leading Republicans, among whom was Ingalls of Kansas.[98] They are now being repudiated by the Republican Party for not supporting this measure. In a speech Mr. Ingalls declared that the Southern people were walking upon dynamite and volcanoes and seeking their own destruction, and then he turns right around and votes against this bill, the same measure which he had seemed to think was a proper one. That is the reason he retired from the U.S. Senate.

Mr. Harrison at every step urged the passage of this bill. Of course, all the South does not want it, but the colored people do, as it is the only thing that will give them equal representation in the Legislature, in Congress and in the Senate. On the one side there is the man who opposed the Force bill which gives you the right to vote and have it counted, and on the other side is the man who favors it, Mr. Harrison, who is working for your rights, and yet you oppose him. I can not see the wisdom and philosophy of it.

By this time we knew pretty well what number of votes would be cast for Harrison. We had the actual count of every man and knew where each one stood. A man came up to me and said he understood that the Texas delegation was breaking from Harrison. I said, "A few moments ago the report came to that the Indiana delegation was breaking. We only had twenty-six votes in the Texas delegation and we have that number yet." I also heard someone say that if the Indiana delegation was breaking, the South Carolina delegation would break.

The Blaine men were working hard, and the Harrison men were losing no time. I would do my hardest work in the largest crowds. One time someone shouted where was I from. I replied from Indiana. The answer came that Indiana was under water. I said then I wished to God all states were under water as Indiana is. "From Indiana," I said, "you can get mineral waters from the earth and all matter of the mineral kingdom are represented in her bowels. Besides the minerals there gushes forth the gas which heats and enlightens the homes of the people." After this I heard nothing more about Indiana being under water.

Many speeches were made by the delegates, also the white and colored men. The Blaine men tried to keep the Harrison men from making speeches or say[ing] anything favorable for their candidate. On Wednesday about noon there was such a crowd and so many men trying to get at me, that Mrs. Dr. Morris[99] of Indiana told her husband that she was uneasy, for fear that I would be mobbed. Often my son, with Mr. Vaughn and Mr. Jones[100] and members of the Columbia Club, stood around me when I made speeches for Mr. Harrison. Often the crowd would get angry and I would say, "you have a right to support your man, but our man is going to be nominated on the first ballot." When asked how I knew, I replied that we had 526 votes which would more than elect Harrison. All that was to be done was to cast the votes. Morris Ross of the Indianapolis News came up to me and asked me what Harrison's chances were. I replied that they were good and he would be nominated. When I told him we had 526 votes, he said I was wild and did not know what I was talking about.

It was known that I was an untiring supporter of Mr. Harrison. A delegation from Indiana whose leader had desired a postmastership under Harrison, and did not receive it, and who opposed Harrison, had a procession one day, and I was asked, "where are your Harrison men now?" and I shouted back that not a delegate in that procession could vote. On Wednesday evening the Indiana delegation held a meeting and discussed how we could best execute our campaign for our candidate.

One of the leaders of the Mississippi delegation asked me, "what about your man Harrison." "He's all right," I said, and when asked what good qualities he possessed, I said that after he had made a trip over the country a committee composed of Indianapolis citizens to receive him to his home was appointed, I being one of the committee. Other members were such prominent men as Gov. Hovey,[101] Gen. Lew Wallace,[102] Judge Woods[103] of the Supreme Bench, Gen. McGinnis,[104] and the Rev. Dr. Haines.[105] When the train arrived at Montezuma, Ind., where we were to meet the President, we went to his car and took seats. I met Mr. Harrison on one of the platforms and shook hands with him, and he called me by name and told me he was glad to get back to his old home again. Mr. Harrison made a speech and said that every where he had been, [he had been] welcomed kindly and enthusiastically, but the welcome given him by his own citizens was the sweetest of all. We had seventy-five miles to ride before we reached Indianapolis and during that time many stops were made at the way stations where speeches were made.

The General at one place was standing up and talking, whereat I offered him my seat. He declined, thanking me. After awhile an ex-banker of this city [Indianapolis] offered the President his seat, which he accepted, and I thought this a mark of distinction accorded one of his humblest citizens. We were assembled in a kind of family circle in the presidential car. To the left of me were Mrs. Harrison, Mrs. McKee[106] and old friends, and to the right were Gen. Lew Wallace, Judge Woods and others, and directly in front of me was the President.

When a pause in the conversation occurred, I said, "General, it was predicted when you left Washington, that you would not speak to the Southern people as to the Northern." He said, "Mr. Knox, when I left Washington, I decided that whatever was my duty that I would do." I told him again it was predicted that he would not speak on questions touching my race, and he told me he had had but one opportunity to do so, and that was in response to a welcome address made by the Mayor of Memphis. In it the mayor declared against Negro domination and supremacy. Mr. Harrison said to the people that "all he asked of the South or any part of the country was that the citizens be given equal rights—a right to cast his vote and have that one vote counted." He said they need not be afraid of Negro supremacy. "You have the power in your hands to make a proper qualification of your voters, and as long as you make the qualification without regard to color or complexion, the Negro will find no fault."[107] "These," I said, to the Mississippi man, "are words which the President of the United States spoke. Moreover, he is the best president we ever had and has given us the purest administration."

On Wednesday I received many invitations to go out carriage riding to see the beauties of the city, etc., but I declined them all, as I had not come to the convention for health or pleasure, but to do all in my power to make Mr. Harrison the nominee of this convention.

On Thursday we had a morning session, after which the Harrison men held a convention of which Chauncey Depew[108] was president. This convention had great influence over the delegates. I was otherwise engaged and could not be present. A delegate from Arkansas came up to me and asked me: "Suppose Harrison is defeated and fails to get the nomination of the convention." "If such be the case," I replied, "we will have to sneak home through a back way, for we dare not let the people know when we get in. They will be indignant."

I then visited the different delegations, and one day had a long argument in presenting my man. A tall, fine looking New Yorker asked me about Mr. Harrison. I said he was very strong. I said he had 22 votes in the New York delegation, and if he can receive that number in a delegation under the influence of such men as Fassett, Clarkson and Platt, he is undoubtedly a strong man. Again, asking me if he was so strong, I replied: "yes, he is a bass; he swims up stream and minnows must get out of his way. He is mighty from the beginning." This same gentleman asked me what he had done, and I retorted "what has he not done." He had made us one of the best presidents of the country and has brought prosperity to it. Take him as a citizen, in his family, as a warrior, as a General, as a Senator, his character stands forth like the Son of Man. As Moses he held up the serpent in the wilderness, so he was sent to man to be held up before the world, and all looking upon him shall be saved. He is so grand and American-like [that] all men will be drawn upon him. While Mr. Blaine is a good man and a statesman, he does not possess the magnetism that Harrison does. Blaine cannot get the votes. In 1884 Mr. [Grover] Cleveland defeated him for the presidency, and to illustrate, Harrison then defeated Mr. Cleveland. This shows to me conclusively that Harrison is the strongest man. Because Harrison could not give all these men positions, they are down on him."

"Well, what position do you hold?" I replied I did not hold any, except the position of American citizen under a prosperous administration. In the parlors at the New York headquarters I was placed upon a chair and asked to make a speech. At the conclusion of it I was given three rousing cheers, and people came to the parlors to learn what caused the noise. When I went into the delegation we had but 22 votes, and when I came out Harrison had 30 votes and I could not but feel that this was the result of some of my hard work. During the speech I was frequently interrupted and Mr. Todd,[109] standing near me, said, "only one speak at a time," but I said they could talk but must not get angry, for no matter who would be nominated they would have to support him anyway. I forgot to mention that on the previous evening I had been approached by four gentlemen from our delegation who informed me that a committee of five had been appointed to call upon the Arkansas delegation and I was selected as chairman. I was thinking to myself that was a distinct honor, and afterwards the thought came to me that perhaps they thought the del-

181

egation was composed of colored men and it would be best to have me as chairman of the committee. When we arrived at the Arkansas headquarters, instead of finding it composed of colored men, they were all white with the exception of Judge Gibbs.[110] I took in the situation at once. We were introduced to each member present, and a number of distinguished men composed the delegation. One of our committee began to speak, saying we had come to find out how the delegation stood for Harrison. I interrupted him and asked to be allowed to speak for a moment. I did not think they should be approached in such a direct manner, as if we had come to electioneer. I asked one man how the delegation stood for Harrison, saying we felt satisfied we could rely upon them. He said: "gentlemen, the New York delegation has been with us for about an hour and a half and has been reading the texts and papers, etc., in favor of Harrison. They have just been gone about fifteen minutes. We took a vote and that vote resulted 15 for Harrison and one for Blaine, sixteen being the number of the delegation members." I stated that we need have no fear of the Arkansas delegation and being introduced to the Blaine supporter, told him he could not be blamed for supporting Blaine as he was a fine man, but requested that if he saw that Blaine would have no show that he give his vote to Harrison. He replied that if he saw things going against Blaine and he had no chances, he would give our man his support. Withdrawing from the delegation we reported to headquarters how things stood.

On Thursday evening I met Gen. Griffin[111] of Hammond, Ind., and he suggested that we go down to dinner together. We did so, but found the dining room rather crowded. At last we espied a table where a delegate and his wife were, and a waiter also seeing us, directed Mr. Griffin to take a seat at that table, thinking I would go to some other table as I was colored, but Mr. Griffin did not care if it was a colored man with him and said: "We will take seats here." The lady's face changed color and she looked very indignant that I should be at a table with her. Presently Sen. Spooner[112] of Wisconsin and Gen. Wallace took seats at our table and we were discussing the convention. Senator Spooner was a staunch supporter of Mr. Harrison and a conspicuous character in the convention. Senator Spooner said there was a majority report to be adopted and that he would go up and move that the convention adopt the majority report which he did. It was unexpected to the Blaine men, and they feared it would give us advantage of the grounds. Senator Spooner suggested that some Indiana delegate second the motion and if my memory serves me right, Gen. Griffin did so, and the motion was carried.

The hall at night was crowded with delegates and spectators, about 12,000 people being present, in fact, the largest number I have seen in one enclosure. You will imagine the surprise of this crowd when at 11 o'clock we found ourselves in utter darkness. The city's contract with the light company was to furnish light until that hour. [I] knew that if the people began to get excited and made for the exits to the hall, there would be a stampede and many persons injured, perhaps crushed to death. Thinking of this I quietly slipped out of the hall and when the lights were turned on again, I returned. About 1 o'clock in the morning some members of our delegation complained of being sleepy, and I told them we were not here to eat, sleep or drink, if necessity demanded, until we nominated Harrison. I suggested that they observe the manner in which other delegations were working, and that we should work more than they, as we were the one presenting the nominee to the convention. The convention adjourned about 2 o'clock.

While I was coming from headquarters about an hour afterwards, I was approached by a colored man who asked me if I was not Mr. Knox of Indiana. I replied that I was. Without much preliminary talk he asked me if I wanted to be a man, and I told him that had always been the ambition of my life, and I desired to know how he could make me a man. He said, "by money," and that by going to a certain room in the hotel I could get all the money I wanted. I asked if he meant by being bought and he replied, "yes." Well, I replied, if there is any buying to do, I am in that business myself, whereupon he immediately left me, saying he had meant no harm.

On Friday morning after eating breakfast at the West House, and counselling at headquarters, our attention was turned to the convention which opened about 10 o'clock. I had received for my part five packs of tickets for admission to the convention, and had frequent requests to sell some, as many had been sold at $25 and $30 a pack, and some as high as $5 a single ticket, but mine were to be given away. After my supply of tickets was exhausted I had requests for more, but

183

did not need them as I had become acquainted with the gatekeeper, and he allowed those to pass whose names I mentioned.

I returned to the convention hall and presently speech-making commenced. The speakers were surrounded by eager reporters who were getting notes for their respective journals. A Senator from Colorado[113] placed Mr. Blaine in nomination, and Chauncey Depew placed Mr. Harrison in nomination, and it is needless to pay any tribute to the eloquent manner in which he did so. The nomination was seconded by Col. Richard W. Thompson of Indiana. Several colored men made speeches for Mr. Blaine, and others for Mr. Harrison.[114] After the speeches, a Cincinnati club marched in with a banner for Blaine. Presently I noticed what seemed to be a moving picture of Mr. Harrison coming from the west. It was being carried by three men. This surprise was prepared by Hardy Martin, a young man of Indianapolis. The picture was greeted with a loud chorus of cheers from all over the house. Confusion reigned for a time, and when all had been quieted, a woman in the western part of the building raised a white umbrella and shouted for Blaine. She held it for about thirty minutes, assisted by the men about her, waving it all the time. Just in front of us was Gov. Foraker[115] of Ohio, who seemed to be in complete control of the Ohio delegation, his object being to have them support McKinley.[116] Mr. McKinley arose and said he did not want the delegates to vote for him, as he was not a candidate and had not come for the purpose of having his name brought before the convention. I believe that if McKinley had been a candidate he would have been the nominee of the convention, as when the Blaine men saw there was no hope for their man, they would have given Mr. McKinley their support, but as it was the Blaine men had no chance.

When order was again restored, a ballot was taken which resulted in the nomination of Harrison. The convention then proceeded to nominate the vice-president and Whitelaw Reid[117] was unanimously chosen. Some talk was made of Thomas Reed[118] of Maine, but his friends from Maine said that he did not desire the nomination. After the nomination of the vice-president the convention adjourned.

We were informed that our train would leave for Indianapolis at 11 o'clock that night, and we began to make preparations. Congratulations were much in order among us, after we started for home, traveling the entire night. When we reached Lafayette, we were given a warm reception by the citizens. As our train came through Illinois, a gentleman on the train came to me and said he wished me to address the citizens of his town, Lebanon. When we got there, however, we found that this gentleman's plans had been disarranged and that Mr. Fairbanks[119] was the man selected to speak.

After a number of speeches by different gentlemen, we again took the train for Indianapolis. Mr. Gordon told me that I should have the honor of leading the Columbia Club through the streets of our city as I had in Minneapolis. The club formed in rank and I supposed I was to lead, I asked one gentleman where my position would be, and he said in the rear. I said nothing but finally took my place about the middle of the rank. The streets were lined with people who welcomed us home.

On arriving at the club, speech-making was again in order, and Mr. Smiley N. Chambers[120] was first introduced. Afterward a call was made for Mr. Shiel, but as he remained in Minneapolis, he could not respond. After several had spoken, a call was made for "Knox." I went forward and made a short talk. My speech was made in these few words: "Fellow citizens. We have been selected by you as delegates to the National Convention and you entrusted to us the interests of the state and the Nation to see that Gen. Harrison was nominated, and this we have done, and we believe in the work that is to follow, you will equally join us. We have supported him because we believe that he is for the best interests of all, not only for us Republicans, but equally well for the Democrats. Mr. Harrison has given to the nation an administration that speaks for itself. The country has never prospered as it has done under his administration. Therefore we believe that his nomination and his work should speak for him. (I was so hoarse from continual speaking that I did not attempt to address them at length.) Gentlemen, before I stop speaking, I wish to predict the nominee of the Democratic convention: that will be Mr. Cleveland, as will be shown when the convention meets in Chicago." My prediction came true, as he was not only nominated but elected.

Now to business, especially to The Freeman. While I was away, the first issue made its appearance, and Mr. Cooper, the manager, sent me two hundred copies to distribute to the delegates. The Freeman put in some good work for Mr. Harrison during the campaign.

When I first employed Mr. Cooper he did not seem to be choice as to what salary he should have, but said he was satisfied with $12 per week. For secretary and treasurer of the company, I had employed Mr. F. B. Allen,[121] and altogether had Mr. E. E. Cooper, Mr. Allen, Mr. Allison W. Sweeney, Mrs. Lillian Thomas and my son[122] besides the force in the composing room, in all about twelve people. Everything went along smoothly for awhile, but I afterwards found out that there was one trouble—there were too many "big" men employed. One always seemed to have it in for the other. Finally I hired a Mr. Stapp[123] to take charge of the city work, to take subscriptions, etc. Mr. Cooper, as I went into my private office one day, stated that he was entitled to more consideration. I told him I thought so too, and it was agreed that he be paid $15 per week. At another time he seemed dissatisfied. I asked what would satisfy him. He said that he thought he should receive more money, as workmen in my [barber] shop made from $11 to $15 per week. He wanted $25. I told him that men in the shop received what they earned and I would agree to pay him that if he earned it.

Everything as I supposed was going along smoothly now, but one day Mr. Cooper came to me complaining of Mr. Sweeney's treatment of him, stating that if he had anything to say to him, he must first tell Mrs. Thomas, who would then have to break it gently to Mr. Sweeney. I told him I would look into the matter. Mr. Cooper recommended Mr. Sweeney's discharge, but I told him I did not desire to take any advantage of Mr. Sweeney, as I supposed this was something that could be readily adjusted, so I told Mr. Cooper we would meet Mr. Sweeney in the morning and talk over the matter.

At 9 o'clock the next morning, Mr. Cooper and myself went into the editorial room, and I spoke to Mr. Sweeney, telling him of Mr. Cooper's complaints, and Mr. Cooper substantiated them. I thought that Mr. Cooper was at least entitled to respect from the under-employees. As I finished, Mr. Cooper told the story in paragraphs, being interrupted at the end of each by Mr. Sweeney saying, "is that all." There were no changes in Mr. Sweeney's countenance and he nearly annihilated Mr. Cooper. Mr. Sweeney said that he gave the manager

186

due respect, and as for the charges made by Mr. Cooper, they were not true, as there was no man in the office more easily approached than him. I told Mr. Cooper that he could see Mr. Sweeney [had] put himself in an attitude where he could be readily approached without a third party. They grew quite indignant at each other, and I thought they would not even speak to each other any more. I suppose I had no more gotten to my shop when Mr. Cooper went into the editorial room and shook Mr. Sweeney by the hand, saying, "Allison, do you know we are two of the biggest Negroes in the country. The idea of you and I suffering this old 'handkerchief-headed' Negro to make a fool of two of the biggest Negroes in the land is not to be tolerated." When I heard of this, I knew that Mr. Cooper was one of the "ten greatest Negroes" and had made no exception to it, but as Mr. Sweeney had never been entered on that roll of honor as one of the "ten greatest," I did not know what place he would occupy. On this same day, I noticed Mr. Sweeney and Mr. Cooper on an electric car looking as happy and gay as larks. I thought to myself, surely I am mocked by these two men and the conference we had this morning is nothing but a farce. These things I would not stand. Mr. Cooper made the remark, "Mr. Knox is running The Freeman, but I am the manager."

Everything went along quietly for awhile until one morning, when I least expected it, Mr. Cooper informed me that he wished to see me. I told him very well. He said that as he was the founder of the paper he thought he should receive more consideration than others employed on the paper. I told him that I thought so too, and asked him what the trouble was. He then stated that I had hired a man by the name of Stapp, and the man had done something that displeased him. I asked him what it was about, as I thought perhaps Mr. Stapp might not be wholly in fault and that I might call on the gentleman and make an investigation, and if I should find things as Mr. Cooper stated I would then discharge Mr. Stapp as I did not intend he should not recognize Mr. Cooper's authority as manager of the paper. I talked the matter over with Mr. Stapp and he said that Mr. Cooper had tried to discharge him, and he had told Mr. Cooper that not he, but I, had hired him, and therefore Mr. Cooper had no power to discharge him. I then told Mr. Stapp that I did not wish to encourage him in disobedience to the manager and felt that obedience was due him as long as he was right, but I never had and never would relegate all my powers to any man, that I always reserved enough authority myself to enable me to fulfill my own wishes and desires in my business in regard to those who worked for me. I told Mr. Cooper that I thought he acted too hasty in trying to discharge Mr. Stapp, and that there seemed to be something back of it all that he did not care to mention. Mr. Cooper said that if I employed Mr. Stapp he would quit. I then said: "Mr. Cooper, I never allow anyone to dictate to me about who[m] I shall and shall not employ. I pay you your salary for your work and you should attend to your own business. As far as this matter is concerned, I will accept your resignation here." Here Mr. Stapp tried to interfere, but I told him to attend to his own business as I was attending to this matter myself. I presume Mr. Cooper thought the storm would pass over and he would go on. Another idea had presented itself to him which he thought would be a great scheme and bring in a good deal of money to The Freeman and that my profits would be materially increased. The next day he came to me and said he had been working hard and desired to take a vacation. I told him very well. He asked for transportation which was furnished him. He made a trip down about Missouri through Arkansas and Indian Territory. In about three weeks he returned[124] and asked me if he still held his old position, but I informed him that he had resigned once and I had put in his place Mr. F. B. Allen. He asked me what I meant—if it meant I let him out. I answered that it did; at the same time I told him that at any time he wished to buy the paper he could have it for the same amount of money it cost me.

This was in '92. The campaign began to wax warm and The Indianapolis Freeman took an active part, taking its stand in favor of Harrison and the Republican Party. Fifteen to twenty thousand copies were run off during each week, I, being a member of the State Executive Committee [of the Republican party], took quite an active part in the campaign, attending different meetings of committees, state and county conventions. One day Mr. Cooper came to me and said that he desired to buy The Freeman. I said, "very well, I will sell it, but you must come on with the money." He did not buy it. The campaign ended, the Republicans were defeated, and the tidal wave of the Dem-

188

ocratic Party swept the country. The legislature convened and was strongly Democratic. At this time we were having some trouble with our mail. Mr. Cooper claimed that all mail that had his name on it should be returned to him, but I thought that all mail with The Freeman on it should now be mine. I went to the postmaster and told him to turn over to me all mail directed to Ed. Cooper and The Freeman. He said he thought it belonged to me but he could not act in the matter until he had conferred with the postoffice in Washington. He conferred with the authorities there and received the reply that I was entitled to all letters directed to The Freeman.

Mr. Cooper obtained a position in the legislature,[125] in which position he considered himself the head of all. In the meantime advertising bills came due, and some remittance came in before I had gotten the letters and other mail turned over into my hands. Mr. Cooper and I had some words about this. One day he informed me that he had received a check for $100 from a certain publishing house, and I stated that we had been looking for this letter, and concluded that it must be in his possession. He finally came down and paid me $100, for which I was very thankful. The idea now struck him of going to Washington and going into the newspaper business there with a capital of $25,000.

As time went on The Indianapolis Freeman had a great many obstacles to overcome on account of its past management, which made anything but smooth sailing for it. I had many obligations to meet and much money had to be expended in order to get everything running in a businesslike manner.

Mr. Cooper had not long been off the paper when Ralph St. Julius Perry[126] made a contract with him for thirty letters at $5.00 each, containing sketches of his experiences of "Travels in Guinea Land." At the time I had objected to this and said I would not accept the contract, because I did not want the letters. I told Mr. Cooper not to make the contract, but regardless of my wishes in the matter, he went ahead and made the contract, and as one of the conditions, the letters were to be copyrighted. Mr. Perry instructed his lawyer to bring suit for $150 which I refused to pay. I counseled with my lawyer, and the lawyer said that he thought from the contract he had the best of me. I then said that if he thought that, we must look around and find the easiest way out, as the easiest way is always the best way. He told me

189

to offer a compromise. I told him that in order to keep out of a law suit I was willing to compromise on half the amount—$75. He went to see them and they at once rejected the compromise and informed my lawyer that they intended to collect the full amount—$150. They tendered us the letters and we refused them. An idea presented itself to me that they had not [had] the letters copyrighted. I telegraphed to Hon. John R. Lynch of the treasury department, asking him if he would not go over to the patents rights office and find out if there were any letters there copyrighted from sketches of R. St. Julius's [Perry's] "Travels in Guinea Land." Receiving no reply, I telegraphed Hon. Dan Ransdell, marshal of the District of Columbia. My lawyer told me that if the letters had not been copyrighted we would have the best of the case. I got an answer that "there was nothing there"—he had investigated the records thoroughly and found no "Letters of Travels in Guinea Land by R. St. Julian Perry." The court held the contract was not valid. Mr. Van Buren, Mr. Perry's lawyer, said he would bring it up before another term. It came before Judge Walker[127] who held that since they had not carried out their part of the agreement, we could not carry out our part of the contract, and that they had forfeited all right to the money. The costs of the suit all came to about $200, so I felt we had made a successful battle. This is but one of the obstacles we had to encounter. The case was in court from '92 to '94, at which time it was decided. In the meantime we had moved our office.

In '93 my editor had some trouble and it placed me in a somewhat awkward position for the time being. Mr. Allen was then manager. When the storms and tempests were raging, I had hoped that he would stand by me and The Freeman. One evening about 7 o'clock he came into the shop. I saw from his countenance that he had something to say and asked him what it was. He said nothing. I looked at him again and said that I knew he must have something to say and asked him what it was, but he said that he had not. I had an engagement that evening to attend a banquet given for a sick man, dying of consumption, at which entertainment I was to make a speech. He walked out with me and said he was going in that direction. He then told me that he thought he would go over to Crawfordsville on Saturday night (this was on Friday night). I asked if he would be back in time to look after the work on the paper. He said yes, he would be back, but he did not intend to stay as he felt tired and needed a vacation, and he did not feel that $12 per week justified him in devoting his entire time to the paper. I said to him, "What do you mean? Are you going to quit?" He said he meant that he could not go on working for $12 per week. I told him that it was all right, that I would accept his resignation. This rather unnerved me for a moment, but I admonished myself inwardly not to let these troubles worry me, but to stand up and be a man. I only had fifteen minutes in which to go three miles to make my speech. My subject that evening was "How to put yourself in a position to obtain the good things of this life that God intended you to have." The house was packed when I got there and everybody expressed themselves as believing that it was the greatest effort of my life.

The next morning I went to the office. Mr. Allen was there, and I informed him that I wanted to talk with him in the private office. I said to him: "Last evening I accepted your resignation; I want you to prepare your books and turn them over to me." He said, "Oh, I did not mean that." I replied that I did mean it—if he was playing, I was not, but meant what I said. I saw that he wished to take advantage of me and whenever I see that anyone wishes to take advantage of me I am up in arms—my ambition and pride are aroused and I will not allow them to take such advantage if I can avoid it. I told him that I had accepted his resignation and that I meant it. I then put in Mr. Julius Cox[128] as manager.

Mr. Cox assumed the management of The Freeman: he had been looking after the firm's advertising previous to this. This was '93. Everything went along smoothly until October, when things did not move along so smoothly, and I found it necessary to make a change. The World's Fair was then over and the hard-times of '93 which were felt by everybody were felt by the newspaper people perhaps more than any other class. But by energy and push we were able to keep The Freeman to the front.

During the World's Fair the [National Negro] Press Association met at Chicago. John Mitchell[129] of the [Richmond, Virginia] Planet, then president of the association, was re-elected. During the convention there was a great many warm discussions and debates, and many ideas were suggested that are likely to come up when a body of distinguished men and women meet together. In this convention resolutions were passed that no one could have a vote but the editors of papers. As my editor was Mr. Sweeney, these resolutions closed my mouth and opened his. This state of affairs was not at all satisfactory to me. I finally got the eye of the chair and being recognized, stated that I could not understand why the proprietor and publisher of a paper should have no right to have a voice in matters; that I thought as I bore all the expenses of my paper that I should have something to say in regards to the methods and in fact in anything concerning newspapers, and I further stated that I would withdraw The Freeman from the Association unless publishers were given a voice. They held a two days' session in the Art Building and many distinguished ladies and gentlemen were present. This was in August [1892].

After the convention adjourned, a reception was held and speeches were made. I also visited a number of other places of interest, among them the Quinn's Chapel Literary Society, where I made a short address. Mr. [W. D.] Driver[130] representing The Freeman in Chicago, showed me things of different interest. We went to the M.E. Church where they were having a banquet for bishops assembled from all over the United States. On this occasion some were given the power of the pulpit, and I myself was given the power of the press. Much attention was given to the Negro Problem, and here I give a few of my remarks on that subject:

"The Negro journal of the country is the one thing that can bring about the true status of the Afro-American. When the white people take us up, it is but to ridicule us, to tell us how we have stolen a chicken, or a shawl or dress. They pay attention only to our misdemeanors and we get no credit for any good we may do. If we expect to get justice, we must expect to get it through our own race, and how so well can this be done than through the journals of our own people? If we expect to see in the papers that Mr. So and So gave a reception and so and so were there, we must see it in the Negro journal because blood is thicker than water, and one touch of nature makes us kin. It makes no difference what petty disagreements we may have, when it comes to the great question of justice, we all must agree that we must depend upon our race to attain it. If we desire good things said of us, if we desire praise where praise is due, we must accept it from our own papers, otherwise we may be held up in an unfair and unjust light. If we expect to receive the true history of the people of our race, it must come from the pen of the black man, for only he can have in his heart a feeling of justice and entire loyalty to his people. The Negro is like Moses, who although raised in the house of Pharoah, when he found that his own country needed his aid, he went to its assistance. And though on the following day they blamed and criticized him for having killed an Israelite and buried him in the sand, and he went away, yet he came back and delivered them out of the hands of their enemies. So the Negro must be given justice by his own race, and the "Negro Question" must be solved by the black man, for he is the one who is vitally interested. It is the same with the artists. If we expect true pictures of our ladies, expect their features drawn as they are without exaggeration, we look to the Negro artist to accomplish it. If we expect to have portraits without the lips being too thick, the nose too flat, if we expect them drawn as God made them, it must be done by the hand of Negro artists. This is true about any race no matter what their color or condition."

"You can readily see why the Negro journal should be encouraged and should be patronized by our own people, and why we should encourage artists and historians in order to get things represented as they really are, so that our pictures will not be caricatures and our histories falsely exaggerated, and the questions which interest us as a people distorted and ridiculed. We should encourage everything that tends toward the improvement of our race, that tends to enlighten it, or will assist in making it more intelligent."

During this visit I took in the sights at the World's Fair but it was too stupendous for me to undertake to describe it. It could not be described by tongue or pen; it was something that had to be seen to be realized and appreciated. When I returned the second time I found it necessary to change the arrangements of The Freeman somewhat, and I thought that it would be best to change the management. Mr. Cox was assigned other duties as city man, and Mr. Sweeney was made manager and editor of The Freeman. Things now went along quite smoothly. '94 brought the campaign for the election of county and state officers, and the Republicans made a hard fight to get their candidates elected. The County Convention met and nominated their men and then the convention was held to nominate the judges and representatives. At the convention there were two colored men who aspired to the nomination of representative, Mr. Bagby[131] and Mr. Shaffer,[132] but neither received the nomination. Mr. Bagby felt very much displeased and dissatisfied at his defeat, and though he had several engagements to make speeches at different places throughout the state, he failed to make them, and I was never able to learn the cause of his failure to do so. I got a letter from Mr. Gowdy asking me to call on the State Central Committee at their headquarters immediately as they had business of interest. At this council they asked me if I could not go out into the state and make some campaign speeches or if I could not go, if I could recommend someone else. I suggested Mr. Bagby but they said he had failed and they did not want him. I suggested several others but they did not please the committee. I told them that I was busy and that my business would hardly admit of my leaving home, but that if they could not get anyone else to suit them and if they thought it for the interest of the party, I would go myself. So an appointment was made for me to speak at Columbus, Ind. I arrived there and was met at the depot by Prof. Stewart[133] of that place and another gentleman. They escorted me to the hotel where I was to stop during my stay. The county officers and different white representatives call[ed] on me at the hotel and we conversed about the condition of affairs, and talked over the political aspect and the situation in general. I asked the chairman whom I was to talk to and he said that I was there for the purpose of speaking to the colored people, that a number of colored people were dissatisfied and were sulking, so that they wished me to speak to them as it might be the means of pacifying them and leading them to understand the situation better. The club, headed by the band, then marched down the street to the hotel and I was escorted to the court house. The streets were thronged with people and Mr. Stewart suggested we stop on the outside and wait until the crowd was settled, after which we went in. The house was crowded, the galleries filled and people standing. I talked for an hour and a half. I discussed the tariff question, the slave question, the attitude of the Democratic party towards the Negro, and the attitude of the Republican Party towards the Negro, what the party had done for the race, and what the Cleveland administration had done for the country. In beginning my speech I said: "I

194

was sent here by the State Central Committee for the purpose of speaking to the colored people. This is true, and before beginning I will say to you all that there are but two great parties in this country—the Democratic and Republican parties. We must acknowledge this, for the other parties are mere sideshows, springing up like mushrooms in the night time; they cannot last. Their reason for existing I cannot state here. I have come to speak to the colored, the doctors, the lawyers, the mechanics, the farmers, the laborers, to the clerks, to all who may be here, you can not harm one of the least of these without doing yourself an injury, for our interests are one—your interests are mine and my interests are yours." Mr. Stewart said to me he was afraid we would have trouble keeping order owing to the crowd, but I informed him I always had order wherever I spoke and I thought I would have no trouble here. I suppose he thought there would be trouble, owing to the fact of my being a colored speaker. But we had good order, and Mr. Stewart told me afterwards that such order had never been kept there before. After the speaking I went to my hotel and took lunch, after which the committee escorted me to my train, and I returned home. The chairman of the committee [in Columbus, Ind.] wrote the chairman of the State Central Committee congratulating him upon the good work I have done.

NOTES

INTRODUCTION

1. *Freeman* (Indianapolis), November 9, 1895.
2. Ibid., July 1, 1910.
3. For an analysis of this address see Louis R. Harlan, *Booker T. Washington: The Making of a Black Leader, 1856-1901* (Urbana: University of Illinois Press, 1972), pp. 204-28.
4. Dixon Merritt, ed., *The History of Wilson County, Tennessee: Its Land and People* (Nashville: Benson Printery, 1961), pp. 1, 32, 37, 238; *Agriculture of the United States: The Eighth Census* (Washington, D.C.: Government Printing Office, 1864), pp. 136-39; *Sixth Census or Enumeration of the Inhabitants of the United States in 1840* (Washington, D.C.: Blair and River, 1841), pp. 260-69.
5. *Goodspeed's History of Tennessee: Maury, Williamson, Rutherford, Wilson, Bedford and Marshall Counties* (Nashville: n.p., 1886), pp. 842, 856.
6. "George L. Knox," in John H. Binford, *History of Hancock County, Indiana* (Greenfield, Ind.: King and Binford, 1882), p. 411; "George L. Knox," in W. N. Hartshorn, *An Era of Progress and Promise* (Boston: Priscilla Publishing Co., 1910), p. 430.
7. Wills and Inventories, Wilson County, Tennessee, vol. 1843-1848, pp. 403-5 (Wilson County Courthouse, Lebanon, Tennessee).
8. Population Census of 1860, Wilson County, Tennessee, Free Inhabitants, p. 216, National Archives (Microfilm Copy); Population Census of 1860, Wilson County, Tennessee, Slaves, p. 43, National Archives (Microfilm Copy).
9. *Tennesseans in the Civil War: A Military History of Confederate and Union Units with Available Rosters of Personnel,* 2 vols. (Nashville: Civil War Centennial Commission, 1964), 1: 71-73, 440, 2: 240.
10. *Indianapolis Freeman,* October 6, 1894.
11. *Hancock Democrat* (Greenfield, Indiana), April 12, August 2, 1883; *World* (Indianapolis), May 7, 1887; *Indianapolis Freeman,* June 27, July 11, 1891.

12. Wills and Inventories, Wilson County, Tennessee, vol. 1866-1871, p. 31.

13. *Indianapolis Freeman,* March 13, 1920.

14. Binford, *Hancock County,* p. 411; *Indianapolis Freeman,* May 9, 1891.

15. *Indianapolis Freeman,* October 6, 1894.

16. Ibid.

17. For sketches of his life as a slave, see Binford, *Hancock County,* pp. 411-12; *Indianapolis Freeman,* June 5, 1889, May 9, 1891.

18. For a history of this regiment see A. L. Kerwood, *Annals of the Fifty-seventh Regiment: Indiana Volunteers* (Dayton, Ohio: W. J. Shuey, 1868); Knox regularly attended the reunions of this regiment.

19. *Indianapolis Freeman,* May 9, 1891.

20. Cyrus F. Adams, "George L. Knox: His Life and Work," *Colored American Magazine* 5 (October 1902): 466; for biographical data on Aurilla Harvey Knox, see *Indianapolis Freeman,* November 22, 1894.

21. *Indianapolis Freeman,* December 2, 1899; for a description of Greenfield in the period of Knox's residence there, see Minnie Belle Mitchell, *James Whitcomb Riley as I Knew Him: Real Incidents in the Early Life of America's Beloved Poet* (Greenfield: Ole Swimmin' Hole Press, 1949).

22. Binford, *Hancock County,* p. 412; *Indianapolis Freeman,* May 9, 1891; Population Census of 1870, Hancock County, Indiana, p. 110, National Archives (Microfilm Copy).

23. *Hancock Democrat,* June 29, August 3, October 5, 1865, March 1, April 5, 26, August 2, 16, 30, 1866, January 31, August 27, December 19, 1867, July 23, 1868; George J. Richman, *History of Hancock County, Indiana* (Indianapolis: Federal Publishing Co., 1916), pp. 359-71.

24. *Hancock Democrat,* February 2, April 20, 1871, June 27, August 1, 1872, October 16, 1873, March 2, April 9, May 14, 1874, September 19, 1878, September 29, 1883.

25. Ibid., March 29, 1883.

26. This poem appears in *The Complete Works of James Whitcomb Riley,* ed. Edmund H. Eitel, 6 vols. (Indianapolis: Bobbs-Merrill, 1913), 3: 377-80; *Indianapolis Freeman,* January 6, 1906, July 29, 1916.

27. Richman, *History of Hancock County,* pp. 619, 632-33; *Hancock Democrat,* November 4, 1873.

28. *Hancock Democrat,* February 26, 1874; Richman, *History of Hancock County,* p. 633.

29. Richman, *History of Hancock County,* pp. 633-34; *Hancock Democrat,* August 31, 1882, August 16, 1883.

30. *Hancock Democrat,* August 12, 1880; Adams, "George L. Knox," p. 467.

31. *Hancock Democrat,* May 6, 15, 1879; *People's Advocate* (Washington), May 17, 1879; *Louisianian* (New Orleans), May 17, 1879.

32. For a description of the controversy over the exodus in Indiana, see Emma L. Thornbrough, *The Negro in Indiana before 1900* (Indianapolis: Indiana Historical Bureau, 1957), pp. 212-24, and Nell Irvin Painter, *Exodusters: Black Migration to Kansas after Reconstruction* (New York: Alfred Knopf, 1977), pp. 251-53.

33. *Hancock Democrat,* November 13, December 4, 1879, January 1, 8, 15, 29, February 12, August 12, September 30, 1880.

34. Ibid., January 8, 1880.

35. *Indianapolis Freeman,* May 9, 1891.

36. For the most comprehensive statement of Knox's views on race relations, see his "The American Negro and His Possibilities" in *Twentieth Century Negro Literature,* ed. D. W. Culp (Atlanta: J. L. Nichols, 1902), pp. 454-63.

37. *Hancock Democrat,* February 21, 1884; Adams, "George L. Knox," pp. 467-68.

38. *Indianapolis Freeman,* July 20, 1889, May 9, 1891; *Indianapolis Star,* August 26, 1927; Thornbrough, *The Negro in Indiana,* pp. 360-61; *Indianapolis World,* March 1, 1890.

39. On Myers's career see John A. Garraty, ed., *The Barber and the Historian: The Correspondence of George A. Myers and James Ford Rhodes, 1910-1923* (Columbus: Ohio Historical Society, 1956), pp. xi-xxiv; Felix James, "The Civic and Political Activities of George A. Myers," *Journal of Negro History* 58 (April 1973): 166-73.

40. *Eleventh Census, 1890,* vol. 1, Part 2, pp. 131, 347; *Thirteenth Census, 1910,* vol. 4, p. 557.

41. *Indianapolis World,* January 6, 1892; *Indianapolis Freeman,* January 9, 1892.

42. Quoted in *Indianapolis Freeman,* June 13, 1896.

43. The *Plaindealer* (Detroit), July 15, 1892, described Knox as the wealthiest black in Indianapolis, claiming that he was worth $25,000; Adams placed his worth at $50,000 in 1902, see Adams, "George L. Knox," p. 468.

44. *Indianapolis Freeman,* October 8, 1892, July 5, 1903.

45. Data on the elite families of Indianapolis can be found in Thornbrough, *The Negro in Indiana,* and the extant files of the city's three black newspapers, the *Freeman,* the *World,* and the *Recorder.*

46. *Indianapolis World,* September 3, 10, 24, 1892.

47. Emory Bucke, *The History of Methodism,* 3 vols. (New York: Abingdon Press, 1964), 2: 11-15; *Indianapolis World,* April 16, 1887; *Indianapolis Freeman,* May 7, 1892, April 7, 1894, December 3, 1898, August 26, 1899,

March 10, 1900, March 30, November 30, 1901, August 20, 1910; see also Joseph C. Hartzell, "Methodism and the Negro in the United States," *Journal of Negro History* 7 (July 1923): 301-15; David E. Skelton, *History of the Lexington Conference* (n.p.: n.p., 1950), pp. 8-9; Walter H. Riley, *Forty Years in the Lap of Methodism* (Louisville: Mayes Printing Co., 1915), pp. 26-27.

48. *Journal of the General Conference of the Methodist Episcopal Church Held in New York, May 1-31, 1888* (New York: Phillips and Hunt, 1888), pp. 380, 384, 385; *Indianapolis News,* May 26, 1888; *New York Daily Tribune,* May 6, 8, 23, 29, 1888; *Bee* (Omaha), April 30, May 5, 7, 12, 13, 20, 1892; *Indianapolis Freeman,* May 21, June 11, 1892; Bucke, *History of Methodism,* 2: 16.

49. *Freeman* (New York), April 9; see also ibid., May 21, 1887; L. M. Hagood, *The Colored Man in the Methodist Episcopal Church* (Cincinnati: Cranston and Stowe, 1890); Bucke, *History of Methodism,* 2: 13-14.

50. *Indianapolis Freeman,* February 23, 1895, October 19, November 2, 9, 23, 30, 1901.

51. *Indianapolis World,* January 8, February 19, 1887; *Indianapolis Freeman,* January 5, 1889.

52. *Indianapolis Star,* August 26, 1927; *Indianapolis Freeman,* January 11, 1890, December 21, 1895, January 11, 1896, December 12, 1914.

53. *Indianapolis Freeman,* November 16, 1888, February 15, 1890, December 12, 1896, July 24, 1897, March 26, 1898.

54. Thornbrough, *The Negro in Indiana,* pp. 302-7.

55. Martin Kilson, "Political Change in the Negro Ghetto, 1900-1940's," in Nathan Huggins et al., *Key Issues in the Afro-American Experience,* 2 vols. (New York: Harcourt, Brace, Jovanovich, 1971), 2: 171-72.

56. *Indianapolis World,* July 16, 1892.

57. Ibid., September 10, 24, 1892.

58. *Indianapolis Freeman,* March 19, April 2, 1892.

59. *Indianapolis World,* September 24, 1892; a correspondent of the *Cleveland Gazette* (January 14, 1888) wrote in reference to Knox: "As to shaving an Afro-American, he does not like for one even to get his shoes blackened . . . , let alone a shave. And they can only get a bath after work hours. That is the way he treats his own color. I know as I have been employed by him."

60. *Detroit Plaindealer,* August 19, 1892; *Indianapolis Freeman,* August 13, 1892, January 18, 1895, March 2, 1902; *Cleveland Gazette,* August 16, 1902; *Plaindealer* (Topeka), June 26, 1903.

61. *Indianapolis Freeman,* August 13, 1892; Knox, *Twentieth Century Negro Literature,* p. 456.

62. *Indianapolis News,* May 30, 1892.

63. *Indianapolis Freeman,* April 16, 1892.

64. Ibid., March 19, June 11, 1892; *Chicago Herald,* quoted in the *Indianapolis News,* June 8, 1892; see also *Indianapolis Freeman,* June 10, 13, 1892;

Indianapolis World, March 12, July 16, September 24, October 22, 1892.

65. For Cooper's checkered career see *New York Freeman,* March 6, 1886; *Indianapolis World,* December 7, 1889; *Indianapolis Freeman,* July 18, 1908; "Edward Elder Cooper," *Alexander's Magazine* 6 (August 15, 1908): 155; I. Garland Penn, *The Afro-American Press and Its Editors* (Springfield, Mass.: Willey, 1891), pp. 336-37.

66. *Indianapolis Freeman,* May 16, 1896; Thornbrough, *The Negro in Indiana,* pp. 315-16.

67. *Indianapolis Freeman,* February 17, 1900.

68. *Recorder* (Indianapolis), September 3, 1904.

69. Ibid.

70. Ibid., October 8, 1904; *Indianapolis Star,* October 26, 29, 1904.

71. The information concerning Knox's attempt to become a candidate for Congress has been drawn from four newspapers, two white and two black, representing both Republican and Democratic biases. See *Indianapolis Star,* October 18, 23-25, 28-31, November 1-6, 1904; *Sentinel,* August 24, 30, September 26, 28, 30, October 22, 23, 26, 28, 29, 31, November 1, 4, 5, 7, 8, 1904; *Indianapolis Recorder,* September 3, October 1, 8, 15, 22, 29, 1904; *Indianapolis Freeman,* October 1, 8, 15, 22, 29, November 12, 1904; August Meier, *Negro Thought in America, 1880-1915: Racial Ideologies in the Age of Booker T. Washington* (Ann Arbor: University of Michigan Press, 1968), p. 186.

72. For a discussion of the *Freeman's* editorial position regarding the Brownsville affair, see Ann J. Lane, *The Brownsville Affair: National Crisis and Black Reaction* (Port Washington, N.Y.: Kennikat Press, 1971), pp. 113-17.

73. *Indianapolis News,* September 26, 1907; *Indianapolis Recorder,* September 28, 1907.

74. *Indianapolis Freeman,* July 6, 1907, June 27, October 17, November 7, 1908, September 10, 1910, October 26, 1916, April 24, 1920, June 23, July 5, 12, August 2, September 27, October 4, November 1, 1924; in 1916 the *Freeman* endorsed Thomas Taggart, a Democrat, for the United States Senate. See Emma Lou Thornbrough, *Since Emancipation: A Short History of Indiana Negroes, 1863-1963* (Indianapolis: Indiana Division, American Negro Emancipation Centennial Authority, n.d.), p. 30.

75. See Emma Lou Thornbrough, "American Negro Newspapers, 1880-1914," *Business History Review* 40 (Winter 1966): 475, 483; *Colored American* (Washington), January 4, 1899; Frederick G. Detweiler, *The Negro Press in the United States* (Chicago: University of Chicago Press, 1922), pp. 7-8, 57; *Indianapolis Recorder,* May 11, 1901; Luther P. Jackson, Jr., "The Popular Media: The Mission of Black Newsmen," in Mabel M. Smyth, *The Black American Reference Book* (Englewood Cliffs, N.J.: Prentice-Hall, 1976), p. 850.

201

76. See Thornbrough, "American Negro Newspapers," pp. 475, 477; George L. Knox to John P. Green, December 7, 1895, John P. Green Papers, Western Reserve Historical Society, Cleveland, Ohio.

77. *Indianapolis Freeman,* September 28, 1895; see also L. M. Hershaw, "The Negro Press in America," *Charities* 15 (October 1905): 68.

78. *Indianapolis Freeman,* October 12, 1907; George L. Knox to Booker T. Washington, August 20, 1901, February 6, 1904, Booker T. Washington Papers, Library of Congress.

79. *Indianapolis Freeman,* July 18, 1896, January 21, November 25, 1899, June 8, 1901, January 4, 1902, January 23, June 2, 1917, May 11, 31, 1924.

80. Ibid., June 4, 1892, April 23, September 10, 17, 1904, June 10, 1911, August 23, 1913; George L. Knox to Booker T. Washington, August 20, 1901, January 20, 1904, November 21, 1908; Washington to Knox, September 20, 1904, Washington Papers.

81. Emmett Scott to George L. Knox, January 4, 1904; Knox to Booker T. Washington, February 6, 1904, May 25, 1905; Washington to Knox, March 23, 1904 (telegram), October 11, 1908, Washington Papers.

82. Knox to Washington, November 18, 1911, Washington Papers.

83. Ibid., January 3, 1901, Washington Papers.

84. Washington to Knox, February 2, 1904, September 17, 1908; Knox to Washington, October 31, 1905, Washington Papers.

85. *Correspondence of W. E. B. Du Bois,* ed. Herbert Aptheker (Amherst: University of Massachusetts Press, 1973), 1: 101; Thornbrough, "American Negro Newspapers," p. 483; Meier, *Negro Thought in America,* pp. 230-31.

86. *Indianapolis Freeman,* March 7, 1896, September 27, 1902.

87. Ibid., January 23, February 6, 20, 27, 1897; John W. Lyda, *The Negro in Indiana History* (Terre Haute: n.p., 1953), p. 87.

88. *Detroit Plaindealer,* August 19, 1892; *Chicago Conservator,* quoted in *Indianapolis Freeman,* March 15, 1902.

89. *Indianapolis Freeman,* December 30, 1899.

90. Culp, *Twentieth Century Negro Literature,* pp. 454-63.

91. *Indianapolis Freeman,* March 3, 1917, September 20, 1919, February 7, September 27, 1920.

92. Ibid., January 24, July 17, 1920, February 2, July 21, September 27, 1924; Emma Lou Thornbrough, "Segregation in Indiana during the Klan Era," *Mississippi Valley Historical Review* 48 (March 1961): 612.

93. *Indianapolis Freeman,* September 11, November 8, 1919.

94. Ibid., March 13, 1920.

95. Ibid., September 1, 1900, April 14, December 26, 1914, April 17, 1915, October 4, 1924.

96. Ibid., December 10, 1892, December 31, 1904, September 17, 1910, November 14, 1914, February 3, 17, 1917.

97. See Willard B. Gatewood, Jr., *Black Americans and the White Man's Burden, 1898-1903* (Urbana: University of Illinois Press, 1975), pp. 110, 192-93, 203-4, 218.

98. *Indianapolis Freeman*, March 17, 24, 1917, June 22, July 6, 20, September 18, 1918; see also Clement Richardson, *The National Cyclopedia of the Colored Race* (Montgomery, Ala.: National Publishing Co., 1919), pp. 507, 613-14.

99. *Indianapolis Freeman*, October 13, 1917, February 9, June 27, December 28, 1918.

100. For obituaries see *Indianapolis News*, August 25, 1927; *Indianapolis Star*, August 26, 1927; *Chicago Defender*, September 3, 1927; *Chicago Broad-Ax*, September 3, 1927; *Cleveland Gazette*, September 10, 1927.

101. *Indianapolis Freeman*, June 14, 1924.

PART ONE

1. Huldah Knox remained in Tennessee after the Civil War. In 1891 she was in such poor health that she moved to Indianapolis to live with her brother George L. Knox.

2. Charles Knox died shortly after he escaped from slavery and entered the Union lines.

3. Statesville was a small town in Wilson County, Tennessee, the county in which Knox was born.

4. For discussion of the difficulties in establishing the identity of Knox's "young master," see above pp. 5-7.

5. Knox undoubtedly refers here to Dr. Thomas H. Knight, a physician in Statesville, who according to the federal Census of 1850 was thirty-six years old, a native of Tennessee, and a man of means.

6. Daniel Boyd, age twenty-one in 1850, was in the tanning business with his brother, William R. Boyd.

7. This is obviously a reference to W. H. McConnikin, a well-known physician in Wilson County, Tennessee.

8. Chase C. Mooney wrote that the concern about a slave insurrection in Tennessee in 1856 "was directly associated with the election of that year." "Most of the trouble," he concluded, "was in the panic realm and not in actual insurrection." See Mooney, *Slavery in Tennessee* (Bloomington: Indiana University Press, 1957), p. 63.

9. According to official election returns, Lincoln received no votes in Wilson County in 1860, while John Bell (Constitutional Union) received 2,223; John C. Breckinridge (Southern Democrat), 1,165; Stephen A. Douglas (Democrat), 63.

10. Robert Hopkins Hatton (1826-1862), known as "the American

Whig-Know-Nothing Demosthenes," was a native of Ohio who served in the Tennessee legislature (1855-1857) and was an unsuccessful candidate for governor in 1857. He was elected to Congress in 1858 on the American party ticket; he became colonel of the Seventh Regiment, Tennessee Volunteer Infantry in May 1861 and was made brigadier general in the Confederate army a year later. Hatton was killed in May 1862. See Charles M. Cummings, "Robert Hopkins Hatton: Reluctant Rebel," *Tennessee Historical Quarterly* 23 (June 1964): 169-81.

11. Albert G. Carden, a resident of Cainsville, Tennessee, raised a company of volunteers in Wilson County which became part of the Eighteenth Tennessee Infantry. Carden ultimately became lieutenant colonel of the regiment which first saw action in Kentucky in 1861 and took part in the Tennessee campaign in the following year; see *The Military Annals of Tennessee, Confederate*, ed. John B. Lindsley (Nashville: Lindsley and Co., 1886), pp. 359-72.

12. No such county existed in Tennessee, so apparently Knox is referring to Rutherford County which adjoined Wilson County on the south.

13. The first battle of Bull Run or Manassas (Virginia) took place on July 21, 1861.

14. The battle of Fishing Creek, Kentucky, which occurred on January 19, 1862, was also called the battle of Logan's Cross Roads or Mill Springs.

15. Battle of Fort Donelson (Tennessee), February 14, 16, 1862.

16. Governor Isham G. Harris of Tennessee, following the fall of Nashville, fled to Memphis and later to Mississippi.

17. In 1861 Knox's master joined a state volunteer unit which was to serve for twelve months. The first compulsory conscription act, passed by the Confederate Congress in April 1862, made able-bodied white males between the ages of eighteen and thirty-five liable for a maximum of three years of military service. Among those exempted under this law were teachers of schools of twenty or more pupils. For Confederate conscription see Albert B. Moore, *Conscription and Conflict in the Confederacy* (New York: Macmillan, 1924).

18. Battle of Stones River, Tennessee, from December 31, 1862, to January 3, 1863.

19. Knox has reference to the Second Conscription Act, passed by the Confederate Congress in September 1862, which extended the age limit to forty-five and modified the exemption system.

20. James Madison Phillips, of Wilson County, Tennessee, was captain in Company D, Fourth Tennessee Cavalry, sometimes also called Eighth Tennessee Cavalry, which took regimental form in November 1862 but was reorganized on January 23, 1863. Known as "Baxter Smith's regiment" to distinguish it from other regiments also called the Fourth Cavalry and Eighth

Cavalry, it saw action at Shiloh, Perryville, Chickamauga, and other battles. Captain Phillips was wounded at Perryville on October 8, 1862, and at Murfreesboro on December 31, 1862. W. C. Knox was a private in Company D under the command of Captain Phillips. See Lindsley, ed., *The Military Annals of Tennessee*, pp. 629-35; George B. Guild, *A Brief Narrative of the Fourth Tennessee Cavalry Regiment* (Nashville: n.p., 1913); Civil War Centennial Commission, *Tennesseans in the Civil War*, 2 vols. (Nashville: Civil War Centennial Commission, 1964), 1: 71-73, 440; 2: 240.

21. Milton, Tennessee, a village established in 1820, was located on Bradley's Creek in Rutherford County.

22. Whites in Wilson County after whom this individual presumably took his name spelled it "Biggles."

23. George D. Wagner, formerly colonel of the Fifteenth Indiana Regiment who was promoted to brigadier general late in 1862, was in command of a brigade which included that regiment.

24. Knox and his comrades were in the camp of the Fifteenth Indiana Regiment which had been mustered into federal service on June 14, 1861, for three years. In November 1862 the unit arrived in Nashville, Tennessee, and thereafter played a conspicuous part in the battle of Stones River (December 31, 1862 – January 2, 1863). It remained at Murfreesboro until June 24, 1863, then marched to Tullahoma.

25. The Fifty-seventh Indiana Regiment was mustered into service at Richmond, Indiana, on November 18, 1861. Early in 1862 it arrived in Nashville, Tennessee, then moved south, taking part in the siege of Corinth (Mississippi). Later in 1862 and 1863 it participated in various engagements in Middle Tennessee and in the battles at Chickamauga and Missionary Ridge.

26. Knox arrived immediately following the bitter fighting which occurred in the vicinity of Tullahoma between June 24 and July 3, 1863.

27. This is obviously a reference to James Ayres of Cherry Valley, Tennessee, a small settlement near Statesville. According to the Census of 1860, Ayres was seventy-four years old and a well-to-do farmer.

28. This raid by Confederate General John Hunt Morgan took place in July 1863.

29. Knox's reference here should read Walden's Ridge, a mountain range named for Elisha Walden who ventured into the Tennessee country in the 1760s.

30. The Sequatchie Valley, named for a Cherokee Indian chief, is west of Chattanooga.

31. The reference is to Wagner's brigade, named for its commander, George D. Wagner. Wagner's brigade was the first unit of the Union Army to enter Chattanooga.

32. Gustavus A. Wood assumed command of the Fifteenth Indiana Infan-

try on November 29, 1862, when Colonel George D. Wagner was promoted to brigadier general.

33. Captain John F. Monroe of the Fifteenth Indiana Infantry.

34. For a brief account of the battle of Chattanooga, see Gilbert E. Govan and James W. Livengood, *The Chattanooga Country* (New York: E. P. Dutton, 1952), Chapt. 11.

35. Captain Monroe died on November 25, 1863, as a result of wounds received in the battle of Missionary Ridge.

36. Lieutenant William G. Humphreys of Company A, Fifty-seventh Indiana Volunteer Regiment was from Madison, Indiana. Mustered in on June 17, 1863, he resigned February 11, 1864. For the story of this regiment, see A. L. Kerwood, *Annals of the Fifty-seventh Regiment, Indiana Volunteers* (Dayton, Ohio: W. J. Shuey, 1868).

37. Greeneville, Tennessee.

38. Colonel George W. Leonard, of New Castle, Indiana, was commissioned colonel of the Fifty-seventh Regiment, Indiana Volunteers, on July 28, 1863, and died on May 15, 1864, of wounds received at Resacca, Georgia. He was described as "a most brave and accomplished officer."

39. Addison M. Dunn of Boxleytown, captain of Company E, Fifty-seventh Regiment, Indiana Volunteers, was commissioned on October 30, 1861, and ultimately promoted to major. He was killed in battle at Franklin, Tennessee, on November 30, 1864.

40. Samuel T. Smith, of Ligonier, Indiana, was adjutant in the Fifty-seventh Indiana Regiment. Mustered in on January 25, 1863, he remained in military service for a little more than a year.

41. For a time the *Freeman* contained a column devoted exclusively to inquiries concerning lost relatives.

PART TWO

1. This village which Knox calls Boxville Town was listed in the 1860 census as Boxley and was apparently called Boxleytown later. The town was named for George Boxley. See Joseph C. Carroll, "George Boxley, Prototype of John Brown," *Negro History Bulletin* 5 (June 1942):198-200.

2. Isaac Collins was a thirty-four-year-old physician, who lived in the Hamilton County, Indiana, village with his wife, Caroline, and three children.

3. Elijah Bishop Martindale (1828-1910), lawyer, businessman, and publisher, was born in Wayne County, Indiana. Admitted to the bar in 1850, he practiced law for eleven years in New Castle where he published the *Courier* (1857-1858). After serving as judge of the district court of common pleas (1861-1862), Martindale moved to Indianapolis and devoted his attention to

real estate and business interests rather than law. A founder of the Union Fire Insurance Company, he was owner and publisher of the *Indianapolis Journal* (1875-1880), the state's leading Republican newspaper.

4. John Freeman, who came to Indianapolis from Georgia in 1844 and acquired considerable real estate including a restaurant, was the wealthiest black man in Indiana prior to the Civil War.

5. The Bates House was one of the leading hotels in Indianapolis.

6. While in Kokomo, Knox apparently first met Aurilla Harvey, the daughter of a prosperous black farmer in Howard County. See Joseph C. Carroll, "George Levi Knox," *Negro History Bulletin* 5 (May 1942): 186-88.

7. Knox first became acquainted with Thomas Orr during the Civil War. Orr was a member of the Fifty-seventh Infantry, Indiana Volunteers (Company A). Thomas was a painter, while Smith, Marsh, and Boyer were farmers. All resided in Hancock County.

8. Anti-Negro themes appeared frequently in Greenfield's Democratic newspaper throughout the late 1860s and early 1870s. The *Hancock Democrat*, for example, proclaimed in its issue of July 20, 1868, that the South was "dominated by ignorant and depraved Negroes" as a result of Radical Republican policies and warned that Indiana would be subjected to such heresies as racially mixed schools unless the Radicals were defeated.

9. John Williams, a native of South Carolina, was a well-known farmer in Center Township, Hancock County.

10. John C. Rardin, a Democrat and a former captain in the Ninth Indiana Cavalry during the Civil War, was elected justice of the peace of Center Township in Hancock County shortly after being mustered out of military service in 1865. After failing to win the Democratic nomination for sheriff in 1867, he embarked upon several business enterprises including the "ice cream and soda water trade." In 1868 he became a liquor dealer, a business in which he prospered.

11. William Sebastian, a native of Kentucky, was a well-known farmer who had lived for many years in Hancock County and whose residence was one of the most imposing structures in Greenfield. He served as postmaster of Greenfield in the early 1840s and as Hancock County clerk from 1849 to 1855.

12. Alexander K. Branham, a well-known merchant who at one time owned the Bragg House, a local hotel, was long prominent in the civic life of the community. His military title derived for his role as commander of Company E, Regiment 105, mustered into service in July 1863 during Morgan's raid into southern Indiana.

13. Solomon T. Kauble, a veteran of the Mexican War, served as private in the Eighth Indiana Infantry at the beginning of the Civil War and later as first lieutenant in the Fifth Indiana Cavalry. After the war, he returned to Hancock County for a few years and finally settled in Missouri.

14. Taylor W. Thomas, a native of Ohio who had long resided in Hancock County, was a retired farmer.

15. The family of Irvin and Jane Hunt which lived in a cabin on Brandywine Creek. Irvin Hunt was employed for many years by the *Hancock Democrat*.

16. James F. Sloan was minister of the Christian Church in Greenfield from 1867 to 1869 and in 1875.

17. This is obviously a reference to William R. Hartpence, editor of the *Greenfield Commercial.*

18. It is virtually impossible to identify "Jobe" Tindall, later referred to as "Joe," among the numerous Tindalls who lived in Greenfield and Hancock County. Knox may have reference to John T. Tindall, a liveryman, who resided in the town.

19. Presumably Elmer T. Swope, a young attorney.

20. Dr. Edwin B. Howard was a dentist in Greenfield.

21. Benjamin Raines, Jr., was the son of Benjamin Raines, a barber in Greenfield.

22. Joseph Baldwin was a hardware dealer and John R. Windsor, a blacksmith and policeman. While several families of Thomases resided in Greenfield at the time, the census records include no one by the name of Oscar Thomas.

23. The Thayer family was prominent in the life of Greenfield. One of its best-known members was Captain E. P. Thayer, a meat merchant, who at various times owned the Star Grocery and the Premium Meat Market, both of which were located on the town square near Knox's barbershop.

24. Daniel Wolsey Voorhees (1827-1897), a powerful figure in Indiana's Democratic party, was a member of the United States House of Representatives (1861-1865, 1869-1873) and the United States Senate (1877-1897). Born in Ohio, he was educated at DePauw University.

25. Newton W. Ray delivered his first sermon at the Methodist church in Greenfield in mid-November 1879. See *Hancock Democrat*, November 20, 1879.

26. Morris Pierson, one of the earliest settlers of Greenfield, was born on April 26, 1799, in Vermont. He served in several positions of trust including those of county treasurer, county school commissioner, and surveyor. Prominent in Republican and Masonic affairs, Pierson was an enthusiastic promoter of pikes and railroads and was president of a woolen mill. He died on May 22, 1879.

27. James Whitcomb Riley (1849-1916), born in Greenfield on October 7, 1849, was the son of Reuben A. Riley, the town's first mayor. His most popular works were written in the dialect of his home state. His poems first appeared in the local press, the *Hancock Democrat* and the *Greenfield Commercial.*

28. John Keefer was "the village sign painter" in Greenfield. For the James Whitcomb Riley apprenticeship to Keefer, see Minnie Belle Mitchell, *James Whitcomb Riley as I Knew Him* (Greenfield: Ole Swimmin' Hole Press, 1949), p. 118.

29. Samuel R. Milligan, a prominent physician of Greenfield, was the father of Edward Milligan, one of Riley's youthful companions.

30. A variation of this quip appears in Mitchell, *James Whitcomb Riley as I Knew Him*, p. 192.

31. Benjamin R. Raines, a blacksmith in Greenfield before the Civil War, served for a time with the Union forces. Because he "had his hand terribly mutilated" during an encounter with the Confederate forces of General John Hunt Morgan in southern Indiana in 1863, Raines abandoned his old trade and opened a barbershop in Greenfield in 1864. See *Hancock Democrat* (Greenfield, Indiana), March 3, 1864.

32. Moses Broyles, born a slave in Maryland, purchased his freedom in 1854 and moved to Indiana where he enrolled in the Eleutherian Institute. He became pastor of the Second Baptist Church in Indianapolis in 1857 and for many years was considered one of the most influential members of the Negro community in Indiana.

33. Aurilla S. Harvey (1840-1910) was born in Halifax County, North Carolina, the daughter of Preston and Martha Harvey, who migrated to Indiana when she was only four years old. The Harveys were proud of their heritage, often noting that they were among "the first families" of Indiana's black community.

34. The family of Irvin Hunt.

35. The reference here is to Samuel E. Gapen, a young saddler and harnessmaker.

36. Gooding Corner was located in the heart of Greenfield at the corner of State and Main streets. It was formerly the site of the Gooding Tavern where Henry Clay reputedly stayed overnight in 1844. See George J. Richman, *History of Hancock County* (Indianapolis: Federal Publishing Co., 1916), pp. 651-52.

37. The first public school for Negroes in Greenfield opened on November 4, 1873, with John Bailey as the teacher in charge. There is some evidence that Negro residents of the town had maintained a private school for their children prior to this date, and Knox may have reference to such a school here. On the first public schools for blacks, see Richman, *Hancock County*, p. 619.

38. Thomas P. Snow, born in London and a shoemaker by trade, came to the United States in 1828. Disembarking at New Orleans, he made his way north and settled in Shelbyville, Kentucky. Around 1850 he moved to Greenfield, Indiana, where he organized the Pickwick Club, a literary society for young men. The local newspapers described him as "a man of notions general-

ly, and also an antiquarian of deep research . . . a humanitarian as well as an antiquarian." In his old age Snow not only made shoes but also became a "seller of books." He died in 1870. See Marcus Dickey, *The Youth of James Whitcomb Riley* (Indianapolis: Bobbs-Merrill, 1919), pp. 96-103; B. F. Bowen, *Biographical Memoirs of Hancock County, Indiana* (Logansport, Ind.: B. F. Bowen, Publisher, 1902), p. 350; *Hancock Democrat*, December 3, 1868.

39. Calvin B. Gilliam, a former slave, arrived in Boone County, Indiana, in 1869 and received most of his education at Spiceland, Indiana. A Republican and a Methodist, Gilliam joined the Grange in 1873 and served for a time as chaplain.

40. William J. Sparks, born March 11, 1853, in Morgan County, Indiana, worked for a time in the Commercial Mills on Blue River, which were owned by his father. He ultimately settled in Greenfield where he was an agent for a sewing machine company. In 1879 he was elected clerk of the city of Greenfield and served in that capacity until he became mayor. A dedicated Republican, Sparks was a faithful member of the Greenfield Christian Church and was superintendent of its Sunday school. See J. H. Binford, *History of Hancock County, Indiana* (Greenfield: William Mitchell, Printer, 1882), pp. 367-68.

41. Sparks was elected mayor of Greenfield in 1881.

42. In the city election in 1883 there were three tickets: the Republican candidate for mayor was Sparks; the Democrats nominated the Reverend W. K. Williams as their candidate, but when he refused to accept the nomination, they chose Israel Poulson, a prominent attorney; the so-called citizens ticket was headed by Reuben A. Riley.

43. Reuben A. Riley, an attorney, was born in Redford County, Pennsylvania, on June 7, 1819. Settling in Greenfield, Indiana, in 1844, he became the town's first mayor in 1852 and later served as a member of the state legislature from Hancock County. At the outbreak of the Civil War, Riley raised a company of volunteers and served in the military forces for four years. Prior to the war he had been a Democrat, but after 1865 he pursued an independent course in politics and for a time was allied with the Greenback party.

44. John Spangler, a teamster and a native of Pennsylvania, was active in Republican circles in Greenfield.

45. Ephraim Marsh, born in Hancock County, Indiana, on June 2, 1845, graduated from Asbury University in 1870. He served for a time as a clerk in the United States Treasury Department before being elected clerk of the Hancock County Circuit Court in 1874. Long prominent in Democratic politics he was chairman of the Hancock County Democratic Committee in the early 1880s and closely allied with Daniel S. Gooding.

46. See below, pp. 109-10.

47. Indiana ratified the Fifteenth Amendment in 1869. For an account of

the political struggle over ratification, see Emma Lou Thornbrough, *The Negro in Indiana: A Study of a Minority* (Indianapolis: Indiana Historical Bureau, 1957), pp. 243-49.

48. John Addison, a native of Ohio, moved to Greenfield in 1854. Seven years later, he was elected Hancock County treasurer. In 1868 he was elected on the Democratic ticket to represent the county in the state legislature. Thereafter, he held various elective posts including that of county commissioner. For Addison's resignation from the legislature in 1869 and his subsequent reelection, see *Hancock Democrat*, March 11, 23, 1869.

49. Thomas Andrews Hendricks (1819-1885), born in Ohio, was a lawyer and Democratic politician in Shelbyville, Indiana, who served in the lower house of the state legislature and in the state senate prior to his election to Congress in 1850. Leaving Congress in 1855, he was appointed commissioner of the General Land Office, a post he held until 1859. In 1868 during the debate over the Fifteenth Amendment he was a powerful advocate of white supremacy. Hendricks served as vice president of the United States in 1885, but died after serving eight months.

50. Oliver P. Morton (1823-1877), lawyer and Republican politician who was Indiana's famous "war governor" (1861-1864) and a United States Senator (1867-1877), at first appeared to oppose Negro suffrage but ultimately was largely instrumental in having Indiana ratify the Fifteenth Amendment.

51. Adams L. Ogg, a well-to-do farmer and lawyer active in Hancock County politics, was described in 1880 as "a venerable specimen of antique Republicanism." A veteran of both the Mexican War and the Civil War, Ogg was known as a friend of the freedmen. His law practice was devoted to the pension claims of ex-soldiers. Following his espousal of the Liberal Republican cause in 1872, Ogg supported the regular party ticket until 1884 when, because of his objections to James G. Blaine, he voted for Democrat Grover Cleveland. He remained in the Democratic party for the remainder of his life.

52. John Dobbins appears to have been something of a local character known principally for his talent as a "fiddler." In 1872 Dobbins was fined for assaulting Irvin Hunt, a black employee of the print shop of the *Hancock Democrat*. See *Hancock Democrat*, July 12, 1872.

53. David S. Gooding was born in Fleming County, Kentucky, on January 10, 1824, but his family moved to Greenfield in 1836. Elected to the state legislature on the Whig ticket in 1847, he later switched allegiance to the Democratic party and for many years was the most influential figure in the party in Hancock County. He served for a time as judge of the Court of Common Pleas and as marshal of the District of Columbia (1865-1869). Defeated in 1870 and 1872 in his races for Congress, he returned to the state legislature in 1885.

54. Jeremiah Morrow Wilson (1828-1910), a lawyer, was a native of

Ohio who served as judge of the Court of Common Pleas in Indiana (1865-1871) and as a congressman (1871-1875). For many years Wilson was prominent in the Republican party in Indiana.

55. On the contested election between Gooding and Wilson, see *House Miscellaneous Documents*, No. 36, 42d Cong., 1st sess., pp. 1-368; *House Reports*, No. 41, 42d Cong., 2d sess., pp. 1-4.

56. Morgan Chandler, banker and Democratic leader in Hancock County, was born in Owen County, Kentucky, in 1827 and settled in Greenfield in 1850. During his first decade in the town he served as sheriff of Hancock County and as county court clerk. Following his tenure as county chairman of the Democratic party (1878-1880), he was elected to the lower house of the state legislature in 1880 and a decade later served two terms as state senator. A founder of a private bank in 1871, known as the Greenfield Banking Company, Chandler was its first cashier.

57. Probably John S. Gibbs, a farmer in Hancock County.

58. Charles Fischer, born in France of German parents, owned a tailor shop on the town square in Greenfield.

59. William S. Wilkins, a native of Ohio, was a prosperous farmer in Hancock County, whose real property, according to the Census of 1870, was valued at $10,000. See *Hancock Democrat*, February 15, 1872.

60. William N. Craig, a native of Ohio, was a schoolteacher in Greenfield.

61. Shelton Osborn, a native of Kentucky, was a tailor in Greenfield.

62. Henry Wright, born in Hancock County, Indiana, on November 28, 1833, belonged to one of the pioneer families of the area. A schoolteacher for twenty years, he abandoned that profession early in the 1870s to serve as deputy auditor of Hancock County. In 1875 he was elected auditor and was reelected to a second term in 1879. See Binford, *History of Hancock County*, p. 416; Bowen, *Biographical Memoirs of Hancock County*, p. 201.

63. Cook's candidacy was obviously harmed by the publicity lavished upon an altercation that occurred between him and A. B. Lineback, a Greenfield resident, during the campaign. A political argument between them led to a fistfight and knifing in which both were wounded. Defeated in his campaign for sheriff, Cook traded his farm in Hancock County for one near Knightstown owned by Matthew Hinchman and moved to that village shortly after the election. See *Hancock Democrat*, May 2, October 24, 1878.

64. Literary work refers to the debating club organized in Greenfield's black community by Knox in 1878. Its members included James Kelly, Cook White, Lewis Brazelton, and other locally prominent blacks. Their debating club was an adjunct to the black Methodist church and proceeds from the admission fee charged to witness debates were donated to the church. See Rich-

man, *Hancock County*, pp. 633, 660; *Hancock Democrat*, November 7, 14, 21, 1878.

65. John Ward Walker, a well-known merchant in Greenfield, was the owner of J. Ward Walker and Company, a business established by his father in 1858. Walker was a founder of the Greenfield Banking Company in 1871 and served for a time as its cashier. A Mason and a faithful member of Greenfield's Methodist church, he was active in Republican politics and was the party's candidate for county auditor in 1878. See Bowen, *Biographical Memoirs of Hancock County*, pp. 260-61; *Hancock Democrat*, September 19, 1878.

66. Presumably this is Dr. Noble P. Howard, a prominent physician in Greenfield or his son Noble P. Howard, Jr., who was also a physician in the town. The elder Howard, born in Warren County, Ohio, September 11, 1822, and a graduate of the Indiana Medical College, settled in Greenfield in 1843. A Civil War veteran, Howard was an active Methodist layman. Originally a Whig, he was "an earnest Union man during the Civil War," then became identified with the Republican party until 1872. Following the "Liberal Republican" movement in that year, he switched his allegiance to the Democratic party, the party of his brother-in-law, David S. Gooding.

67. According to the election returns published in the *Hancock Democrat* (October 10, 1878), Wright received 1,751 votes and Walker, 1,149 votes.

68. Prompted by the "exodus" of blacks from the South to Kansas and other western states such as Indiana, the National Conference of Colored Men which met in Nashville, Tennessee, on May 6, 1879, "enthusiastically and almost unanimously supported the exodus." See August Meier, *Negro Thought in America, 1880-1915: Racial Ideologies in the Age of Booker T. Washington* (Ann Arbor: University of Michigan Press, 1966), pp. 59-61.

69. Knox was one of eleven delegates from Indiana attending the Nashville meeting. The remark that prompted the negative reaction from the gallery was Knox's observation: "There is an impression abroad that the Northern delegates have come here [Nashville] to take away the colored people in the southern states from their homes. This is not so." See *Louisianian* (New Orleans), May 17, 1879; *People's Advocate* (Washington), May 17, 1879.

70. For the reaction to the "Negro exodus" in Indiana, see Emma Lou Thornbrough, *The Negro in Indiana before 1900* (Indianapolis: Indiana Historical Bureau, 1957), pp. 212-23.

71. John W. Jones was a lawyer and real estate dealer in Greenfield who was active in local Republican politics as well as in temperance and fraternal organizations.

72. The Democratic organ in Greenfield, the *Hancock Democrat*, castigated local Republicans for encouraging the "pauperized exodusters" from the South to settle in Indiana, claiming that it was merely a political scheme to

strengthen the Republican party. Knox was singled out for special criticism as one of the principal "bosses of de emigration." For hostile editorials with specific references to Knox, see *Hancock Democrat*, December 25, 1879, January 1, 8, February 4, 12, September 30, 1880.

73. For a similar piece of verse on emigration see ibid., January 29, 1880.

74. On January 8, 1880, the *Hancock Democrat* reported the arrival of "another lot of North Carolina Negroes," twenty-five in number, at Greenfield.

75. Local Democrats vehemently denied any involvement in the burning of Moore's store. See *Hancock Democrat*, January 22, 1880.

76. In January 1880, at the height of the agitation over the "exodusters," Lou Young opened a barbershop in the Guymon House, Greenfield's principal hotel.

77. William Thomas, born in 1840 in Indiana, was a farmer of moderate means who resided in Brandywine Township of Hancock County. First elected sheriff in 1874, he was reelected two years later. Thomas did not seek reelection in 1878, but supported his deputy William H. Thompson, a Democrat, who was elected in that year.

78. Charles Downing, born in New York City on August 7, 1857, was orphaned at the age of four. In 1867 he was "taken in by William S. Wood," a well-known citizen of Greenfield. Downing served as deputy county clerk under Ephraim Marsh. In 1882 he was elected on the Democratic ticket to succeed Marsh as clerk. Downing was also a loyal member of the Odd Fellows. On October 8, 1879, he married Angie B. Williams of Bradford Junction, Ohio, whose father, Arthur Williams, had formerly resided in Greenfield. See Binford, *History of Hancock County*, pp. 370-71.

79. William McBane was a lawyer in Greenfield who ran unsuccessfully for mayor in 1878.

80. Stephen T. Dickerson, born October 27, 1830, in Shelby County, Indiana, moved to Greenfield when he was twenty-two years old. For a generation he was the preeminent stock trader (steers and sheep) in the area. A civic-minded individual, Dickerson was a prominent layman in the Christian Church, an advocate of good roads, and a key figure in the Hancock County Agricultural Society for many years.

81. Stanton J. Peelle (1843-1928), a native of Indiana who served in the Union army during the Civil War, settled in Indianapolis in 1869. Prominent in Republican affairs, Peelle was deputy district attorney of Marion County (1872-1873) and a member of the state legislature (1877-1879) before being elected to Congress in 1880.

82. William Easton English (1850-1926), son of the 1880 Democratic vice-presidential candidate, William H. English, was a native of Indiana and a graduate of Butler University. English successfully contested the election of Peelle in 1882 and served briefly as a member of the Forty-eighth Congress.

83. During the congressional campaign the Democrats made much of Peelle's vote in favor of a high tariff on wool.

84. Presumably Erick Swope is a reference to Elmer T. Swope, a graduate of the University of Michigan, who was a young lawyer.

85. James J. Walsh was a lawyer in Greenfield who served for a time early in the 1880s as prosecuting attorney of Hancock County.

86. Presumably, the name "Jaunty Tauge" refers to Jonathan Tague who, according to the Census of 1880, was a fifty-eight-year-old farmer. A Republican, Tague was active in Hancock County politics for many years, having been elected county auditor in 1867. See *Hancock Democrat*, October 10, 1867.

87. William S. Wood, a native of Virginia, was a hardware merchant and prominent citizen of Greenfield. His hardware store was located on the town square near Knox's barbershop. A prime mover in erecting the Citizens' Bank, he was the owner of extensive real estate and president of the Greenfield Manufacturing Association (flax). An active member of the Christian Church and the Knights of Pythias, he was president of the local school board.

88. Arthur P. Williams, a railway express agent in Greenfield, was a prominent figure in the civic life of the town, who later moved to Ohio.

89. Philander H. Boyd was one of the seven largest taxpayers in Greenfield in 1879. A banker and the owner of extensive real estate, Boyd was also prominent in local Democratic politics and in 1881 was elected to the city council. He was one of the founders of the Citizens' Bank (1873) and served as its president for many years. See Bowen, *Biographical Memoirs of Hancock County*, p. 264.

90. John B. Simmons (1813-1888), born near Harrisburg, Pennsylvania, migrated to Indiana as a young man and ultimately settled in Hancock County near Greenfield. A blacksmith and a farmer, he owned 600 fertile acres in the county. Simmons was one of the organizers and principal stockholders in the Citizens' Bank of Greenfield.

91. Israel Poulson, a lawyer and large property owner in Greenfield, was active in Democratic circles and ran unsuccessfully for mayor in 1883.

92. "William S. Wood committed suicide by taking sulphate of morphia and chloroform, at the Union Depot, Indianapolis, September 30, 1875, aged thirty-seven years. The cause of this sad occurrence was financial difficulties and large forgeries, a full account of which were given by him in his dying statement and confession." Quoted in Binford, *History of Hancock County*, p. 163.

93. No such person appears in the records of Hancock County, but undoubtedly Knox is referring to Richard A. Black, a Greenfield attorney who was an active Republican, serving as the party's county chairman in 1888.

94. Lafayette Reynolds was a young attorney who resided in Center Township, a short distance from Greenfield.

95. "General Order No. 40" refers to the order issued by General W. S. Hancock on November 29, 1867, restoring civil rule to Texas and Louisiana. His action created a sensation and a sense of outrage among Radical Republicans. In the election of 1880 when Hancock was the Democratic presidential candidate, Republicans incorporated references to "General Order No. 40" into their "bloody shirt" rhetoric.

96. Albert Gallatin Porter (1824-1897), born in Lawrenceburg, Indiana, and educated at DePauw University, was a lawyer and Republican leader in Indianapolis where he served as city attorney (1851-1853) and as a member of the city council (1857-1859). Following two terms in Congress (1859-1863) and two years as comptroller of the treasury (1878-1880), Porter was elected governor of Indiana on the Republican ticket in 1880.

97. Franklin Landers (1825-1901), born in Morgan County, Indiana, was a merchant, cattleman, and pork-packer whose political career included membership in the Indiana senate (1860-1864) and in the United States Congress (1875-1877). He was the unsuccessful Democratic candidate for governor of Indiana in 1880.

98. James T. V. Hill (1855-1928), a native of Chillicothe, Ohio, came to Indianapolis as a young man. He worked as a barber and postal clerk to earn enough to attend Central Law School, from which he graduated in 1882. Hill, "the first Negro lawyer in Indianapolis," was an active churchman and a civic leader who was identified for many years with the Democratic party.

99. Frederick Douglass (1817-1895), born a slave in Maryland, escaped bondage in 1838 and became active in the abolitionist cause. Douglass held a succession of federal appointments including those of recorder of deeds in the District of Columbia and minister to Haiti. He was generally viewed as the preeminent black American in the late nineteenth century.

100. William Mitchell (1823-1899), one of Greenfield's best-known citizens, was born in Montgomery County, Kentucky, where he learned the printing trade. He worked for various newspapers, including the *Cincinnati Dollar Times*, and in 1859 established the *Hancock Democrat* in Greenfield. Originally a Whig, he later affiliated with the Democratic party and was active in party affairs in Hancock County for many years. See Bowen, *Biographical Memoirs of Hancock County*, pp. 267-69; Richman, *Hancock County*, pp. 643-44.

101. Mitchell's *Hancock Democrat* often referred to Knox as "our popular barber" and "famous tonsorial artist." But while it was generous toward Knox personally, it was a bitter foe of "Negro equality" and editorially denounced legislative efforts to protect the civil rights of black citizens.

102. Orlando M. Edwards was a physician and "dry goods merchant" in Greenfield, who owned Edwards' Emporium on the town square. He was a prominent layman in the Greenfield Methodist Church.

216

103. The Lexington Conference was an exclusively black conference within the predominantly white Methodist Episcopal Church (Northern Methodist). All-Negro conferences, presided over by white bishops, were first organized in the 1860s and received the official sanction of the General Conference in 1876. By 1900 the all-black Lexington Conference which embraced congregations in Kentucky, Indiana, Ohio, and Illinois possessed a membership of 12,000 served by 145 ministers. Knox was an important figure in the organization of a Negro Methodist church in 1874 in Greenfield which became known as the Second Methodist Church. For the early history of the "colored M. E. Church" in Greenfield, see Binford, *History of Hancock County*, p. 421; for the origins of the Lexington Conference, see David E. Skelton, *History of the Lexington Conference* (n.p., 1950), pp. 8-9.

104. Marshall William Taylor (1846-1887) was born free in Lexington, Kentucky, of "Scotch, Irish and Indian descent on his father's side and African-Arabian on his mother's." He grew up in Louisville where he "attended such schools as were accessible." In 1870 he was licensed to preach by the Methodist Episcopal Church. Although he wrote several volumes, he was best known for his pulpit eloquence. Following service as a minister and presiding elder in Indiana and Ohio, he was elected editor of the *Southwestern Christian Advocate* in 1884 and retained that position until his death three years later. A delegate to two general conferences of the Methodist Church and to the Ecumenical Conference in London in 1881, Marshall was regarded as one of the most eminent Negro clergymen in America.

105. Martha Hunt was the sixteen-year-old daughter of Irvin and Jane Hunt, who were among the earliest black settlers in Greenfield. Irvin Hunt was employed for many years as "a roller boy" in the press rooms of the *Hancock Democrat*.

106. Brandywine Creek was a small stream on the eastern edge of Greenfield.

107. Edward W. S. Hammond (1850-1920), born in Baltimore and educated at Lincoln University, was recognized as one of the most erudite and eloquent black clergymen in the Methodist Episcopal Church. He served various pastorates in Indiana including Simpson Chapel in Indianapolis and was at different times presiding elder of districts within the Lexington Conference. The author of several books, he was elected editor of the *Southwestern Christian Advocate* (New Orleans) in 1892 and was for a time dean of the theological department of Walden University, a Methodist institution in Nashville, Tennessee. At the time of his death in 1920, Hammond was minister of Barnes Chapel M. E. Church in Indianapolis.

108. For a brief account of the first camp meeting in 1881 and subsequent ones through 1884, see Richman, *Hancock County*, p. 633.

109. Jesse Mundy was a respected black Methodist minister who served

various churches within the Lexington Conference, including those at Princeton and Evansville, Indiana.

110. W. H. Vaughn was a widely known black minister of the Methodist Episcopal Church who later occupied the pulpit of Coke's Chapel in Louisville, Kentucky, one of the most important appointments within the Lexington Conference.

111. Henry Steen was a Methodist minister stationed at Shelbyville, Indiana. Earlier he served congregations in Ohio and was the founder of the Dirr Avenue Methodist Church in Cincinnati in 1873.

112. Marie B. Woodworth-Etter, a member of the United Brethren Church, began her healing ministry in 1876. She later associated with the Methodist Holiness Church and held racially integrated revivals in the South in the 1880s. A well-known itinerant evangelist until the 1920s, she built a famous tabernacle in Indianapolis and wrote several books of prophecy.

113. Knox was in charge of the camp meetings of 1884, 1885, and 1886, although he had moved to Indianapolis early in 1884.

114. Lawrence was a town in northeastern Marion County near Indianapolis.

PART THREE

1. Knox appears to be confused about dates. The Morton Monument was unveiled on January 15, 1884, not in February.

2. Allen W. Conduitt, born in Mooresville, Indiana, on August 28, 1849, and educated at Butler University, was engaged for a time in the general merchandise business in various towns in the state. In 1875 he moved to Indianapolis and became a junior partner in the wholesale grocery firm of Conduitt and Son which his father had established several years earlier. In 1893 Conduitt abandoned the wholesale grocery business for various enterprises including coal, asphalt and street improvement, and automobiles. An Episcopalian prominent in several fraternal orders, he was active in the Democratic party.

3. James M. Morgan engaged in a variety of enterprises and was usually included among the list of "largest taxpayers" in Greenfield published periodically in the local newspaper. His principal businesses were livery stables, a feed store, and the selling of buggies and carriages.

4. Andrew T. Hart, born on July 7, 1811, was the senior member of Hart and Thayer, Greenfield's leading mercantile firm. Apprenticed as a saddler at the age of eighteen, he followed that occupation until he moved to Greenfield from Liberty, Indiana, in 1833. In addition to his business interests as a dry goods merchant, Hart served in a number of public offices including those of county treasurer and assistant assessor. Prominent in the Masons and

Odd Fellows, he was first a Whig and later a Republican. According to one writer, he was "connected with almost all public enterprises in the county during his residence therein." Binford, *History of Hancock County*, pp. 369-70.

5. James A. New, born in Hancock County, Indiana, on October 18, 1850, was the son of William New, one of the county's most prosperous farmers. Following graduation from Indiana University in 1872, he read law with Hamilton J. Dunbar whose law firm he later joined. He served a term as county examiner of schools but thereafter devoted his attention solely to the practice of law. New was a loyal Democrat and active in the Methodist Church.

6. The Bates House was built in 1853 by Hervey Bates.

7. E. F. Claypool, a member of one of Indiana's most prominent families, became president of the First National Bank in Indianapolis in 1886. The bank was organized in 1863 by William H. English and ten associates.

8. Of this group of barbers the only one who became prominent in Indianapolis's black community was Henry Moore. Born in Kentucky in 1837, he migrated to Indianapolis in 1873 and obtained employment as a porter in the Bates House. In 1891 he purchased a half-interest in the Denison House barbershop. His partner was Charles Lanier. Moore was active in the Masonic order and in the Ninth Presbyterian Church.

9. Knox conceded that the "shaving parlors" of the Palmer House in Chicago were more elaborately outfitted than his Bates House shop in Indianapolis.

10. Simpson Chapel Methodist Episcopal Church, organized as a mission in 1874 and originally called Coke Chapel, was the leading black congregation in Indianapolis connected with the predominantly white Northern Methodist Church. Affiliated with the Lexington (Kentucky) Conference, it was served by a succession of able ministers including Marshall W. Taylor, M. S. Johnson, and George A. Sissle who later became prominent in denominational affairs. For a brief, though somewhat garbled, history of Simpson Chapel, see Jacob P. Dunn, *Greater Indianapolis: The History, the Industries, the Institutions, and the People of a City of Homes*, 2 vols. (Chicago: Lewis Publishing Company, 1910), 1: 603

11. The ladies' department was opened in 1890 and Knox's daughter, Nellie, served for a time as its manager.

12. Eli Foster Ritter (1838-1913), a Civil War veteran and well-known attorney in Indianapolis, abandoned the Republican party for the Prohibition party, serving as chairman of its National Convention in 1892. A writer on legal and moral subjects, Ritter was one of the organizers of the Central Avenue Methodist Episcopal Church in Indianapolis, a frequent contributor to church publications, and an active layman in denominational affairs.

13. Daniel Jones and Thomas R. Fletcher, ministerial and lay delegates re-

spectively, represented the Lexington Conference in the General Conference of the Methodist Episcopal Church in 1888. Jones was presiding elder of the Bowling Green District.

14. The Committee on Itinerancy of the Methodist General Conference of 1888 recommended in its majority report that the period of ministerial appointments be extended from three to four years. A minority report which recommended five years was overwhelmingly adopted. Knox was in favor of the minority report.

15. James Monroe Buckley, born in New Jersey in 1836, was educated at Wesleyan University and entered the Methodist ministry in 1858. Five times elected a delegate to the church's quadrennial conference, he was selected editor of the *Christian Advocate* in 1880.

16. William Swindells was a Methodist minister in Philadelphia.

17. The "Woman Question" arose at the Methodist General Conference in 1888 when five women presented themselves as lay delegates. After four days of impassioned debate, the conference decided, by a close vote, not to seat the women. Knox voted in favor of seating them.

18. Willard Francis Mallalieu, born in Massachusetts in 1828 and educated at Wesleyan University, was admitted to the New England Methodist Conference in 1858. After serving as an assistant secretary of the church's Freedman's Aid Society, he was elected bishop in 1884.

19. The *Tribune* did not mention Knox by name but simply stated: "A colored lay delegate from the Lexington Conference said Methodism was 'almost comparatively dead' in New York City because of the short limit of itinerancy." See *New York Daily Tribune*, May 23, 1888.

20. John Philip Newman, born in New York City in 1826, entered the Methodist ministry in 1848. Between 1864 and 1869 he labored in the South primarily among blacks and created three conferences, two colleges, and a journal. He was chaplain to the United States Senate (1869-1874) and "spiritual adviser" to President Ulysses S. Grant. He was elected bishop in 1888.

21. James N. Fitzgerald, born in Newark, New Jersey, in 1838 and educated at Princeton, entered the Methodist ministry when he was thirty years old after abandoning the study of law. He served as secretary of the church's mission society and was elected bishop in 1888.

22. Daniel Ayres Goodsell, born in Newburgh, New York, in 1840 and a graduate of the University of the City of New York, entered the Methodist ministry in 1859. He served for a time as secretary of the Methodist Board of Education and was elected bishop in 1888.

23. John William Hamilton, born in West Virginia and educated at Boston University, entered the Methodist ministry in 1868. He was the founder of the People's Church in Boston and served as editor of the *Christian Educator*. He was elected bishop in 1900.

24. Amos Shinkle, a banker in Covington, Kentucky, located across the Ohio River from Cincinnati, was a prominent lay leader in the Methodist Church. The General Conference of 1888 was the fourth which he had attended as the delegate from his conference.

25. Newman was a controversial figure closely identified politically with the Grant administration. Knox claimed that his support for Newman was based on the clergyman's good works among the freedmen in the post-Civil War South.

26. It is impossible to identify the "influential persons" to whom Knox refers.

27. Alexander A. Jones, a native of Massachusetts who served with distinction as a private in a Negro regiment during the Civil War, was for a time active in Republican politics and the Grand Army of the Republic in that state. He moved to Indianapolis in the 1880s and as a result of his services to the Republican party there received an appointment as a janitor in the office of the State Auditor in 1887. Veteran black Republicans resented the party's recognition of a newcomer whom they viewed as a mere political opportunist. Late in 1887, Jones was dismissed from his post in the Auditor's office, charged with stealing official documents, and arrested. He attempted in vain to recoup his standing among black Republicans and finally in 1892 shifted his allegiance to the Populist party.

28. William Wesley Walden (1859-1917), a well-known member of Indianapolis's black community, was a lay leader in Bethel A.M.E. Church and a member of the Grand United Order of Odd Fellows in which he served as secretary for many years. A staunch Republican, he was active in the party in Marion County and "filled various important positions in the courthouse," including that of deputy sheriff.

29. George W. Cheatham usually described his occupation as that of a "merchant policeman" or "night patrolman." A perennial aspirant for political office, Cheatham was always active in local Republican campaigns.

30. W. Allison Sweeney, born in Superior, Michigan, in 1852, was educated in the public schools of Ann Arbor. For a time he edited a weekly in Wheeling, West Virginia, known as *The People*, but early in the 1880s moved it to Detroit and changed its name to *The National People*. After a few years in Detroit, he moved to Indianapolis where he was associated with a variety of newspapers, both black and white. A writer of ability and an eloquent speaker, Sweeney joined the *Freeman* as editor in 1888.

31. According to the account of the proceedings of the Marion County Republican Convention which appeared in the *Indianapolis News* (May 26, 27, 1888) there were six black candidates for the nomination for state representative; in addition to the four mentioned by Knox, Harry P. Hill, a little-known black resident of Indianapolis and Dr. S. A. Elbert, a prominent black

physician, were also candidates. On the first ballot the vote was as follows: Hill, 16; Knox, 80; Elbert, 72; Sweeney, 19; and Walden, 219. The vote for Cheatham was not recorded in the *News* which stated: "On the second ballot all the colored men threw their support to Mr. Walden."

32. William D. McCoy (1854-1893), born in Cambridge City, Indiana, was brought to Indianapolis by his parents when only five years old. At the age of eighteen he secured employment as a schoolteacher in Sidney, Ohio, and afterward taught for a few months in Indianapolis. In 1872 he migrated to Helena, Arkansas, where he lived for eight years. In Helena he served on the city council for four years, was city recorder for two years, and occupied the office of superintendent of schools for one year. In 1879 he returned to Indianapolis. A popular schoolteacher in the city, McCoy became active in Republican politics and was the party's candidate for the state legislature from Marion County (Indianapolis) in 1890. Defeated in the Democratic sweep of that year, he shortly afterward succeeded in securing an appointment as minister to Liberia where he died from African fever. For revealing correspondence concerning McCoy's appointment to the Liberian Mission, see the following letters in the Benjamin Harrison Papers (Library of Congress): W. D. McCoy to Benjamin Harrison, June 12, 1890; W. D. McCoy to Benjamin Harrison, September 25, 1890; W. D. McCoy to E. W. Halford, January 17, 1891; L. T. Michener to W. D. McCoy, September 29, 1891 (copy); William Morris to Benjamin Harrison, November 6, 1891.

33. Daniel Moore Ransdell (1842-1912), an Indianapolis native who lost an arm in the Civil War, was active in Republican politics and held a succession of elective and appointive positions: deputy recorder of Marion County, 1866-1867; city clerk of Indianapolis, 1867-1871; member of the Indianapolis city council, 1871-1873; clerk of the Marion County Court, 1878-1882; member of the Indiana Republican State Committee, 1884-1889. President Harrison appointed him marshal of the District of Columbia (1889-1894).

34. Celeste H. McCoy, the daughter of William S. and Myria A. Walker, was born in Quebec, Canada, but the family settled in Cincinnati shortly after Lincoln issued the Emancipation Proclamation. Following the death of William Walker, the family moved to Helena, Arkansas, in 1866. There Celeste Walker met William D. McCoy. They were married on December 10, 1879.

35. William G. Brownlow (1805-1877), born in Wytheville, Virginia, entered the Methodist ministry in 1826 and two years later moved to Elizabethton, Tennessee, where he continued his ministerial duties and edited a Whig newspaper. Moving his paper to Jonesboro in 1839 and to Knoxville ten years later, Brownlow was known as "the fighting parson" because of his caustic editorials. Elected governor of Tennessee in 1865, he was reelected in 1867. Elected to the United States Senate in 1869, he served there until his retirement in 1875.

36. The Metropolitan African Methodist Church was organized in 1836 under the leadership of A. W. Wayman who later became a bishop. In 1881 the building of a new structure was begun. Completed five years later, the church had a seating capacity of 3,000 and was adorned by large stained glass windows donated by annual conferences outside Washington. See the *Washington Bee*, May 29, 1886.

37. Presumably the Dr. St. Clair mentioned here refers to the Reverend Matthew Wesley Clair, who was born in Virginia in 1865 and graduated from Morgan College in 1887. Clair was a well-known black minister in the Northern Methodist Church (Knox's denomination). In 1890 he was elected editor of the *Methodist Banner*, a publication of the Washington Annual Conference.

38. Thomas DeWitt Talmage (1832-1902), a clergyman of the Reformed Dutch Church, held pastorates in Philadelphia and other cities before being called to Brooklyn at the Central Presbyterian Church. Talmage was considered one of the most dramatic preachers of the late nineteenth century and his tabernacle in Brooklyn, a large, imposing structure, was completed in time for Easter services in 1890.

39. Edward Elder Cooper (1859-1908) was a resourceful and innovative newspaperman who founded three well-known Negro journals. Born in Duval County, Florida, he grew up in Tennessee. Migrating to Indianapolis in 1877, he graduated from the city's public high school five years later. In 1882 he secured a job in the Railway Mail Service. Accused of tampering with the mail, he was ultimately dismissed from the service. During his tenure in the RMS, he and Edwin F. Horn, a schoolteacher, launched the *Colored World*, a weekly published in Indianapolis. Plagued by a series of financial difficulties, Cooper was forced to turn the paper over to his creditors. In 1888 he launched another journal, *The Freeman*, a venture in "illustrated journalism" which was described as "the Harper's Weekly of the colored race." The *Freeman*'s editorial position reflected the political opportunism of its publisher who at various times embraced Democracy, Republicanism, and independence. W. Allison Sweeney, a talented writer, served as editor of the *Freeman*. Within four years after its appearance, Cooper's questionable business practices had brought the paper to the brink of financial disaster. Moving to Washington in 1893 he launched a third paper, *The Colored American*, which lasted until 1904.

40. Cooper's enemies in the black community (who were numerous) conceded that he "had a way with words" and possessed a "genial personality," but they repeatedly accused him of unethical business practices. The *Indianapolis World* (October 4, December 26, 1891) claimed that his life of "tricking here, cheating there" made him "a positive detriment to the race."

41. According to reports in the black press, a Mr. Hover of Cincinnati

brought suit against Cooper and the *Freeman* to collect a debt of $418. See *Gazette* (Cleveland), June 11, 1892.

42. In 1890 Cooper had sponsored a contest in the *Freeman* to determine "the Ten Greatest Negroes in America." The results, which presumably reflected the sentiments of the *Freeman's* readers, indicated that Cooper, along with Frederick Douglass, Blanche K. Bruce, and Daniel Payne, belonged among "the ten greatest Negroes."

43. Thomas Rogister was the owner of an ice cream parlor in Indianapolis and a lay leader in Simpson Chapel Methodist Episcopal Church.

44. John T. Leggett, a lay preacher, was active in Simpson Chapel Church, serving for a time as superintendent of its Sunday school. He ultimately became a licensed Methodist minister.

45. Actually Knox was elected an alternate delegate-at-large to the Republican National Convention in 1892. The delegate-at-large was Stanton J. Peelle whom Harrison had appointed judge of the District of Columbia Court of Claims. When Peelle declined to attend the convention, Knox functioned as a full-fledged delegate.

46. Although Knox often made this claim, it was disputed by various contemporaries, one suggesting that the "first Negro delegate-at-large to represent a northern state in a national political convention" was Samuel E. Watson of Michigan at the Republican Convention in 1884.

47. W. S. Rollins, a black clergyman of the Methodist Episcopal Church, served as presiding elder of the Indiana District of the Lexington Conference. In 1894 he was tried and acquitted by a church court for "immoral language and unchristianlike conduct." See *Freeman*, February 10, 1894.

48. George A. Sissle, born in Lexington, Kentucky, on August 28, 1852, was a well-known black clergyman in the Northern Methodist Church, who twice served as minister of Knox's church, Simpson Chapel in Indianapolis.

49. Louis M. Hagood, born of slave parents in Missouri, studied at Lincoln Institute (Missouri) and entered the Saint Louis Conference of the Methodist Episcopal Church in 1874. He graduated from the theological school of Central Tennessee College ten years later, attended Meharry Medical College in Nashville, Tennessee, and received the M.D. degree from the Louisville Medical College. Hagood apparently never practiced medicine but was a Methodist minister of recognized ability. Perhaps his best-known publication was *The Colored Man in the Methodist Episcopal Church* (Cincinnati: Cranston and Stowe, 1890), an eloquent defense of Negroes who chose to remain with the predominantly white denomination rather than leave it for one of the all-black Methodist organizations.

50. John Morgan Walden, born in Lebanon, Ohio, on February 11, 1831, was a journalist and politician before entering the Methodist ministry in 1858.

He was a founder of the church's Freeman's Aid Society in 1866 and served as its president for many years. Walden was elected bishop in 1884.

51. Jeremiah M. Peters was a black physician in Owensboro, Kentucky, and a prominent lay leader in the Lexington Conference of the Methodist Episcopal Church.

52. James T. V. Hill, the Negro attorney, was a member of Simpson Chapel Methodist Episcopal Church.

53. Presumably E. D. Collins, a black Methodist minister.

54. Benjamin J. Morgan, a well-known black chiropodist in Indianapolis, was an active layman in Simpson Chapel Methodist Episcopal Church and a prominent figure in the social life of the city's Negro community. Born in Kentucky in 1861, Morgan was the son of Thomas and Amanda Grayson, but assumed the name of his mother's second husband. For a number of years he was employed by a real estate firm in Cincinnati where he studied chiropody under the well-known Dr. Jared Carey. Morgan began his practice in Indianapolis and was "patronized by the city's best" citizens including Governor Claude Matthews, Thomas Taggart, and Louis Reibold.

55. Benjamin Tobias Thornton (1849-1900), born a slave in Winchester, Virginia, was for a quarter of a century a member of the Indianapolis police force and an influential figure in the city's black community. Promoted to detective in 1886, Thornton held that rank until his death.

56. Ezra D. Miller, a Methodist minister who had served various churches in the Lexington Conference including the one in Jeffersonville, Indiana, occupied the pulpit of Simpson Chapel in Indianapolis in 1892.

57. According to the proceedings of the General Conference of 1888, printed in the *New York Daily Tribune* (May 30, 1888), a "report was finally adopted by which the name of the [Freedman's Aid] Society became 'The Freedman's Aid and Southern Educational Society of the Methodist Episcopal Church.' "

58. E. R. Overall, born in Saint Charles County, Missouri, on August 25, 1835, moved to Chicago at the age of twenty. There he engaged in abolitionist activities and at the outbreak of the Civil War recruited Negro troops for the Union army. Settling in Omaha in 1886, he became active in political and civil rights causes and organized the first black literary society in the city. Appointed general delivery clerk in the Omaha post office in 1869, he held the position for more than a quarter of a century. Overall acquired considerable property and was considered one of Omaha's most prosperous black citizens by 1890, when he became the first Negro in Nebraska to be nominated for the legislature on the Republican ticket. Though defeated in the election, Overall paved the way for the success of his friend, Dr. M. O. Ricketts, who was elected two years later.

225

59. A. D. White and Dr. Matthew Oliver Ricketts were two well-known members of Omaha's black community in the 1890s. White was a realtor and businessman who was prominent in fraternal and church affairs. Ricketts, born in Henry County, Kentucky, on April 3, 1858, grew up in Missouri where he graduated from Lincoln Institute in 1876. After teaching school for three years, he migrated to Omaha and entered the Omaha Medical School. In 1892 he became the first Negro to be elected to the Nebraska legislature. Reelected in 1894, he served with considerable distinction and secured the passage of a civil rights bill. Later, Ricketts moved to Kansas and devoted most of his time to fraternal affairs.

60. Charles Nelson Grandison, a well-known Methodist clergyman, served as president of Bennett College from 1890 to 1892. This institution, founded in 1873, and located in Greensboro, North Carolina, was one of a series of black colleges sponsored by the Northern Methodist Church in the South. For an interesting account of Grandison, see James D. Corrothers, *In Spite of Handicap: An Autobiography* (Westport, Conn.: Negro Universities Press, 1970), pp. 101-18.

61. The election of Negro bishops within the Northern Methodist Church was proposed by black delegates as early as 1872. Despite declarations by general conferences that race and color were not barriers to the episcopacy, no Negro bishop was elected until 1920. See Reimers, *White Protestantism and the Negro*, pp. 71-75.

62. Aristides Alphonso Peter Albert, the son of a slave woman and Pierre Albert, a Frenchman, was born in Saint Charles Parish, Louisiana, on December 10, 1853. Graduating from Straight University in New Orleans in 1881, he entered the ministry of the Methodist Episcopal Church and held a succession of posts in the Louisiana Conference of the church. In 1888 he was elected editor of the *Southwestern Christian Advocate*, the church's journal devoted to the interests of its black constituency.

63. Isaac Wilson Joyce, born near Cincinnati on October 11, 1836, began his ministry in Indiana in 1859 and was elected a bishop in the Methodist Church in 1888.

64. John Franklin Goucher (1854-1890), a native of Pennsylvania and a graduate of Dickinson College, entered the Methodist ministry in 1869 and served for many years as pastor of the First Methodist Church in Baltimore. He was president of the board of trustees of Centenary Biblical Institute for the Education of Colored Youth, an institution which developed into Morgan College. He was also a founder of the Women's College of Baltimore in 1884 and became its second president six years later. The college later was named in his honor, Goucher College.

65. William Nast (1807-1899), a native of Germany who settled in the United States in 1828, taught German at the Military Academy at West Point

and at Kenyon College until 1835, when he entered the Methodist ministry. Nast created the German Methodist Society in Cincinnati in 1838 and began the publication of *Der Christlicke Apologete* the following year. He served as its editor until 1892 when his son Albert Nast succeeded him. See Carl Wittke, *William Nast: Patriarch of German Methodism* (Detroit: Wayne State University, 1959).

66. Knox obviously refers here to Alpha Jefferson Kynett, a native of Pennsylvania and well-known Methodist clergyman, who was one of the founders of the Church Extension Society. He served for many years as a secretary of church extension and was reelected to that position in 1892.

67. The comment in the *Omaha Daily Bee* (May 20, 1892) read: "Mr. Knox . . . made a speech that sailed away into the clouds and part of it never came down again."

68. Lillian Thomas, born in Chicago and reared in Wisconsin, settled in Indianapolis early in the 1880s. A well-known writer and elocutionist, she served on the staff of various white newspapers including the *Indianapolis News* as well as that of the *Freeman*. Upon her marriage to James E. Fox, a merchant tailor of Pensacola, Florida, in May 1893, she severed her connection with the *Freeman*. She died in 1917.

69. Randolph Sinks Foster, born in Williamsburg, Ohio, on February 22, 1820, entered the Methodist ministry in 1837. In 1856 he became president of Northwestern University and later served as head of Drew Theological Seminary. Foster was elected bishop in 1872.

70. William Conrad Bobbs (1861-1926) entered the employ of Merrill, Meigs and Company, booksellers of Indianapolis, in 1879 and became a director of the company in 1890. He served for many years as president of its successor, the Bobbs-Merrill Company.

71. The Columbia Club, organized in 1888 by a group of young Indianapolis Republicans to promote Harrison's candidacy, became a permanent society whose membership included the Republican elite of Indiana. Its uniform consisted of blue flannel coat and trousers, white vest, pearl-colored derby, and a walking stick. The avowed purpose of the club was "to inculcate, teach and secure high appreciation of the fundamental principles of the Republican Party." No Negroes belonged to the club but a succession of organizations, such as the Herculean Club, performed a similar function among black Republicans in Indianapolis.

72. I. S. Gordon was a conspicuous figure in the Indianapolis business community. He was president of Gordon-Kurtz Company, jobbers and manufacturers of saddlery hardware, and was a director of the Industrial Life Association, which claimed to be the oldest life insurance company in Indiana.

73. James G. Blaine (1830-1893) represented Maine in the House of Representatives (1863-1876), where he was Speaker for three terms, and in the

227

Senate from 1876 to 1881, when he resigned to become secretary of state. He was the unsuccessful Republican candidate for president in 1884 and served as Benjamin Harrison's secretary of state until his resignation on June 4, 1892, on the eve of the Republican National Convention. A perennially popular figure in the party, he was backed by those Republicans disenchanted with Harrison and bent upon preventing his renomination in 1892. On the Blaine-Harrison contest of that year, see Robert D. Marcus, *Grand Old Party: Political Structure in the Gilded Age, 1880-1896* (New York: Oxford University Press, 1871), pp. 160-72.

74. Benjamin Harrison (1833-1901), grandson of President William Henry Harrison, was born in Ohio and settled in Indianapolis to practice law in 1854. He served in the Union army and was brevetted brigadier general in 1865. Unsuccessful as Republican candidate for governor of Indiana in 1876, he was elected United States Senator in 1880 and served in the Senate from 1881 to 1887. Elected president in 1888, Harrison was defeated for reelection in 1892 by Grover Cleveland.

75. Hervey Bates, born in Indianapolis in 1834, was a member of an old and distinguished Indiana family. His father, the first sheriff of Marion County, was a well-known businessman whose numerous enterprises included the building of the Bates House, Indianapolis's leading hotel. Hervey Bates, the second of five generations to bear that name, was prominent in various mercantile and banking ventures and was a founder of the American Hominy Company.

76. Roger R. ("Rhody") Shiel (1843-1910), born in Strawtown, Indiana, served in the Eighth Indiana Cavalry during the Civil War. Following the war, Shiel entered the business of buying and shipping livestock. Although his livestock enterprise was headquartered in Indianapolis, he did not actually establish his home in the city until 1892. A zealous Republican, he was influential in party affairs in Indiana and was an enthusiastic supporter of his friend Benjamin Harrison. Shiel was a key member of the Indiana delegation to the Republican National Convention in 1892, where he attracted national attention for his flamboyant antics in Harrison's behalf.

77. Richard Wigginton Thompson (1809-1900), born in Virginia, rose to political prominence in Indiana as a Whig and ultimately became a power in the Republican party. He served in the Indiana legislature, as a congressman (1841-1843, 1847-1849), as internal revenue collector and judge, and as secretary of the navy under President Rutherford B. Hayes. By the time he placed Harrison's name in nomination in 1892, he was generally considered "the grand old man" of the Republican party in Indiana.

78. It is impossible to determine whether this is a reference to C. S. Dearborn or H. W. Dearborn.

79. William Murrell, born a slave in Georgia, was valet to Confederate

General James Longstreet. After Longstreet's death, he enlisted as a soldier in the Union army (Forty-fourth Regiment). At the end of the Civil War, Murrell settled in Louisiana where he served in the legislature and edited the Delta, Louisiana, *Madison Vindicator*. In the administration of Governor W. P. Kellogg, he was assigned command of the Louisiana National Guard. Murrell moved to Jersey City, New Jersey, in 1883. There he edited a black weekly, *The New Jersey Trumpet*, and held a minor post in the Interior Department. An alternate delegate-at-large to the Republican National Convention in 1892, he became a center of controversy because of the effort to contest his credentials and his attempt to function as the delegate-at-large in the absence of John I. Blair. See *New York Times*, June 9, 11, 12, 1892.

80. James S. Clarkson, journalist and Republican politician, was born in Indiana and grew up in Iowa. He owned the *Daily State Register* of Des Moines (1870-1891); was a member of the Republican National Committee from 1876 to 1896, serving as its chairman in 1890-1892; and was appointed first assistant postmaster general by Harrison in 1889 and resigned the following year. Clarkson was generally considered the leader of the anti-Harrison movement in the Republican National Convention in 1892.

81. Thomas Collier Platt (1833-1910) of New York was for many years a power in the Republican party. Following two terms in the House of Representatives, he was elected to the Senate in 1881 but served only a few months. Returned to the Senate in 1897, he remained there until 1909. In 1892 Platt was one of the leaders of the anti-Harrison movement during the preconvention campaign.

82. Jacob Sloat Fassett (1853-1924) of New York, who was in the banking and lumbering business, was secretary of the Republican National Committee between 1888 and 1892 and served as temporary chairman of the Republican National Convention of 1892. An important member of Senator Thomas C. Platt's New York Republican organization, Fassett was appointed collector of the Port of New York in 1891 by Harrison in an effort to win Platt's support for his renomination as president.

83. Norris Wright Cuney (1849-1898) was the leading black Republican in Texas for more than a quarter of a century after the Civil War. During the Harrison administration he served as collector of customs at Galveston. See Maud Cuney Hare, *Norris Wright Cuney: Tribune of the Black People* (Austin, Texas: Steck-Vaughn Co., 1968).

84. Mifflin W. Gibbs (1823-1915), born in Philadelphia, settled in San Francisco during the California Gold Rush. Ten years later he migrated to Canada where he acquired considerable wealth from various business ventures. Returning to the United States, he took up residence in Arkansas and was elected city judge in Little Rock in 1873. He held a succession of federal patronage posts including that of receiver of public moneys in the Land Office to

which he was appointed by Harrison in 1889. See Tom Dillard, "Black Moses of the West: A Biography of Mifflin Wistar Gibbs, 1823-1915" (Master's thesis, University of Arkansas, 1974).

85. Robert Smalls (1839-1915), a black Republican prominent in South Carolina during Reconstruction, first attracted attention because of his daring capture of the Confederate ship *The Planter* during the Civil War. A member of the South Carolina legislature, Smalls also had a relatively long tenure in Congress (1875-1879, 1882-1883, 1884-1887). See Okon Edit Aya, *From Slavery to Public Service: Robert Smalls, 1839-1915* (New York: Oxford University Press, 1971).

86. Thomas E. Miller (1849-1938), born in South Carolina and a leading Negro Republican in the state in the late nineteenth century, was a lawyer, state legislator, a member of Congress (1890-1891), and president of the state college for Negroes (1896-1911).

87. Blanche Kelso Bruce (1841-1898), born in Virginia and educated at Oberlin College, settled in Mississippi in 1868 and became a leading black Republican in the state. He served as United States Senator from Mississippi (1875-1881) and thereafter held a succession of federal appointments. Harrison appointed him recorder of deeds (1891-1893).

88. Pinckney Benton Stewart Pinchback (1837-1921), born in Mississippi, became a key black Republican in Louisiana during Reconstruction, serving as a state senator and as lieutenant governor. In 1873 he was elected to the United States Senate but was not allowed to take his seat. Thereafter, Pinchback held various appointive posts in the federal government and lived for many years in Washington and New York. See James Haskins, *Pinckney Benton Stewart Pinchback* (New York: Macmillan, 1973).

89. John Mercer Langston (1829-1897), lawyer, educator, and politician, was born in Virginia and educated at Oberlin College. He practiced law in Ohio for a time and was active in Republican politics there until 1868 when he returned to Virginia as a school inspector for the Freedman's Bureau. He served as dean of the law school at Howard University (1869-1876), as minister to Haiti, as president of Virginia Normal and Collegiate Institute, and as Republican congressman from Virginia (1890-1891). Langston's opposition to Harrison apparently resulted from his failure to receive an appointment as a federal judge.

90. Langston delivered an address in Indianapolis on September 3, 1891. It was entitled "The Negro Problem: The Method of Its Solution." Knox presented the "welcome address."

91. James M. Townsend (1841-1913), born in Ohio and educated at Oberlin College, was an outstanding minister of the African Methodist Episcopal Church in Indiana whose tenure in the state legislature was marked by a futile struggle to repeal the state's discriminatory "black laws." A veteran of

the Civil War and prominent politician as well as a churchman, Townsend was appointed to a position in the General Land Office by Harrison in 1889.

92. John Roy Lynch (1847-1939), born in Louisiana, was an influential black Republican in Mississippi for more than a quarter of a century after the Civil War. He was a member of the state house (1869-1873), serving one term as Speaker, a member of Congress (1873-1877, 1882-1883), and chairman of the Republican State Executive Committee (1881-1889). In the Harrison administration Lynch held the position of fourth auditor of the treasury for the Navy Department (1889-1893). See John R. Lynch, *Reminiscences of an Active Life: The Autobiography of John Roy Lynch*, ed. John Hope Franklin (Chicago: University of Chicago, 1970).

93. This is a reference to Langston's unsuccessful attempt to persuade President Harrison to appoint him to a federal judgeship.

94. John K. Gowdy (1843-1918), born and reared in Rush County, Indiana, was a veteran of the Civil War who became chairman of the Rush County Republican Committee in 1879. Active in the Methodist Church, the Grand Army of the Republic, and the Masonic Order, he served as chairman of the Republican State Committee in Indiana from 1890 to 1897. In recognition of his services to the party, Gowdy was appointed consul-general to Paris in 1897.

95. Russell Alexander Alger (1836-1907), born in Ohio, settled in Grand Rapids, Michigan, where he engaged in the lumber business and took an active part in Republican affairs. A Civil War veteran, he was elected governor of Michigan in 1884 and became head of the Grand Army of the Republic in 1889. Alger was Michigan's favorite-son candidate for the Republican nomination for president in 1892.

96. The "force bill" refers to the measure introduced in the House in 1890 by Henry Cabot Lodge. It provided for federal supervision of federal elections upon petition by a specified number of voters and, according to its advocates, was designed to guarantee implementation of the Fifteenth Amendment. On the Lodge bill see Richard E. Welch, Jr., "The Federal Elections Bill of 1890: Postscripts and Prelude," *Journal of American History* 52 (December 1965): 511-26.

97. Harrison was a strong advocate of the federal elections bill in 1890. Knox's reference regarding Blaine's opposition to such a measure concerns a federal elections bill introduced in 1875.

98. John James Ingalls (1833-1900), born in Massachusetts and educated at Williams College, settled in Kansas in 1858. A lawyer by profession, he participated in the territorial government and made several unsuccessful attempts in the 1860s to win state office. A staunch Republican, Ingalls finally was elected to the Senate in 1873 and was reelected twice. Skilled in the use of colorful, vitriolic language and in waving the "bloody shirt," he was an ardent

supporter of the Civil Rights Act of 1875. But by the time of the Force bill of 1890 he publicly expressed doubt about the wisdom of enfranchising blacks and opposed federal legislation to protect their voting rights. For comments on the "inexplicable mystery" of Ingalls's about-face on the race question by a prominent black political figure, see Lynch, *Reminiscenses*, pp. 452-54.

99. Laura Hull Morris, the wife of Dr. Minor Morris who was a professor of pathology at Central College of Physicians and Surgeons in Indianapolis, was active in the social life of the city, a music teacher, and a key figure in the Matinee Musicale. The Morrises moved to Washington in 1901 where Dr. Morris held a position in the War Department. For an account of the sensation created by Mrs. Morris's expulsion from the White House in 1906, see Willard B. Gatewood, Jr., "Theodore Roosevelt and the Case of Mrs. Minor Morris," *Mid-America* 48 (January 1966): 3-18.

100. Edward W. Vaughn and Gabriel L. Jones were among a sizable group of black Republicans from Indianapolis who attended the National Convention in 1892. Born in Memphis, Tennessee, in 1854, Vaughn spent much of his life in Iowa where he received considerable formal education. He taught school for a time in Arkansas and later, after learning the trade of pressman, published a journal in Moline, Illinois. Returning to Iowa, he published a newspaper in Des Moines and served as a messenger for Governor William Larrabee (1886-1890). Sometime later he settled in Indianapolis and during the presidential campaign of 1892 edited a political sheet called the *Republican Line*. The election was scarcely over when the newspaper "suspended," and Vaughn moved to Lexington, Kentucky, to assume direction of another journal. Jones (1858-1915), also a native of Tennessee, grew up in Indianapolis where for seven years he taught school. During the Harrison administration he held a minor post in the Internal Revenue Service and later served as a deputy clerk in the Marion County Recorder's Office. In 1896 he was elected to the lower house of the Indiana legislature.

101. Alvin P. Hovey (1812-1891), originally a Democrat who switched his allegiance to the Republican party, was an attorney and veteran of the Civil War. In 1851 he became a judge on the state's supreme court and in 1856 was appointed United States attorney for Indiana. He served as minister to Peru (1865-1870) and as a member of Congress (1887-1889). Hovey was governor of Indiana from 1889 to 1891.

102. Lew Wallace (1827-1905), born Lewis Wallace in Brookville, Indiana, served in both the Mexican and Civil wars, as governor of the New Mexico Territory (1878-1881), and as minister to Turkey (1881-1885). He was the author of the immensely popular novel *Ben-Hur*. An influential Republican, Wallace was a delegate to the party's National Convention in 1892.

103. William Allen Woods was born in Tennessee in 1837 and admitted to the bar in Indiana in 1861. He was a member of the Indiana legislature

(1867), state circuit court judge (1873-1880), judge of the state supreme court (1881-1883), and United States district judge (1883-1892). Woods was an active Republican who lived in Indianapolis.

104. George Francis McGinnis, born in 1826, was a veteran of the Mexican War who rose to the rank of brigadier general during the Civil War. Settling in Indianapolis in 1850, he served as auditor of Marion County (1867-1871) and for many years was a fixture in the Republican party in Indiana.

105. Matthias Loring Haines (1850-1941) was pastor of the First Presbyterian Church of Indianapolis from 1885 to 1920. President Harrison was an elder in this church.

106. Presumably Mrs. J. Robert McKee, nee Mary ("Mamie") Harrison, daughter of Benjamin Harrison.

107. For an analysis of Harrison's relations with southern Republicans, see Vincent De Santis, "Benjamin Harrison and the Republican Party in the South, 1889-1893," *Indiana Magazine of History* 51 (December 1955): 279-302.

108. Chauncey Mitchell Depew (1834-1928), a New York attorney and Republican politician, was president of the New York Central Railroad from 1885 to 1899. A member of the state legislature in 1861 and 1862, Depew was an unsuccessful candidate for the United States Senate in 1881. Elected senator in 1899, he served until 1911.

109. Jacob Jefferson Todd, born in Pennsylvania in 1843 and educated in Indiana where he settled, was a Civil War veteran and prominent attorney who practiced in Bluffton. Long active in the Republican party, Todd was a delegate to the National Convention in 1880 and was present at the Minneapolis convention in 1892 as a member of the Columbia Club.

110. Gibbs may have been the only black man present at the Arkansas headquarters, but the state's delegation included three other well-known black Republicans: Ferd Havis of Pine Bluff, a delegate; William LaPorte of Little Rock, an alternate delegate; and Jesse C. Duke of Pine Bluff, an alternate delegate-at-large.

111. Charles F. Griffin, a delegate-at-large from Indiana to the Republican National Convention in 1892, had been elected secretary of state in 1886 and reelected two years later. Born in Indiana in 1857, he was considered a "skillful lawyer and powerful advocate" who occupied positions of prominence in the Masonic Order, Presbyterian Church, and the National Guard.

112. John Coit Spooner (1843-1919), born in Indiana, settled in Wisconsin and graduated from the state university there. A Civil War veteran, Spooner began the practice of law in 1867 and was elected to the Wisconsin legislature in 1872. An active Republican, he went to the United States Senate in 1885 for one term. Unsuccessful in his bid for the governorship of Wisconsin in 1892, he returned to the Senate in 1897 and remained there until 1907.

113. Edward Oliver Wolcott (1848-1905) was the Republican senator

from Colorado (1889-1901) who placed Blaine's name in nomination.

114. The Negro delegate who seconded the nomination of Blaine was William E. Mollison of Mississippi, a lawyer and businessman in Vicksburg; Henry Plummer Cheatham, a black Republican congressman from North Carolina (1889-1893), seconded Harrison's nomination.

115. John Benson Foraker (1846-1917), a Civil War veteran and attorney in Cincinnati, served as judge of superior court (1879-1882) and was the unsuccessful Republican candidate for governor of Ohio in 1883. Elected governor in 1885, he was defeated for reelection in 1889. He was elected senator in 1896.

116. William McKinley, Jr. (1843-1901), a Civil War veteran and an attorney in Canton, Ohio, was a Republican congressman from 1877 to 1884 and from 1885 to 1891 and governor of Ohio from 1892 to 1896, when he was elected president of the United States. In 1892 McKinley was a favorite-son candidate for president from Ohio, who garnered considerable support from the anti-Harrison forces.

117. Whitelaw Reid (1837-1912), journalist and diplomat, was a dedicated Republican and publisher of the influential *New York Tribune*.

118. Thomas Brackett Reed (1839-1902) of Maine, a graduate of Bowdoin College and a paymaster in the Union army (1864-1865), began the practice of law in Portland in 1865. Following election to a succession of state offices on the Republican ticket, Reed went to Congress in 1877 and remained there for twenty years. For three terms he served as Speaker of the House of Representatives.

119. Charles Warren Fairbanks (1852-1918) of Indiana, born in Ohio and educated at Ohio Wesleyan University, settled in Indianapolis in 1874 where he practiced law. He was chairman of the Republican State Convention in 1892. He served in the United States Senate (1897-1905) and as vice president (1905-1909).

120. Smiley N. Chambers, an aspirant for the Republican gubernatorial nomination in Indiana in 1892, was a veteran of the Civil War. A graduate of Shurtleff College in Illinois, he was a prominent attorney in Vincennes, who had long been active in the Republican party. President Harrison appointed him federal attorney for Indiana in 1889.

121. Frank B. Allen was principal of a school in Crawfordsville, Indiana, for seven years prior to taking up residence in Indianapolis in 1890. He first joined the staff of the *Freeman*, then became an editorial writer for the *World*, another black weekly in the city. In 1892 Knox brought him back to the *Freeman* where he remained for less than a year. Allen later moved to Mound City, Illinois.

122. Elwood Knox.

123. After a year with the *Freeman*, Charles C. Stapp, a veteran newspa-

perman and a favorite of Indianapolis's various black literary societies, also severed his connection with the journal.

124. Upon his return to Indianapolis, Cooper announced that he had purchased 160 acres of land in the Indian Territory (Oklahoma) and planned to settle in the town of Guthrie where he would publish a newspaper with the aim of attracting Negro settlers to the area. He spoke enthusiastically of making Oklahoma a "black state." See *Indianapolis News*, September 8, 1892.

125. Cooper was in charge of the cloakroom in the legislative building until he moved to Washington, D.C., in 1893 and launched the *Colored American*.

126. Ralph St. Julius Perry was a physician and surgeon in Indianapolis who occasionally contributed articles to the press based upon his medical experiences in Africa in the early 1880s.

127. Lewis C. Walker, born in Ohio in 1837 and educated at the Southwestern Normal School in Lebanon, served as mayor of Wilmington, Ohio, for a time before moving to Richmond, Indiana, in 1869. He served two terms in the Indiana legislature from Wayne County. Moving to Indianapolis in 1873, Walker was elected judge of the superior court seven years later. Prominent in fraternal circles and an elder in the Presbyterian Church, he was long active in the Republican party.

128. Julius R. Cox, a graduate of Fisk University, remained in charge of the *Freeman* until 1895 when he took a job in the Indianapolis post office. In 1904 Cox became a "traveling secretary" to Booker T. Washington. His successor on the *Freeman* was William M. Lewis, a teacher and civic leader in Indianapolis's black community.

129. John Mitchell, Jr., of Richmond, Virginia, was born a slave in 1863 and attended the Richmond Normal School. Active in fraternal and church affairs, he was editor of the *Richmond Planet* and a prominent black Republican who served on the Richmond City Council.

130. W. D. Driver was for a time foreman of the composing rooms of the *Freeman* and served as the paper's representative in Chicago during the Columbian Exposition. He later edited the short-lived *Weekly Review* and occasionally wrote for the *Indianapolis News*. In the mid-1890s Driver left Indianapolis and settled in Coffeyville, Kansas, where he died in 1897.

131. Robert Bruce Bagby (1846-1903), born in Virginia and educated at Oberlin, was a veteran of the Civil War. After the war, he served as a school principal in Crawfordsville, then spent six years in Washington as a government clerk. Returning to Indianapolis, he practiced law, served in the office of the Marion County clerk and was the first Negro member of the city council.

132. Although Knox apparently is referring to George W. Shaffer, the principal black aspirants for nomination to the state legislature in 1894 were Bagby and Dr. William M. Chavis (1854-1898), a native of Princeton, Indi-

235

ana, and a former schoolteacher in Noblesville and Bloomington, who had studied medicine and recently begun to practice in Indianapolis.

133. Arthur Lutheral Stewart, born on a farm in Warren County, Ohio, December 11, 1872, came "from a well-known and exceptional family—all teachers, save the mother and two sons." At the age of nineteen he became principal of the Negro school in Columbus, Indiana, and, after four years in that position, accepted a teaching assignment in the schools of Indianapolis.

BIBLIOGRAPHY

UNPUBLISHED SOURCES

John P. Green Papers, Western Reserve Historical Society, Cleveland, Ohio.
Benjamin Harrison Papers, Library of Congress.
Booker T. Washington Papers, Manuscript Division, Library of Congress, Washington, D.C.
Wills and Inventories, Wilson County Tennessee, vol. 1843-1848, vol. 1866-1871, Wilson County Courthouse, Lebanon, Tennessee.

NEWSPAPERS

Broad-Ax, Chicago, Illinois
Chicago Defender
Cleveland Gazette
The Colored American, Washington, D.C.
The Freeman, Indianapolis, Indiana
Hancock Democrat, Greenfield, Indiana
Indianapolis News
Indianapolis Star
Indianapolis World
The Louisianian, New Orleans, Louisiana
New York Daily Tribune
New York Times
Omaha Daily Bee
The People's Advocate, Washington, D.C.
The Plaindealer, Detroit, Michigan
Plaindealer, Topeka, Kansas
The Recorder, Indianapolis, Indiana
The Sentinel, Indianapolis, Indiana
Washington Bee

ARTICLES

Adams, Cyrus F. "George L. Knox: His Life and Work." *Colored American Magazine* 5 (October 1902): 465-68.

Carroll, Joseph C. "George Boxley, Prototype of John Brown." *Negro History Bulletin* 5 (June 1942): 198-200.

_____. "George Levi Knox." *Negro History Bulletin* 5 (May 1942): 186-88.

Cummings, Charles M. "Robert Hopkins Hatton: Reluctant Rebel." *Tennessee Historical Quarterly* 23 (June 1964): 169-81.

De Santis, Vincent. "Benjamin Harrison and the Republican Party in the South, 1889-1893." *Indiana Magazine of History* 51 (December 1955): 279-302.

"Edward Elder Cooper." *Alexander's Magazine* 6 (August 15, 1908): 155.

Gatewood, Willard B. "Theodore Roosevelt and the Case of Mrs. Minor Morris." *Mid-America* 48 (January 1966): 3-18.

Hartzell, Joseph C. "Methodism and the Negro in the United States." *Journal of Negro History* 7 (July 1932): 301-15.

Hershaw, L. M. "The Negro Press in America." *Charities* 15 (October 1905): 66-68.

James, Felix. "The Civic and Political Activities of George A. Myers." *Journal of Negro History* 58 (April 1973): 166-73.

Thornbrough, Emma Lou. "American Negro Newspapers, 1880-1914." *Business History Review* 40 (Winter 1966): 467-90.

_____. "Segregation in Indiana during the Klan Era." *Mississippi Valley Historical Review* 48 (March 1961): 594-618.

Welch, Richard E. "The Federal Elections Bill of 1890: Postscripts and Prelude." *Journal of American History* 52 (December 1965): 511-26.

OTHER SOURCES

Aptheker, Herbert, ed. *Correspondence of W. E. B. Du Bois*. Amherst: University of Massachusetts Press, 1973.

Aya, Okon Edit. *From Slavery to Public Service: Robert Smalls, 1839-1915*. New York: Oxford University Press, 1971.

Binford, J. H. *History of Hancock County, Indiana*. Greenfield, Indiana: William Mitchell, 1882.

Bowen, B. F. *Biographical Memoirs of Hancock County, Indiana*. Logansport, Ind.: B. F. Bowen, 1902.

Bucke, Emory, ed. *The History of Methodism*. 3 vols. New York: Abingdon Press, 1964.

Civil War Centennial Commission. *Tennesseans in the Civil War.* 2 vols. Nashville: Civil War Centennial Commission, 1964.

Corrothers, James D. *In Spite of Handicap: An Autobiography.* Westport, Conn.: Negro Universities Press, 1970.

Culp, D. W., ed. *Twentieth Century Negro Literature.* Atlanta: J. L. Nichols, 1902.

Detweiler, Frederick G. *The Negro Press in the United States.* Chicago: University of Chicago Press, 1922.

Dickey, Marcus. *The Youth of James Whitcomb Riley.* Indianapolis: Bobbs-Merrill Co., 1919.

Dillard, Tom. "Black Moses of the West: A Biography of Mifflin Westar Gibbs, 1823-1915." Master's thesis, University of Arkansas, 1974.

Dunn, Jacob P. *Greater Indianapolis: The History, the Industries, the Institutions, and the People of a City of Homes.* 2 vols. Chicago: Lewis Publishing Co., 1910.

Eitel, Edmund H., ed. *The Complete Works of James Whitcomb Riley.* 6 vols. Indianapolis: Bobbs-Merrill, 1913.

Garraty, John A., ed. *The Barber and the Historian: The Correspondence of George A. Myers and James Ford Rhodes, 1910-1932.* Columbus: Ohio Historical Society, 1956.

Gatewood, Willard B. *Black Americans and the White Man's Burden, 1898-1903.* Urbana: University of Illinois Press, 1975.

Goodspeed's History of Tennessee: Maury, Williamson, Rutherford, Wilson, Bedford and Marshall Counties. Nashville: n.p., 1886.

Guild, George B. *A Brief Narrative of the Fourth Tennessee Cavalry Regiment.* Nashville: n.p., 1913.

Hagood, Louis M. *The Colored Man in the Methodist Episcopal Church.* Cincinnati: Cranston and Howe, 1890.

Hare, Maud Cuney. *Norris Wright Cuney: Tribune of the Black People.* Austin, Texas: Steck-Vaughn Co., 1968.

Harlan, Louis R. *Booker T. Washington: The Making of a Black Leader, 1856-1901.* Urbana: University of Illinois Press, 1972.

Hartshorn, W. N. *An Era of Progress and Promise.* Boston: Priscilla Publishing Co., 1910.

Haskins, James. *Pinckney Benton Stewart Pinchback.* New York: Macmillan, 1973.

Huggins, Nathan, et al. *Key Issues in the Afro-American Experience.* 2 vols. New York: Harcourt, Brace, Jovanovich, 1971.

Journal of the General Conference of the Methodist Episcopal Church, May 1-31, 1888. New York: Phillips and Hunt, 1888.

Kerwood, A. L. *Annals of the Fifty-seventh Regiment, Indiana Volunteers.* Dayton, Ohio: W. J. Shuey, 1868.

239

Lane, Ann J. *The Brownsville Affair: National Crisis and Black Reaction*. Port Washington, N. Y.: Kennikat Press, 1971.

Lindsley, John B., ed. *The Military Annals of Tennessee, Confederate*. Nashville: Lindsley and Co., 1886.

Lynch, John Roy. *Reminiscences of an Active Life: The Autobiography of John Roy Lynch*. Edited by John Hope Franklin. Chicago: University of Chicago Press, 1970.

Marcus, Robert D. *Grand Old Party: Political Structure in the Gilded Age, 1880-1896*. New York: Oxford University Press, 1971.

Meier, August. *Negro Thought in America, 1880-1915: Racial Ideologies in the Age of Booker T. Washington*. Ann Arbor: University of Michigan Press, 1966.

Merrett, Dixon, ed. *The History of Wilson County, Tennessee*. Nashville: Benson Printery, 1961.

Mitchell, Minnie Belle. *James Whitcomb Riley as I Knew Him*. Greenfield, Ind.: Ole Swimmin' Hole Press, 1949.

Mooney, Chase C. *Slavery in Tennessee*. Bloomington: Indiana University Press, 1957.

Moore, Albert B. *Conscription and Conflict in the Confederacy*. New York: Macmillan, 1924.

Penn, Irving Garland. *The Afro-American Press and Its Editors*. Springfield, Mass.: Willey, 1891.

Richardson, Clement. *The National Cyclopedia of the Colored Race*. Montgomery, Ala. National Publishing Co., 1919.

Richman, George J. *History of Hancock County*. Indianapolis: Federal Publishing Co., 1916.

Riley, Walter H. *Forty Years in the Lap of Methodism*. Louisville: Mayes Printing Co., 1915.

Skelton, David E. *History of the Lexington Conference*. N.p.: n.p., 1950.

Smyth, Mabel, ed. *The Black American Reference Book*. Englewood Cliffs, N. J.: Prentice-Hall, 1976.

Thornbrough, Emma Lou. *Since Emancipation: A Short History of Indiana Negroes, 1863-1963*. Indianapolis: Indiana Division, American Negro Emancipation Centennial Authority, n.d.

_____. *The Negro in Indiana: A Study of a Minority*. Indianapolis: Indiana Historical Bureau, 1957.

United States Congress. *House Miscellaneous Documents*. 42d Congress, 1st Session, No. 36.

Wittke, Carl. *William Nast: Patriarch of German Methodism*. Detroit: Wayne State University Press, 1959.

INDEX

243